Politics, Literature, and National Character

Germaine de Staël

Politics, Literature, and National Character

Translated and edited by Morroe Berger

LONDON AND NEW YORK

Originally published as Madame de Staël on Politics, Literature, and National Character in 1964 by Doubleday & Company, Inc.

Published in 2000 by Transaction Publishers

Published 2017 by Routledge
4 Park Square, Milton Park, Abingdon, Oxon OX14 4RN
605 Third Avenue, New York, NY 10017

Routledge is an imprint of the Taylor & Francis Group, an informa business

Library of Congress Catalog Number: 00-023400

Library of Congress Cataloging-in-Publication Data

Staël, Madame de (Anne-Louise-Germaine), 1766-1817.
Politics, literature, and national character / translated, edited, and with an introduction by Morroe Berger.
p. cm.
Originally published: Madame de Stäel on politics, literature, and national character. Garden City, N.Y.: Doubleday, 1964.
Includes bibliographical references.
ISBN 0-7658-0645-2 (alk. paper)
1. Title: Politics, literature, and national character. II. Berger, Morroe. III. Title.

PQ2431 .A23 2000
848' .609—dc21 00-023400

ISBN 13: 978-0-7658-0645-1 (pbk)

Contents

Preface

An editor and translator is likely to irritate people on both counts. My purpose in presenting this anthology is to make available in English a correct translation of Madame de Staël's contributions to what is today called political sociology, the sociology of literature, and the study of national character. In the first of these subjects she displayed perspicacity in all her writings but mostly in *Considerations on the Principal Events of the French Revolution* (1818). The second she treated mainly in *Literature Considered in Its Relation to Social Institutions* (1800). The third subject she wrote about frequently, but it is best exemplified in her book *On Germany* (1813) and in others dealing in part with England and Russia. This anthology comes mainly from these three books.

I think that Madame de Staël's work has value for us not only as a part of the history of ideas but also as an inspiration to liberal thought. In the Introduction I try to show why I think so, and to tell something about her relation to the United States. Richmond L. Hawkins opened the subject of her relations with some Americans in his *Madame de Staël and the United States* (1930), but her intellectual influence has not yet had even such a brief and preliminary survey. I hope that American scholars will be stimulated to make further studies.

In translating Madame de Staël I tried to adhere to a literal translation whenever possible, but I freely abandoned this goal whenever it was necessary in order to convey her meaning correctly.

It is a pleasure to acknowledge the help I have received. My greatest debt is to my friend and colleague, Professor Francois Hoffmann, who went over the entire translation with me and also made the first translation of two essays (Sections III and IV of this anthology). He often saved me from misapprehension of the original and clumsiness in the translation. Another colleague and friend, Professor Rudolf Mach, helped me trace several references in Madame de Staël's text. I am very grateful to the Comtesse Jean de Pange for her encouragement and help in interpreting the works of her illustrious ancestor. To the Comte Othenin d'Haussonville and to M. Jean-René Bory I am grateful for the opportunity to visit Madame de Staël's chateau at Coppet. I want to express my thanks to the Princeton University Committee on Research in the Humanities and Social Sciences for financial assistance.

Virtually all of Madame de Staël's work is included in her collected writings, *Oeuvres Complètes de Madame la Baronne de Staël-Holstein,* edited by her son Auguste de Staël, various printings beginning in 1820; the printing referred to in this book is that of 1836 and 1838, three volumes in two, published in Paris by Didot and Treuttel and Würtz. For the translations in this anthology, however, I have used critical editions wherever possible, and the *Oeuvres Complètes* only in the absence of a critical edition. The sources are, therefore, as follows:

Section I. *Considérations sur les principaux événements de la Révolution française.* (Completed in 1816, published posthumously, in 1818.) New edition, two volumes, Charpentier, Paris, 1876.

Section II. Same as Section I above.

Section III. *Des circonstances actuelles qui peuvent terminer la Révolution et des principes qui doivent fonder la République en France.* (Written in 1799, published posthumously in 1906.) Introduction and notes by John Viénot. Fischbacher, Paris, 1906. Part One, Chapter III, "De l'opinion publique."

Section IV. "A quels signes peut-on connaître quelle est l'opinion de la majorité de la nation?" (1791.) Reprinted in Vol. III, *Oeuvres Inédites de Mme. la Baronne de Staël.* (Edited by Auguste de Staël.) Three volumes, Treuttel and Würtz, Paris, 1821.

Section V. *De la Littérature considérée dans ses rapports avec les institutions sociales.* (First edition, 1800.) Critical edition by Paul van Tieghem. Two volumes, Minard, Paris, and Droz, Geneva, 1959.

Section VI. *Essai sur les Fictions.* (First edition, 1795.) Reprinted in Vol. I, *Oeuvres Complètes.*

Section VII. *De l'Allemagne.* (First edition, 1813.) New edition based upon the manuscripts and original editions by the Comtesse Jean de Pange. Five volumes, Hachette, Paris, 1958–60.

Section VIII. Same as Section I above.

Section IX. *Dix années d'exil.* (Uncompleted manuscript written 1810–13, published posthumously in 1821.) New edition based upon the manuscripts by Paul Gautier. Plon-Nourrit, Paris, 1904.

I have abridged all the works in this anthology, except Section III, which is an entire chapter of a book. I have retained the original numbers and titles Madame de Staël gave to the parts and chapters of her works. Since the reader can thus see the sources of the anthology, I have not used any device to indicate omissions from the original text. The titles of the Sections in the table of Contents are mostly mine; their purpose is to suggest the general subject in each one.

Madame de Staël's own footnotes are indicated by an asterisk and are given in roman type at the bottom of the page. My notes are indicated by numbers (1, 2, 3, etc.), and are given in italics and followed by:—Ed., except, of course, in the Introduction. I have kept my notes to a minimum, usually to identify names and references not likely to be familiar to most readers, and sometimes to help the reader with chronology.

In my Introduction and footnotes, references to the writings of Madame de Staël are to the editions, listed above, used in this translation, unless otherwise stated.

Occasionally I have inserted a few words between brackets [ ] to make an abridged passage read more smoothly.

Morroe Berger

An Introduction to the Life and Thought of Madame de Staël

BY MORROE BERGER

Madame de Staël was often linked with England and Russia as one of the three great "powers" of Europe in the nineteenth century. Many biographers, concentrating on her affairs with Benjamin Constant, Talleyrand, Narbonne, and others, have presented her as a great lover. Each of these portraits contains a germ of truth, for she certainly sought to influence events and one of her means was the men she loved and those who loved her.[1] Yet each portrait misses the real point: the *ideas*

[1] The chief sources for this account of Madame de Staël's life are (1) her own memoirs, *Dix années d'exil,* first published in 1821, four years after her death, (2) her political-biographical study, *Considérations sur les principaux événements de la Révolution française,* published in 1818, a year after her death, (3) the contemporary biography by her cousin, Madame Necker de Saussure, *Notice sur le caractère et les écrits de Madame de Staël* (1820), which appears in Volume III of the *Oeuvres Complètes* of Madame de Staël (various editions since 1820), (4) several collections of her letters, (5) *Le Salon de Madame Necker,* by Paul Othenin d'Haussonville (2 vols., Paris, 1882), and (6) *the* de Staël biography for our time, *Mistress to an Age,* by J. Christopher Herold (New York, 1958). These sources are not cited in the notes to this Introduction but others are. In the discussion of Madame de Staël's thought I do not give page references to her writings included in this anthology but I do give them for her other writings. The editions referred to are those listed

behind her desire to influence events through men of power. Her overriding passion was not love but—as the Comtesse Jean de Pange tells us[2]—liberty. Her chief aim was not power for its own sake but for the sake of liberty and enlightenment.

If others have not understood this point, it is not Madame de Staël's fault, for she herself made it plain in her life and in her brief memoirs, *Ten Years of Exile*. Soon after Napoleon helped overthrow the Directory and became First Consul, he sent his brother Joseph to Madame de Staël to persuade her to stop criticizing the new regime. "My brother," said Joseph Bonaparte, whom Madame de Staël liked and who later helped her often, "is complaining about you." Why didn't Madame de Staël rally to Napoleon like so many others? Did she want the return of the two million francs her father had left in the treasury of the guillotined King Louis XVI? Did she want the cancellation of the order of 1795 exiling her from Paris? Napoleon would give her both. "In short," Joseph reported his brother's plea, "what does she want?" Madame de Staël told the great captain through his brother: "My God, it is not a matter of what I want but of what I think."

While Napoleon expanded a territorial empire, Madame de Staël, as Sainte-Beuve observed,[3] extended her empire of the mind. She most resembled not the political powers of Europe but that great intellectual power, the *Encyclopedia* of Diderot and d'Alembert. She was its true ideological offspring. The last

---

in the editor's preface, unless otherwise indicated. Quotations from and paraphrases of Madame de Staël's writings in this anthology may be roughly placed because the discussion of her thought in this Introduction is divided into three parts. The first part is on political institutions, and refers mainly to Madame de Staël's works in Sections I, II, III, and IV. The second part on literature and society is based mainly on her works in Sections V and VI. The third part on national character refers mainly to her works in Sections VII, VIII, and IX.

[2] Introduction to *De l'Allemagne*, Vol. I, p. XI.

[3] *Portraits of Celebrated Women* (Boston, 1868), p. 155.

volumes of the *Encyclopedia* and Germaine Necker de Staël both made their appearance before the enlightened public of Paris in the spring of 1766. Each sought to encompass and spread knowledge and to influence public opinion. Each took good ideas wherever they might be found, often without acknowledgment. Each aroused the opposition of governments, censorship, suppression, and the ridicule of the paid hacks now remembered in history for nothing more than this minor role. Even in her death, Madame de Staël did not lose her capacity for the dramatic. She died in 1817 at the age of fifty-one, on July fourteenth, Bastille Day—a day of French history significant also in the life of her father and, therefore, in her own life too.

During those years she witnessed the triumph of the intellectual revolution of the eighteenth century, the flowering of the age of democracy in Europe and America, and the degradation of the democratic idea in tyranny followed by reaction. She traveled through Europe, to Russia, Scandinavia, and England, always preaching and seeking to exert influence, yet always observing, listening, and writing. Her interests—material and intellectual—extended to the United States of America which, in the fashion of the time's liberal intellectuals, she regarded as the hope of the future.

What was that hope and that future? Nothing less than the rule of reason guided by morality and right sentiment. Madame de Staël rejected the Old Regime for its superficiality, its failure to reward merit, its hollow values, its arbitrary government. She preferred the Republic once it was established but was suspicious of its demagogy and apprehensive of its tendency to degenerate into tyranny. She held fast to her faith in the rule of law, constitutionalism, and moderation in an era of extremes. She saw human beings shaped by their institutions, and so she studied institutions and wanted to see established those that encouraged reason, morality, and right sentiment.

Life

Madame de Staël inherited a name, Necker, that became famous in French history, and she in turn made famous the name, de Staël, of her first husband.

Jacques Necker was a Swiss banker whose ambition, intelligence, and careful habits made him an unobtrusive young millionaire in Paris in the 1760s. He married, in 1764, a fellow Swiss of similar background. She was Suzanne Curchod, then twenty-seven, a highly educated, dramatic woman on the rebound from a very long but unsatisfactory affair with an Englishman of her own age, Edward Gibbon, known later for his *Decline and Fall of the Roman Empire.* Together, the married couple prospered materially, socially, and intellectually. They gave birth to their only child, Anne Louise Germaine, on April 22, 1766. Necker went into diplomacy and writing, and was successful at both. Three times King Louis XVI called upon him to direct the French treasury, and in 1789 he reached the height of favor with the populace of Paris, who stormed the Bastille on his account.

Madame Necker, meanwhile, established one of the most brilliant intellectual salons of her time. She had often visited Voltaire at Ferney. Rousseau knew and thought so highly of her that he advised her guardian that Gibbon was not good enough for her. At her own salon she collected contemporaries of Rousseau, among whom were Diderot and d'Alembert, who edited the *Encyclopedia,* and others then just as illustrious who contributed to it. For a time Madame Necker even tried to raise her daughter according to the precepts of Rousseau's

Emile, which, published in 1762, four years before the girl's birth, was enjoying a vogue among intellectuals who felt that children ought to be reared in more "natural" surroundings. But this plan was soon dropped. Germaine Necker became a regular member of her mother's salon. She would sit there listening to everything, speaking only when provoked by the celebrated men who enjoyed her serious precocity and the display of her easily aroused passion and earnestness.

Though not reared in accordance with *Emile,* Germaine Necker behaved like the product of an exaggerated "progressive" school of our own day. She was bright because she had a good mind and was in earshot of the clever talk of grownups. She was talkative because "self-expression" was a good thing. She was grave because she took herself very seriously. She was easy to stir up because she was so anxious to show her cleverness and to get her opinions across to others. But such ardor did not please her mother, who admired a congealed hard intelligence that shone like a diamond rather than the warm flowing kind that engulfed everyone in its path. Something of a stylist herself, Madame Necker wrote little essays in the classical French manner. In a fragment on style, she named French as the most precise of languages. "In writing," she admonished, "one must never lose sight of grammatical purity and clarity of expression." Too much emotion, of course, might detract from both. She recommended the style of Buffon, the great naturalist who frequented her salon and who selected style as the subject of his lecture upon his admission to the French Academy. M. Buffon, she said, required of his words that "they should render his thought with precision, without exaggeration and without excess."

It is significant of Madame Necker's approach to style that she wrote to her thirteen-year-old daughter in the same vein as her classical little essays. "Your letter," she wrote Germaine in

1779, "is that of a good child, . . . but your style is a bit too emotional. Do not overreach yourself so much in order to praise and be affectionate toward me. This is a lack of taste rather common at your age. When one has lived longer, one sees that the true way to please and appeal to people is to describe one's thought"—like M. Buffon—"exactly, without exaggeration and without excess . . ."[4]

If Madame Necker treated Germaine at thirteen as though she were an adult, M. Necker was as indulgent toward his daughter at thirty as he had been when she was thirteen. And Germaine responded to him as she never did to her mother. There were no bounds to her admiration for his wisdom or to her estimate of his place among men or to her passionate love for him. This love she often expressed in conjugal as well as filial terms. She never wavered in this devotion. As a girl, she competed with her mother for her father's affections. When Madame Necker wrote an essay on M. Necker, Germaine felt she had to write one too. But the subject overwhelmed her, so she began by explaining: "I choose a subject that exceeds my capacities"—an admission she rarely made after that. "So I ask in advance," she continued, "that I be judged by my heart, and if nature has not granted me that blazing style which transmits the most ardent emotions of the soul, that it be understood that what I write is unequal to what I feel." It is easy to see why the composed Madame Necker was ruffled by her daughter's enthusiasm and her willingness to express it. Asked to choose between the literary portraits offered by his wife and daughter, M. Necker diplomatically refused. But Germaine wrote in her diary: "He admires Mother's very

[4] The quotation from Madame Necker's "Notes on Style," is from *Nouveaux Mélanges extraits des Manuscrits de Mme. Necker* (2 vols., Paris, 1801), Vol. II, p. 222. The quotation from her letter to her daughter is from d'Haussonville, *Le Salon de Madame Necker*, Vol. II, p. 41.

much, but mine compliments him more."[5] So if her mother discouraged Germaine from praising her too warmly, Germaine never in her life felt inhibited in praising her father. This proved annoying even to those who thought well of M. Necker. The American, Gouverneur Morris, who was a critical admirer of Madame de Staël, was led to comment in 1789, at the height of Necker's popularity: "I think that in my life I never saw such exuberant vanity as that of Madame de Staël upon the subject of her father."[6] A decade or so after her father's death and only a few years before her own, Madame de Staël began to write a book published posthumously in 1818 under her own title, *Considerations on the Principal Events of the French Revolution.* In a preface, she explained that her original purpose had been to present her father's political career and writings but that in the course of this work she was led, as she puts it, "by the subject itself," to retrace the principal events of nothing less than the French Revolution and to analyze the national character and institutions of England in order to justify her father's high regard for that country. So this curious juxtaposition of two rather different topics in one book follows from the simple fact that both were in some way related to M. Necker. Madame de Staël's incidental treatment of these two imposing subjects is masterful, a worthy tribute from a loving daughter to an indulgent father.

Madame de Staël's fixation upon her father did not seem to inhibit her in her relations with other men. She was never very pretty, according to the testimony of both men and women. Two years before her marriage Gibbon wrote to a friend, "Mlle. Necker, one of the greatest heiresses in Europe, is now about eighteen, wild, vain, but good-natured, and with a much

[5] *Ibid.*, Vol. II, p. 50.

[6] *The Diary and Letters of Gouverneur Morris*, ed. Anne Cary Morris, (2 vols., New York, 1888), Vol. I, p. 216.

larger provision of wit than of beauty."[7] There were plenty of suitors but the victory went to the handsome scion of a Swedish noble family fallen upon dark days. He was Eric Magnus, Baron de Staël-Holstein. By marrying Germaine Necker he allied himself with wealth and in turn he offered his title and his diplomatic position as Swedish ambassador to Paris. Indeed, the match was made upon diplomatic considerations and involved the royal families of both France and Sweden. But there is no indication that either marriage partner approached the other with enthusiastic affection. They soon were openly unfaithful to each other, and Madame de Staël bore the children of other men as well as those of Baron de Staël. For she attracted men. Though so many thought her far from beautiful and regarded her as intellectually too formidable, often socially inept, and too likely to devour those she sought out or permitted to approach her, a large number could not resist the combination of certain of her physical features which they found attractive and her brilliance and enthusiasm.

But all her relations with men were doomed to be unsatisfactory. She demanded complete fidelity both sexually and ideologically but was not prepared to sign herself over to another in the same way. Not a feminist in the modern sense of the term, she did not argue that women ought to have the *same* rights as men but that they should have those rights corresponding to their status as the sex with greater morality and sensibility. Many years after her marriage she asked, in her book, *On Germany,* why marriage should be so often "profaned" when it is truly "natural" for men and women to seek companionship in their own generation rather than with their parents or children. Her answer was that men and women are

[7] Quoted in Robert C. Whitford, *Madame de Staël's Literary Reputation in England* (University of Illinois Studies in Language and Literature, Urbana, 1918, Vol. IV, pp. 1–62), p. 9.

unequal. "Women," she wrote, "are rightfully excluded from political and public affairs; nothing is more contrary to their natural vocation than anything that would make them the rivals of men. . . . But if the destiny of women must consist in a continual act of devotion to conjugal love, the compensation for this devotion must be the scrupulous fidelity of him who is its object."

This modest claim did not prevent Madame de Staël from becoming precisely what she said women should not be: a political and intellectual rival of men. Soon after her marriage at twenty, in 1786, she leaped wholeheartedly into the political and intellectual life of her time through her salon, her writings, and through the men she attached to herself. And politics, as she came of age and entered society as the rich wife of the Swedish ambassador to Paris, was intriguing (in both senses) and was soon to become dangerous.

Extreme in her personal relations, Madame de Staël was the soul of moderation in politics. As a child of the Enlightenment, she knew the defects of the Old Regime and favored its transformation into a liberal constitutional monarchy. Dreading the possibility of violent revolution even before it occurred, she sought to help France to orderly change. She was interested in change as much as in order, however, so when the French people (in airy disregard of her wishes) made their Revolution and established a Republic, Madame de Staël welcomed its end of old abuses but advocated self-restraint to avoid the creation of new ones. She equated moderation with reason, and reason, she wrote in a passionate defense of both in 1792, was not merely a platitudinous "shade of meaning between extremes but the primary color given off by the purest rays of the sun."

Madame de Staël knew the excesses of right and left from experience. Through the positions of her father and her husband, she was able to see stark epoch-making events from the inside, while through her friends and admirers she tried to influence the course of these events.

In July 1789, Paris crowds demonstrated in front of her residence in the Swedish Embassy and demanded that M. Necker be called back as financial adviser to Louis XVI. Following her father's instructions, Madame de Staël refrained from acting but joined him in Switzerland where they learned that the Bastille had been stormed on the fourteenth and that the King had yielded and recalled Necker. She accompanied her father on his triumphal return to Paris. Writing a quarter-century later of their tumultuous greeting by the Paris crowds, she dwelt fondly upon that day, "the last of good fortune in my life." It was also the beginning of the end of prosperity for France, she added in her characteristic way of identifying the fate of France with that of her father. Necker's popularity declined as the revolutionary mood grew. He was forced to resign in 1790, and Madame de Staël was "condemned," as she put it, to record in her chronicle of France without Necker a succession of "mistakes, crimes, and misfortunes."

As Necker retired from the Paris political scene to Coppet, his daughter moved onto the stage, trying all at once to be actor, director, and prompter (not to mention critic). One of her greatest triumphs was the appointment of Louis de Narbonne, her lover and reputed father of her eldest son, as Minister of War in 1791. Such little victories for the moderate constitutionalists did not stay the Revolution in its plunge toward the Terror.

Madame de Staël knew, before the Terror, the half-menacing embrace of friendly crowds. Shortly after Bastille Day, during the momentous events of October 1789, she saw at first hand the disquieting power of government directed from the streets and courtyards. Learning on the fifth that a Paris crowd was marching on Versailles, where her father and mother were staying with the King and Queen, she hurried to join them. The next morning she saw the raucous confusion of crowd, the royal bodyguard, and the national guard under Lafayette, as some of the enthusiastic marchers forced their way to the Queen's antechamber, killed the guards but missed the Queen, who had just enough time to escape by a secret passage to the King's rooms. The demonstrators in the courtyard shouted their demand that the King go to Paris. There the government could be more directly influenced by both the advocates of a limited monarchy and the more radical groups steadily gaining power. "The populace in rebellion," Madame de Staël wrote in her later account of these events, "is usually deaf to reason and is influenced only by sensations as quick as electric shocks. . . ."

In a few years Madame de Staël also came to know the face of a hostile crowd. In June 1792 she saw twenty thousand armed people marching on the King's palace in the Tuileries "without knowing why." By this time the full force of republican and revolutionary sentiment was felt in the very centers of power. Toward the end of 1792 the Terror began. The King was tried and executed, and the Queen's trial was imminent. From her self-imposed exile in Coppet, Madame de Staël, in the summer of 1793, wrote a defense of the Queen against some of the absurd charges that Madame de Staël regarded as an affront to all women. She was swayed, as usual, by justice and sentiment; there was nothing material to be gained by defending, in a Republic, a helpless, unpopular ex-Queen who, moreover, had usually opposed Necker.

When the Terror fell, Madame de Staël helped her friends to escape the mobs and official hangmen. Then it was her turn to escape. In September of 1792 she had to brave threatening crowds during a long and frightful day as she sought to leave the country, was detained, witnessed the screaming mobs returning with blood-stained arms, and then was finally allowed, through the influence of friends, to go to the refuge her father maintained at Coppet.

She spent the years of the Terror in Switzerland and in England, where several of her friends were gathered at her expense. Most were emigrés she had saved and they lived in a mansion in Surrey, Juniper Hall, which she had rented. When the Terror finally produced its own executioners in 1794, it gave way to a corrupt regime that seemed unable, despite a new constitution, to prevent the descent into anarchy. Madame de Staël's husband, early in 1795, established relations between the French Republic and Sweden. Protected by his diplomatic status, and having seen through the press a number of political and literary articles, Madame de Staël returned to Paris in the spring of 1795. Intellectually and politically fortified by her latest admirer, Benjamin Constant, she had a plan for France which she elaborated in two essays, *Reflections on Peace, Addressed to Mr. Pitt and the French* (1794) and *Reflections on Internal Peace* (1795). The plan was to restore order and good government in France through a constitutional monarchy or a virtuous republic that would not threaten Europe, and to end the war between France and the Allies. The two elements were intimately associated in her mind. External peace could be achieved if Europe would recognize that there could be no going back to the Old Regime in France and if the French could establish a stable government based on the gains of the Revolution but determined to carry the Revolution no further. As she put it in the title of the first chapter of the second part of *Reflections on Internal Peace*, "The principles of the republican friends of order are absolutely the same as the principles of the royalist friends of liberty."

The trouble was that the two parties did not agree. Her activity was an embarrassment to everyone in a political game in which all sides sought total victory. A few months in Paris and Madame de Staël was accused of being an enemy of the Republic. In October 1795 she was ordered to leave France within ten days. Her husband's diplomatic status could only postpone execution of the sentence of exile, which was carried out in December. She spent the following year at Coppet and then the government allowed her to return to France, but only at a distance from Paris of at least twenty miles. The sentence of exile was never revoked, though its application was suspended from time to time, enabling Madame de Staël to spend some time in France, until in 1803 she was banished for more than a decade by Napoleon.

Exile was probably the central fact of Madame de Staël's political and literary existence. Coppet, so attractive to her friends and now so closely linked with her name, was in her mind a way station, a place from which to plan her return to Paris. When she entered Paris in 1814, after Napoleon's fall, she was distressed by the presence of the foreign armies in her beloved city. "The French armies, it is true," she observed condescendingly, "had several times entered almost all the capitals of Europe but none of those cities was so important to its country as Paris was to France. The monuments of fine arts, the memories of men of genius, the brilliance of society, all contributed to make Paris the center of Continental civilization." Banishment from Paris, she wrote, was "a severe punishment in such mild terms that all the flatterers of power easily turned it to ridicule." Yet, she added, the fear of exile made slaves of everyone in Napoleon's realm.

In exile, however, Madame de Staël not only tried to influence events at Paris but also wrote. She is one of those political losers who take their revenge, as Ignazio Silone puts it, in a form of political analysis that "permits them to raise themselves above the immediate historical moment. . . ." It is to such thinkers, Silone remarks—Machiavelli, Bodin, Hobbes, Montesquieu, Marx, Mazzini, Lenin, Trotsky, and Masaryk—that political science in its broadest sense owes its origin and development.[8]

Suspected by the monarchists and exiled by the republicans in 1795, Madame de Staël was to sustain even more damaging blows from the hand of Napoleon, with whom she dueled for seventeen years. Resourceful as she was, she lost every engagement in the running battle. Through her writings and his misdeeds, however, she won the war.

When they first met in 1797, Napoleon and Madame de Staël seemed to take an instantaneous aversion to each other. Being the weaker and hence perhaps the more flexible, Madame de Staël sought to win him over to her stable of men of thought and action. He resisted, repelled by her personally, as he was in general by women intellectually and politically inclined. For her part, Madame de Staël never compromised: she would either get him on her terms (political, of course) or oppose him. It was her personal misfortune that this attitude destined her to oppose the conqueror of Europe. Two years after their first meeting, Napoleon was First Consul, the most powerful man in France. But he could still be criticized openly, and in Madame de Staël's salon his own underlings were encouraged to do so. Napoleon's patience with dissent decreased as his power grew. By early 1800 he had had enough of Madame de Staël's needling. Her political collaborator, Benjamin Constant, was about to attack him in the Tribunate, though the First Consul's reaction to earlier attacks made it clear to everyone that he would not sit back quietly and take it all. At a dinner party given by Madame de Staël,

[8] *The School for Dictators* (New York, 1938), pp. 44–46.

Constant warned her, "Tonight your drawing room is filled with people whom you like. If I make my speech, it will be deserted tomorrow." Her answer was simple: "One must follow one's convictions." He spoke and his prediction proved accurate.

It was not long before the big blow came, preceded by a deceptive calm. In the summer of 1803 Madame de Staël learned that Napoleon would not object if she lived twenty-five miles from Paris. She went in September to Mafliers, northeast of Paris, and from there battered Napoleon with entreaties to permit her to return to Paris itself. So confident was she of a favorable response that she rented a house there. Disturbed by the gathering of her old friends at Mafliers and by reports of her resumption of political activity, Napoleon decided to put her at an even greater distance from Paris—a hundred miles. He sent a policeman in plain clothes to Mafliers to bring the news and facilitate her departure. Upon her insistence that, unlike a conscript, she needed more than twenty-four hours to wind up her affairs, the policeman agreed to accompany her to Paris. "I got into my carriage with my children and this officer," she bitterly commented years later in *Ten Years of Exile,* "who had been selected as the most literary of the *gendarmes.* Indeed, he complimented me on my writings. 'You see, sir,' I told him, 'what being a woman of intellect has brought me to. I pray you, if the occasion arises, to advise members of your family against it.'"

Probably because she appeared to Napoleon simultaneously as dangerous and ridiculous, Madame de Staël seemed to have both a knack for irritating him and a fatal attraction to his path. While awaiting, at Mafliers in 1803, Napoleon's response to her requests for permission to live in Paris, she received an interesting document from England. It was a defense plea in the trial of one Jean-Gabriel Peltier, a royalist emigré who had attacked Napoleon. Jittery about relations with France, the British allowed him to be brought to court and he was defended by Sir James Mackintosh, a famous lawyer and philosopher, whom Benjamin Constant had known as a student in Edinburgh and who was to become Madame de Staël's closest companion in London in 1813. At Mafliers in the "stormy days" of 1803, as Madame de Staël put it in her memoirs, she received a copy of Mackintosh's well-known defense of Napoleon's critic, which she found very moving. A few days later she received Napoleon's unfavorable answer. Crushed, she made her plans to go to Germany, and found time to jab her persecutor by translating Mackintosh's plea into French.[9]

As literary and political enemies bent before Napoleon's growing might and fed his appetite for praise, Madame de Staël refused to mention him by name in her books or to refer to him favorably if indirectly. She did not cease to oppose him or to try to get him to rescind the order of exile. Her books and the gossip about her always reached Napoleon, and he had his own police reports to keep him in touch with her. The only place where she could be happy was Paris, the very center of her adversary's empire. But Paris was too small for these two personalities, and even Europe and all of Russia, it seemed, offered inadequate space for them.

Napoleon's attitude hardened with time. He was less amused or repelled than worried by Madame de Staël and her friends, her popularity in Europe, and her highly regarded books. Harried for years, she seriously considered leaving Europe entirely. Napoleon permitted her to enter France in the spring of 1810 in order to embark for the United States of America. She brought along the manuscript of her *De l'Allemagne*,

[9] *Memoirs of the Life of Sir James Mackintosh*, ed. Robert James Mackintosh (2 vols., Boston, 1853), Vol. I, pp. 181–82.

which she hoped would restore her to life in Paris. It proved, instead, to be the occasion for another blow. After thousands of copies had already been printed, the book was destroyed by order of Napoleon himself. The beaten author lacked the strength to go to America in these circumstances. She returned to Coppet, only to find herself increasingly restricted in her adversary's realm. People were now afraid to visit Coppet, only a few years after its heyday as a center of cultural and intellectual brilliance. Restricted to Geneva and to the area within five miles of Coppet, she decided to escape to England, one of the few places Napoleon had not yet conquered which she felt she could endure.

It is curious that she decided she could get to England only through Russia. For at that time, in the spring of 1812, Napoleon too was planning to enter Russia. He led his Grand Army into Russian territory in June, and a few weeks later Madame de Staël was racing across its vast extent to get to Moscow by another route. She toured Russia triumphantly as Napoleon fought his way through its endless spaces. Three months later she left St. Petersburg for Finland, en route to England, only one week before Napoleon, on September 14, entered abandoned Moscow.

Less than two years later, in May 1814, the familiar roles were reversed: Madame de Staël was in Paris, Napoleon in exile. She was more gracious in victory than he, having no empire to protect. When she heard of a plot to murder him at Elba, she hurried to his brother Joseph and suggested that she herself carry the warning to Napoleon. If she took this proposal seriously, Joseph did not and sent someone less conspicuous. Napoleon conveyed his thanks to his old enemy.

Madame de Staël, as might be expected, had the last word. She devoted many pages of her posthumous *Considerations on the Principal Events of the French Revolution* to Napoleon's character, career, and the damage he caused. She insisted that her judgment was not swayed by his persecution of her, and one may well believe this. Madame de Staël was interested in his public role; she studiously avoided his private life. Knowing herself as well as she knew Napoleon, she remarked that she was even tempted, in his defeat, to defend him now that his erstwhile sycophants vied in their condemnation of him—these calumnies she found viler than the adulation. But she had to criticize him even in his downfall because his ideas still prevailed in the minds of many of his enemies as well as his supporters. All that he left of his "terrible power," she commented with satisfaction and a touch of pity, was the "baneful knowledge of a few more secrets in the art of tyranny."

Back in Paris, Madame de Staël had a more brilliant salon than ever. She was known and admired by those very sovereigns and statesmen of Europe who, like her, had fought Napoleon and who now were settling the future of France. When she had first entered the political scene about a quarter-century earlier, she had to attach brilliant men to herself because, as a woman, she could not enter public life, and her husband proved to be too weak to serve as her instrument. This is why she combined love with politics. In the last three years of her life, however, she could exert influence directly.

She was famous in Europe not only through her books but also through her travels in exile. She had glided through Italy, Germany, Russia, and England, meeting royalty, learning about new intellectual and literary currents, encouraging opposition to Napoleon in the name of liberty—and always talking, talking, talking. Conversation—and the company of people it implied—was both pleasure and necessity to her. She judged individuals, classes and even nations, all too often, by their conversational ability. Of the Russians, for example, she wrote in *Ten Years of Exile* that she found them sincere but not good talkers. In her enlightened way she attributed this deficiency not to innate traits but to environment, so to speak—"as they are in general not highly educated," she explained, "they find little pleasure in serious conversation and do not take pride in a scintillating display of it."

Her power of speech overwhelmed everyone, and she was never inhibited in foreign lands and tongues. Goethe, whom she met in Germany, noted that philosophical talk "was her special delight and passion." This fact aroused his own "evil genius" and, like the great men in her mother's salon thirty years earlier, he enjoyed contradicting her to the point where she became desperate, brilliant, and charming. Another German, the Prussian General Karl von Clausewitz, who fought against Napoleon and wrote on strategy, was likewise impressed when he visited Coppet in 1807. "Mme. de Staël," he noted carefully in a letter to his wife, "speaks a great deal and very interestingly, so that one does not really get tired listening to her. One does not get very far here with stereotyped phrases." He gallantly reported, also, that she could even stop talking, for "nobody makes a witty remark without her pausing to express her delight."[10] Such habits were hard on her friends, but there were compensations. If she taxed them with her talk she at least brought out the best talk in them. Her cousin and first biographer pointed out that Madame de Staël, to whom friendship was sacred though far from indestructible, did not give her friends security of tenure but evaluated their performance every day, and even in their presence. She once said to Madame de Staël, "With you, one must submit to being judged anew each morning." Madame de Staël replied: "What does it matter, if I love the more each evening!"

[10] Letters of Aug. 16 and Oct. 5, 1807, in *Karl und Marie von Clausevitz: Ein Lebensbild in Briefen und Tagebuchblätten,* ed. Karl Linnebach (Berlin, 1917), pp. 132, 146–47.

At the height of her intellectual powers and political influence in Restoration Paris, Madame de Staël had not many mornings and evenings left to live. As always, she was writing, this time her *Considerations on the Principal Events of the French Revolution,* which she was able to complete but not to see published. Her intense emotional life, her travels, her high pitch of activity were all achieved at the expense of her physical strength. Her mental powers remained unimpaired. In 1817 she suffered a stroke, improved slightly and then, just past the age of fifty-one, she succumbed and died, on the twenty-eighth anniversary of the day the Paris crowds took the Bastille and forced Louis XVI to bring back her father. Two weeks later her body was placed at the foot of his, in the tomb at Coppet that he had built to preserve his wife's body. The tomb had been sealed after receiving the body of M. Necker in 1804. His worshipful daughter had had a sculpture made and placed above the iron door, where it remains today, showing M. Necker ascending to heaven guided by an angel (Madame Necker?) as his kneeling daughter weeps below. The sealed iron door was opened again in 1817 to receive the body of Madame de Staël, and it has not been disturbed since.

The stone tomb, surrounded by the graves of Madame de Staël's eldest son and several other descendants, stands today in the shadows of a wood a couple of hundred yards from the chateau of Coppet. Between the tomb and the chateau a road now leads from the railroad station to the main street, which runs for two or three blocks parallel to Lake Leman. The chateau goes back to the thirteenth century but was given its present form in the eighteenth. It stands on a hill several hundred yards from the lake. The little town, which now obstructs the chateau's view of the lake, grew up in the nineteenth century. It is a quiet suburb of Geneva, ten miles away. Along the main street, which has no sidewalks, there are a few shops, the old church, small hotels and restaurants, the post office, and piers. One recent summer the window of a clothing store displayed a poster advertising the brand of the blue jeans worn by a champion rodeo cowboy from Melrose, Montana. Upon the hill the old mansion no longer dominates the surroundings. But inside, many of the rooms, open to the public, remain as they were when Madame de Staël and her friends gave the house its most glorious days.

Relations with Americans

In May 1817, bedridden from her stroke two months earlier and only two months away from death, Madame de Staël received a young American from New England who had come to Europe to seek knowledge in the Germany he had learned about from her book. He was George Ticknor, who was later to revolutionize instruction in languages and literature at Harvard University. Standing before the famous woman, he realized a great ambition. "At last," he wrote in his journal, "I have seen Mad. de Staël." She spoke to him of the United States of America. "You are the vanguard of the human race," she told him, "you are the future of the world."[11]

Madame de Staël never set foot on American soil, but she had varied interests there. Like so many European liberals, she regarded America as a new society unhindered by old impediments to freedom and to individual self-development. In her moments of greatest despair in exile, she frequently contemplated emigration to America. And she had large capital

[11] *Life, Letters, and Journals of George Ticknor* (2 vols., Boston and New York, 1909), Vol. I, pp. 132–33. On Madame de Staël's relationship with Americans, see Richmond L. Hawkins, *Madame de Staël and the United States* (Cambridge, Massachusetts, 1930).

investments there. These three interests—ideological, personal, financial—made her eager to correspond with and meet leading representatives of the young republic that was a model of the moderate republicanism she came to profess. They were Americans who had retained certain ties with Europe through ancestry, ideology, or personal tastes—Thomas Jefferson, Gouverneur Morris, Albert Gallatin, John Quincy Adams, and others. She was content to admire the new country without trying to shape it, though she did make an unsystematic attempt to influence American policy in the War of 1812.

Writing in 1816 of British overseas policy, Madame de Staël predicted: "There is a nation which will one day be very great—the Americans." Only slavery, she felt, marred its perfection but when that was eliminated the world would not be able to withhold the profoundest respect for American institutions. "What is there more honorable for mankind," she asked in her book on the French Revolution, "than this new world which has established itself without the prejudices of the old?—this new world where religion exists in all its fervor without needing the support of the state to maintain it, where the law commands by the respect it inspires although no military power backs it up." She made the same point about the same time in a letter to Thomas Jefferson. "If you succeeded in doing away with slavery in the South," she told him, "there would be at least one government in the world as perfect as human reason can conceive it."[12]

[12] Letter from Pisa, 6 Jan. 1816, in Gilbert Chinard, "La Correspondance de Madame de Staël avec Jefferson," *Révue de Littérature Comparée*, 1922, 2:636. This was not mere flattery and hyperbole. Madame de Staël showed her genuine admiration for the American republic in some notes for a substantial discussion of American government that she planned to include in an unfinished work (discovered and published posthumously): *Des circonstances actuelles qui peuvent terminer la Revolution*, ed. John Viénot (Paris, 1906), Supplement, pp. 335–37.

Many years earlier Madame de Staël had indicated her high expectations for American culture. After reviewing the relations between literature and society down to the French Revolution, she would have liked to consider "what must be the character of the literature of a great nation, an enlightened nation, among whom are established liberty, political equality, and the customs consistent with its institutions." The Revolution might have made France such a nation but it degenerated into tyranny. "There is," however, she pointed out in her major work on literature, "only one nation in the world to which some of these reflections are already appropriate: it is the Americans." Though they did not yet have a well-developed literature in her view, their civil officials had already acquired in their art of governing the "most useful secrets of style." That is to say, in their appeals to public opinion "they are eminently talented in stirring all the emotions by the expression of simple truths and honest sentiments. . . ."

Through her father's and her own investments, Madame de Staël had by her own estimate[13] a fortune of one million and a half francs in United States land, bonds, and banks. It is not known whether these investments were intended only to make money or also to provide property and income in America should Madame de Staël one day find it necessary to emigrate there. And even after she no longer intended to go to America herself, she hoped her son would settle there. On these two matters, her investments and her interest in going to America, she corresponded for many years with Gouverneur Morris, Albert Gallatin, Jefferson, and her American agents (one of whom was the father of James Fenimore Cooper).[14] From time to time she sought reassurance about her invest-

[13] Letter to Albert Gallatin, 30 (23?) Sept. 1814, in Henry Adams, *The Life of Albert Gallatin* (Philadelphia, 1880), p. 532.

[14] Hawkins, p. 26.

ments. In 1805, Morris wrote to her that her interests were in "good hands" and that the value of her land in New York State could not fail to rise because the region was "increasingly sought after by the colonists of New England, whom we call *Yankees* and who are indeed among the best."[15]

When the United States went to war against England in 1812, Madame de Staël was alarmed on two counts. She was concerned about the fate of her investments, and she was disturbed because England's capacity to carry on the war against Napoleon might be reduced. She badgered leading Americans on both points, but it was clear, at least to John Quincy Adams, that the political issue was of the greater consequence to her. They met in September 1812 in St. Petersburg, where Adams was U. S. Minister to Russia and Madame de Staël was en route to England, then already at war with the United States. Adams was not favorably disposed toward the celebrated fugitive because he knew she was an Anglophile. She called him to her hotel to ask him about her American investments. Adams wrote in his diary that she wanted to know "how she could continue to receive her interest in England while there is war between the United States and Great Britain. This introduced a conversation upon the war, which appeared to be to her a topic far more interesting than the affairs upon which she had sent to consult me."[16]

In a letter to his father nearly a year later, Adams recalled that Madame de Staël had demanded to know why America was fighting England and not Napoleon. She did not deny that the United States had a just grievance against England but, Adams comments ironically, she thought that the "knight-errants of the human race" deserved to be indulged because

[15] *Diary and Letters*, Vol. II, p. 465.

[16] *Memoirs of John Quincy Adams*, ed. Charles Francis Adams (12 vols., Philadelphia, 1874–77), Vol. II, p. 400.

they were also fighting Napoleon. Adams told her that Americans regarded Britain not as "the champion for the liberties of mankind but as another tyrant." He agreed Napoleon was likewise a tyrant, but America, he told Madame de Staël, did not join the war against him because it lacked the means, did not want to get into Europe's quarrels, and felt it unnecessary because the Emperor already had enough enemies.[17] Madame de Staël was not satisfied. A month later, in Stockholm, she wrote to Jefferson arguing that the United States, in fighting England, was allowing itself to become Napoleon's tool. She insisted that America, as a free country, must help free Europe from tyranny. Jefferson answered in May 1813, taking a position rather like that of Asian and African leaders today when they are asked why they continue to attack Western imperialism but ignore Russian tyranny over other countries. "Europe," wrote the former President of the young republic, "feels and is writhing under the scorpion whips of Bonaparte, we are assailed by those of England. . . . Each has to grapple with the enemy immediately pressing on itself. We must extinguish the fire kindled in our own house and leave to our friends beyond the water that which is consuming theirs."[18]

Even as Madame de Staël prodded the Americans, an opportunity arose to open negotiations for peace between Britain and the United States, and she was able to play some part in the preliminary arrangements. In the course of the next year she became more sympathetic to the American position.

In March 1813 Secretary of State James Monroe learned that Emperor Alexander of Russia was willing to mediate between Britain and the United States to end the war. Secretary of the Treasury Albert Gallatin, born in Switzerland and a

[17] *Writings of John Quincy Adams,* ed. Worthington Chauncey Ford (7 vols., New York, 1913–17), Vol. IV, pp. 452–53.

[18] Chinard, p. 629.

distant relative of Madame de Staël, persuaded President Madison to send him on the mission to Russia to get in touch with Alexander. But the British representatives in St. Petersburg prevented the Americans from reaching the Emperor. Meanwhile, in March 1814 the Allied armies defeated Napoleon, and the British were even less disposed toward peace with the Americans, and indeed seemed bent upon punishing them. It was thus more important than ever for the American representatives to reach Emperor Alexander, who was now in Paris to discuss the future of defeated France with the other victorious leaders. The British, however, were still able to seal him off from the importunate Americans. The United States Minister in Paris asked General Lafayette for help. Madame de Staël knew the hero of the Americans well. Just a quarter-century earlier, in October 1789, she and he had both been at Versailles when the Paris crowds closed in and forced the King to go to Paris. She also knew Alexander well, having met and won him in St. Petersburg in August 1812.

In London Gallatin anxiously waited to hear whether Alexander could be reached. Lafayette wrote him on May 25, 1814, that he had been able to get a note from the American minister in Paris delivered to Alexander. "I expect this evening," he informed Gallatin, "to meet the Emperor of Russia at a friend's house, and shall try to obtain some conversation on the subject." That night he did see the Emperor—at the house of Madame de Staël.

Three weeks later Gallatin finally met Alexander after more than a year of fruitless attempts. The significance of the meeting is that Russia's intervention was instrumental in diverting Britain from continuing the war against the United States.[19]

Shortly afterward, in July 1814, Madame de Staël offered

[19] Henry Adams, pp. 477–78, 499–516.

Gallatin further aid. In September, not hearing from him, she wrote to him again, this time asking about her American investments and for news of other matters, presumably of the peace negotiations then in progress. "I perhaps merit," she bluntly stated, "some kindness for my efforts to help you. Lord Wellington claims that I never see him without lecturing to him about America." In October Gallatin replied that he could tell her nothing about the peace negotiations, and denounced the British burning of the White House in August, of which he had just heard. The negotiations were set back by this "act of vandalism," he told her, "unequalled during twenty years of war in Europe." As to Madame de Staël's own financial problem, Gallatin assured her that he understood why she might feel concern for American investments. To sell now, he declared, would mean a great loss. If the war continued, he admitted, her investments would decline in value but, he added, his country would always pay the interest on its bonds and their value would climb back to par six months after peace. He took note of her reminder of the help she had extended. "I fully appreciate everything you have done to be of help to America," he wrote.

Just as she had berated the Americans for unintentionally aiding Napoleon by fighting the British, Madame de Staël now reminded them of her help in getting the victorious British to negotiate an end to the war. She wrote Jefferson early in 1816 as she had already written Gallatin: "I do not know whether the newspapers have informed you that I supported your American cause against a very noble adversary, the Duke of Wellington." And she added: "Our family is still a little intellectual island where Franklin, Washington, and Jefferson are revered as in their own country."[20] When she met Henry Clay, who was on the American commission sent to negotiate the

[20] Chinard, p. 636.

end of the war, she reminded him, too, of her help, for which he acknowledged his country's gratitude. She told him that the British had contemplated sending Wellington against the Americans after Napoleon's defeat. Clay replied he was sorry they had not done so because if the Americans had lost to Wellington it would have been no disgrace, whereas if they had defeated him that would have been a great credit. Soon afterward, Madame de Staël entertained Clay at her home. She sat him next to the Duke of Wellington and then told the conqueror of Napoleon what the American had said. Wellington remarked that if he had been sent against the United States and won, he would have considered it the "proudest feather in my cap."[21]

After Napoleon's defeat, Madame de Staël found it possible to sympathize with the American attitude toward Britain. Wishing Gallatin success in his efforts with Emperor Alexander, she told the American, in July 1814, that she now supported the United States against Britain as she had earlier supported the latter against Napoleon. "I now find you oppressed on the side of liberty and you represent the cause that attached me to England a year ago."[22] Two years later she was nearing the end of her *Considerations on the Principal Events of the French Revolution.* In her discussion of British overseas policy, she observed that the Americans had declared war on England at a bad time from the viewpoint of Europe. But no one could suspect America of favoring Napoleon, she hastened to add. It was simply that America, so far away from Europe's concerns, was acting for her own interest. America's ignorance of European affairs, however, did not justify the British burning of the capital. The British destroyed not a

[21] *The Works of Henry Clay,* ed. Calvin Colton (10 vols., New York, 1904), Vol. I, pp. 119–20.

[22] Henry Adams, p. 531.

military target but "peaceful buildings dedicated to national representation, public education, the transplantation of the arts and sciences in a country only recently covered with forests and conquered only by the labors of men against wild nature."

Madame de Staël affected the Americans she met as she did other men of equal reserve and sophistication. They stood a little in awe of her even when they came to know her intimately, fearing she might overwhelm them with her enthusiasm and good will.

High-minded and introspective, John Quincy Adams found her "a little too broad and direct."[23] That was in Russia in 1812. Three years later he visited her in her Paris home, where he met Lafayette and Benjamin Constant. Though he had heard much about her salon, Adams laconically noted in his diary: "The conversation was not very interesting."[24] The more cosmopolitan and pleasure-loving Gouverneur Morris had, a quarter-century before, just after the great events of 1789, found her salon more interesting. "She is a woman of wonderful wit, and above prejudices of every kind," he observed. "Her house is a kind of temple of Apollo, where the men of wit and fashion are collected. . . ." But he did not always find the gathering so stimulating. A few weeks later he noted in his diary: "At Madame de Staël's this evening I meet the world. Stay some time in various conversation, altogether of no consequence."[25]

Yet the Americans knew Madame de Staël herself was "of consequence." Three days after her death in July 1817, Gallatin wrote to Jefferson of this "public loss." He told the former President, who had met Madame de Staël in Paris before 1789: "She was a power by herself, and had more influence on pub-

[23] *Writings*, Vol. IV, p. 451.
[24] *Memoirs*, Vol. III, p. 155.
[25] *Diary and Letters*, Vol. I, pp. 278–79, 371.

lic opinion, and even on the acts of government, than any other person not in the ministry. I may add that she was one of your most sincere admirers."[26]

Madame de Staël's Thought

Madame de Staël absorbed the leading ideas of the Enlightenment on literature, politics, science, and the social order. She turned many of these ideas to her own uses and then bequeathed them to the nineteenth century, which adopted much of the Enlightenment through her works. She had two leading aims, one intellectual and one political, which are almost inseparable in her thought. The first was to explain all literature (both imaginative and analytical) by its relation to social institutions. The second was to guide Europe as it entered the republican era and to help it maintain its cultural legacy and its liberty, for liberty was essential to progress itself.

The three main subjects of this anthology are closely connected in Madame de Staël's thought. Literature, itself shaped by a nation's character, is the measure of the learning of both the best minds and the ordinary ones. Literature in this broad sense in turn helps shape a nation's government and political institutions. In their turn, political institutions, taken as the arrangement of social life in general rather than merely narrow governmental forms, shape the character of a nation. National character, finally is both a determinant and a product of social institutions and thought. How to break into this tight circle? Madame de Staël never dealt with this question explicitly, but her approach suggests that she would have given the role of prime mover to great thinkers and wise rulers who seize a

[26] Henry Adams, p. 566.

propitious time to put forward noble ideas; when there are no special impediments such as tyranny or overwhelming ignorance, society adopts such ideas.

The idea of progress, which she distinguished in several fields, is central in Madame de Staël's thought. She believed that progress in physical science and technology was steady and cumulative. She believed that there was steady progress, also, in "philosophy," that is, in man's understanding of his own social life. Progress in these two domains meant that there was progress in human society itself, for mankind was achieving increasing control and direction of both physical and human nature. There was also progress in the arts, according to Madame de Staël, but here, as in the advance of moral ideas, it was occasionally interrupted by tyranny and the obliteration of freedom. She not only saw progress in the life of the individual and of nations but also looked forward, as had earlier heralds of progress like Condorcet, to progress everywhere in the world of man. One of the main problems of the time, she felt, was the need to remove inequalities between nations too. Following Montesquieu's analysis of the decline of Rome, she warned that Europe could not remain at peace if wide disparities remained between the nations. "The advantages of society," she said of the Northern invasions, "had to become universal, for everything in nature tends toward the same level." The equalizing of economic and cultural advantages, she optimistically believed, would reduce international rivalry.[27]

Not exactly a bourgeoise herself, Madame de Staël believed in the progressive influence of the middle class. In her memoirs, *Ten Years of Exile,* she remarks: "There is no third estate in Russia. This is a great hindrance to the progress of literature

[27] *De la Littérature,* Vol. I, p. 128 (Part One, Ch. VII).

and the fine arts, for it is usually in this middle class that learning is developed." As to the elimination of the French monarchy, she had opposed that rashness but graciously accepted it after the fact. "If I had been asked," she modestly wrote, "I certainly would not have recommended the establishment of a republic in France; but once it was in existence, I did not think it ought to be overturned."[28]

The historical importance Madame de Staël attached to the bourgeoisie is made quite explicit in her delineation of the "stages" of modern history in terms of who has power and who enjoys liberty. This statement, like so many others she made, drew upon ideas frequently expressed or merely suggested by other thinkers, yet her own contribution of clarity and explicitness ought not to be underrated. She began by pointing out that modern history started with the Northern invasions after the decline of Roman civilization. In this she followed a well-established intellectual tradition in which Bodin, for example, preceded her with a kind of racial division of history, and Hegel, her contemporary, offered a national interpretation.

Madame de Staël's interpretation of the three stages within the modern era, however, is probably somewhat more original. She begins with feudalism, the first stage, in which the economy was local, industry and commerce not developed, and land the only important form of property. The lords of the manor exercised power and only they were free. This period was followed by a "partial emancipation," that is, the rise of the bourgeois class in the towns. This class achieved freedom as individuals through their free municipalities and small republics, while the other unfree classes remained so. Because this partial emancipation did not extend beyond these local

[28] *Considérations sur les principaux événements de la Révolution française*, in *Oeuvres Complètes*, Vol. III, p. 193b (Part Three, Ch. XXV, first par.).

realms, Madame de Staël chose not to count this period as a stage in itself.

The second proper stage of the modern era, she said, is that of despotism. The kings increased their power at the expense of the nobles and made alliances with the populace, or third estate. National governments came into being and grew stronger and more centralized. Commerce developed in this period. The clergy's monopoly of learning was ended as intellectual, geographic, and scientific discoveries were made at an increasing pace.

The third stage is that of representative government, the beginning of the royal sharing of power with the people. Thus far, said Madame de Staël, only England had reached that point, but all Europe was moving in the direction indicated by the English and French revolutions of the seventeenth and eighteenth centuries.

Thus did Madame de Staël sketch the "stages" of modern Europe in a way that historiography still follows today (albeit with more qualifications and less confidence): medieval Feudalism, Renaissance and absolutism, and representative government.

Such historical summaries only confirmed Madame de Staël's fundamental optimism about the future of humanity. The great intellectual dispute as to who were superior, the ancients or the moderns, was practically spent in her time, but she entered the battle anyway, and of course came down on the side of the moderns. Many things aroused her ire but one thing that exasperated her was an argument from tradition. "We submit to certain received ideas," she remarked in her book on Germany, "not because they are true but because they are powerful." Guarding against such tendencies, she showed the absurdity of the argument based merely upon the past. "It is humiliating," she wrote in *Considerations on the Principal*

Events of the French Revolution, "to go back to the evidence of history to prove that something as absurd as it is unjust ought to be neither adopted nor maintained. . . . It would be interesting to know which generation among our ancestors was granted infallibility, which is that past era that ought to be a model for the present and from whose course we cannot deviate without falling into pernicious innovations? . . . It will be easy to oppose to the old order of things that you invoke another order of things still older which it replaced."

Though she believed in human perfectibility and the irresistible march of progress, Madame de Staël revealed pessimistic overtones. She associated levity with irresponsibility and superficiality, melancholy with seriousness and profound thought. She believed in progress because it was an article of faith among intellectuals in the eighteenth century, but she believed in the value of melancholy because, she felt, it brought out mankind's higher intellectual and moral talents. Melancholy arose in the cold and dreary climate of the North. It derived from the contemplation of the horrors of history, the impediments to progress, the road that mankind had yet to travel to reach perfection rather than the distance it had already come. Melancholy, according to Madame de Staël, supplied the impetus to continued progress by making the best minds dissatisfied with the state of their world. She seemed to believe that happy people did not strive, that contentment meant stagnation. Melancholy, then, was closely connected with *emulation,* by which she meant that passion of the individual for fame and recognition that stimulates intense efforts to achieve noble goals.

Madame de Staël's fundamental optimism, consisted not in the idea that mankind *ought* to improve or that it was merely *desirable* to eliminate material and intellectual poverty, but that things *could* be improved. This was the faith of the eighteenth century, whether based upon the idea that the road to progress was through governmental action or only the beneficial result of each man seeking his own advantage unhindered by government. The radical nature of this faith in the *possibility* of improvement is emphasized in Disraeli's political novel, *Sybil; or the Two Nations*, written in 1844. A peer is told that the novel's hero has said in the House of Lords that conservatism can retain power only if it promotes the people's happiness. His reply to this warning is another one: "Well, that is sheer radicalism; pretending that the people can be better off than they are, is radicalism and nothing else."[29]

At least one common notion about Madame de Staël is accurate: she was both a "classicist" and a "romantic." Though she did not originate this distinction, it achieved wide currency through her books, *Literature Considered in Its Relation to Social Institutions* and the better-known *On Germany*. She distinguished between the outlook and culture of the warm, sunny South and that of the cold, misty North. The former is rationalist, conventional, clear, witty, imaginative, sensuous. The latter is brooding, introspective, serious, gloomy, emotional. Madame de Staël saw virtues in both, drawing upon various strands of the thought of the Enlightenment as well as upon Rousseau, the great critic of artificiality and conventionality.

Repelled by the courtly emphasis upon form at the expense of feeling and ideas, Madame de Staël extolled sentiment, passion, and enthusiasm in both life and art. She was "romantic," too, in espousing the cause of the most numerous of the disadvantaged minorities of her time, women. In politics, however, she was moderate and "classical," for she believed that order and tranquillity were necessary not only to progress but also

[29] (London, 1926), p. 326 (Book V, Ch. I.).

to the kind of passionate existence she thought individuals and nations should lead. To permit emotional flights, something had to be anchored and the anchor was government. If everything was loose, and mobile, then there would be no virtue and good taste; vulgarity from below and cynicism from above would between them crush noble expression and liberty.

Just as she combined classical with romantic elements, Madame de Staël also believed in a right combination of reason and emotion. In accord with eighteenth-century notions, she believed that the passions checked each other, that passion must activate reason, and that reason must guide emotion and conduct. She believed in the superiority of reason but she did not regard it as adequate in itself, or, indeed, as uniformly triumphant over emotion. Reason had to be accompanied by right sentiment to put wisdom into effect. Commitment, strong feelings, and enthusiasm were necessary to strengthen and humanize reason.

In her major works Madame de Staël spoke for both reason and passion, but in *Literature Considered in Its Relation to Social Institutions* she stressed the former and in *On Germany* the latter. So impressed was she with German imagination and speculation that she asked whether there was not "a germ of truth concealed in all the fables and beliefs branded with the name of madness." She did not want to see thought impeded by either ignorance or sophistication. "Superstitious eras," she remarked, "easily accuse new ideas of impiety and skeptical eras accuse them no less easily of absurdity." Was it not a good thing, too, she asked, that science should exclude itself from some realms? Lest she go too far in this direction, however, Madame de Staël drew back quickly, insisting that reason may impose limits upon itself even when it resists shackles imposed from outside. "Reason," as she had said earlier in *Literature*, "has nothing to fear from reason."

Denunciations of what we now call "mass culture" were already frequent before Madame de Staël's time, when it was feared that literature and art would be debased if they had to appeal to the untrained bourgeoisie. Madame de Staël feared this decline but she did not blame the populace for it. As a "romantic," she defended popular taste, but she believed at the same time that it must be always guided by the best minds. If the masses were without taste, that was the sign of the failure of their betters—the failure of "eloquence." The public's judgment in the arts, according to Madame de Staël in *On Germany*, is usually valid. "When the learned man's ideas," she added, "do not agree with this impression, it is not because these ideas are too profound but rather because they are not profound enough."

"Eloquence," wrote George Santayana, "is a republican art, as conversation is an aristocratic one."[30] Characteristically, Madame de Staël wanted to have both. She saw the revival of eloquence as a means of arousing people to the dangers of the artificial life under the Old Regime, the barbarism of revolution carried to excess, and the tyranny of the Napoleonic reaction. "I still believe," she wrote in *Literature*, "that if speech uttered before a large number of people and books judged by the entire public have no effect whatever, then it is the orators and the writers who are to blame." Conversation, however, was an absolute necessity in her private life. Expression of all kinds became confused in her practice. She would recite to her guests the manuscripts of her books. To her, conversation was not merely an amusing way for clever people to pass the time, but a means of testing ideas and persuading others. Madame de Staël, therefore, did not have the eighteenth-century distrust of eloquence. Believing in the support the

[30] *Character and Opinion in the United States*, (New York, 1920), p. 3.

passions could give to reason, she wanted eloquence in speech and writing to arouse those passions on behalf of truth and moderation.

Madame de Staël's respect for language led her, in *On Germany,* to advocate it, rather than mathematics or natural science, as the basis of education. She believed that mathematics could provide the basis for a science of human affairs but that it inculcated a certain rigidity in children and did not develop the capacity to understand people different from ourselves. Natural science, on the other hand, as taught to children, is only "an erudite toy that accustoms us to systematic amusement and superficial study." Arguing against a trend in her day (similar to one in ours, apparently) toward teaching science as a game, she warned: "Education through amusement dissipates thought. . . . Improvement in infancy depends upon work, in later life upon suffering. . . . You may show your child a lot of things with pictures and cards, but you will not teach him to learn; and the propensity for amusement, which you direct toward the sciences, will soon follow another course when the child is no longer under your control."

Language, according to Madame de Staël, has been the basis of the education of the best minds in Europe. Language lends itself to learning by steps. "The study of grammar," she argued, "requires the same coherence and power of attention as mathematics but it depends much more upon thought." And, she added in one of her frequent analogies that seem pregnant with elusive meaning, "Grammar connects ideas as calculation links numbers."

If Madame de Staël slighted mathematics as a means for the education of children, she certainly elevated its role in the development of a science of politics (or of human affairs in general, that is, social science). She believed that the calculus of probability, developed in the previous century, could one day make an exact science of "philosophy," the analysis and understanding of human behavior and social institutions. She believed, as did other thinkers before her, that the "human sciences" must follow the model of the physical sciences, but she always insisted that human needs and judgments—morality—must be the ultimate criteria, superior even to the calculus of probability.

Much is sometimes made of Madame de Staël's emphasis upon the influence of climate on human dispositions and behavior. In the first place, this element of her thought is usually exaggerated. Though she often pointed to climate as the cause of melancholy, for example, she explicitly subordinated it to social institutions as a molder of attitudes and behavior (as I shall show in a later section of this review of her thought). Second, her emphasis upon climate, following Montesquieu and others, did not imply in her time what it implies in ours. To us it seems to be a rigid limitation upon human self-direction, but to the seventeenth and eighteenth centuries it was "environmental" and therefore something to which man could better adjust and adapt than he could to the divine and occult forces that were formerly believed to shape his fate.

As to divine force itself, Madame de Staël never invoked it as an explanation. She frequently attacked religious fanaticism, yet never doubted the validity and value of religious feeling confined to the supernatural and to morality. She seemed not to need religion herself, however. John Quincy Adams, writing to his father in 1813 after having met Madame de Staël in Russia, reported: "She had much to say about social order, much about universal morality, much about the persecution of *religion,* in which she gave me to understand that she did not herself believe. . . ."[31] She considered that religion need not conflict with science because both are in accord with reason. "Providence," she assured her readers, "has not given us any human faculty of which we are forbidden to make use." Far from detracting from religion, therefore, science increases our appreciation of God. "Philosophy, that is to say, the knowledge of cause and effect, arouses the admiration of all thinkers for the totality of the great work of the Creation; but each separate aspect of it is given an ordinary explanation."

From the exalted role she gave to "philosophy" or social science and the effort she made to practice and promote it, we may infer that Madame de Staël thought of herself as a "philosopher" rather than a literary critic or literary historian. She was, then, one of the French forerunners of sociology who sought, in an age of great change, the principles that might explain how people retained their customary institutions. But her nineteenth-century contemporaries and successors, Maistre, Comte, and Tocqueville, were more conservative than she. Madame de Staël sought not only stability, order, hierarchy, group ties, and religious fidelity, but also progress, free movement of people and ideas, individualism, and secularism.

The study of how these human values develop and may be promoted was, to Madame de Staël, the very highest form of thought, since it tried to penetrate the complex world of mankind, not merely the more regular world of nature. She referred to social science as "that higher philosophy which judges of nations and kings." It is therefore a challenge, not a handmaid, to power. Natural science and imaginative litera-

[31] Letter to John Adams, from St. Petersburg, 22 March 1813, *Writings*, Vol. IV, p. 453.

ture are less dangerous to authority. Indeed, "nothing pleases absolute monarchs more than men so deeply occupied with the physical laws of the world that they leave the human realm to whoever is determined to take it." As to literature: "Poetry has more often been dedicated to the praise of despotic power than to its censure."

Madame de Staël's faith in social science was profound, but she confined her optimism to the kind that followed the model of natural science. On this point, as in her views on probability, she adopted many ideas already well known in her time; her specific debt, however, seems to be to Condorcet. Pure reason was not enough to insure scientific growth. Abstract systems had already been denounced in the *Encyclopedia.* The new method called for observation and experiment as well as deduction and mathematics. Condorcet had stated on his admission to the Académie Française in 1782 (and Madame de Staël agreed): "Contemplating the human sciences, one cannot, indeed, help seeing that, resting like the physical sciences upon the observation of facts, they must follow the same method, acquire a language equally exact and precise, and achieve the same degree of certainty."[32] She seemed to seek a Newton for the social sciences; Condorcet should have had her nomination, judging from her debt to him, but she gave it, according to Gouverneur Morris, to the Abbé Siéyès, whose "writings and opinions will form in politics a new era, as that of Newton in physics."[33] Condorcet opposed her father in politics, while at that time Siéyès was writing a new constitution for France which Madame de Staël undoubtedly wanted to shape. In any case, the new method was everything, she believed. "So by applying, to the extent that it is

[32] *Oeuvres de Condorcet* (12 vols., Paris, 1847–49), Vol. I, p. 392.
[33] *Diary and Letters,* Vol. I, p. 376 (25 Jan. 1791).

possible, the philosophy of the exact sciences to the philosophy of intellectual ideas, we can make effective progress in the human and political domain, where the emotions never cease to block our path."

To Madame de Staël, the method that would put the "human sciences" in such a position was that of the calculus of probabilities, that is, the mathematical formulas that would permit (1) the estimation of the likelihood of a given event, and (2) the prediction of the future on the basis of the past. The leaders of the Enlightenment had already rejected the "esprit de système," that is, the legacy of the Cartesian deductive method, as too remote and highly abstract. In its place they had adopted a more inductive mathematical method based upon discoverable statistical regularities in the real world. They substituted data for system, experience for axioms, probability for certainty.

The mathematical basis of probability theory was laid in the seventeenth century by the Frenchmen Pascal and Fermat and was developed in the eighteenth by the Swiss Bernoulli brothers. Then it began to be applied to social life. Turgot, for example, reasoned that the basic human capacities and traits are the same in all kinds of people. "Talent," he said, "is distributed among mankind very much like gold in a mine. The more ore you extract, the more metal you gather. The more people there are, the more great men you will have or men fit for greatness. The accidents of their upbringing and experience either bring them out or let them remain hidden in obscurity."[34] In 1785 Condorcet dedicated to Turgot his major work of this kind, the *Essay on the Application of the Calculus to the Likelihood of the Correctness of Decisions*

[34] "Ebauche du second discours, dont l'objet sera les Progrès de l'Esprit humain," *Oeuvres de M. Turgot* (9 vols., Paris, 1808), Vol. II, p. 264.

Reached by a Plurality of Votes.[35] This imposing mathematical work, which captivated Madame de Staël in her youth, sought to establish nothing less than a model for determining how likely it is that a given group of people (a legislature, for example) will reach a correct or true decision through voting. An implication of Condorcet's work was that this likelihood of reaching a correct decision could be improved by altering the make-up of the group in accordance with the calculations.

What could probability theory offer? While in hiding in 1793–94, shortly before he died, Condorcet wrote his famous *Outline of a Historical Table of the Progress of the Human Mind.* In it he hailed the "tenth era" of man (which he said was inaugurated by the very Revolution that victimized him) as the one that would lead to the perfection of mankind. In the first paragraph describing this era, he put his answer in the form of a question. "If," he demanded, "man can predict with almost complete certainty the phenomena whose laws he understands, and even if when these laws are unknown to him he can predict future events with great probability on the basis of the past, why should it be regarded as a chimerical undertaking to delineate, with some degree of truth, the future of mankind from the results of its past?"[36]

In another essay, written around the same time and also published after his death, Condorcet gave a popular summary of his "social mathematics." He deplored the fact that the decisions that guide our conduct are based upon vague and unconscious estimates. Though probability theory could not, he conceded, handle all opinions and judgments it never-

[35] *Essai sur l'application de l'analyse à la probabilité des décisions rendues à la pluralité des voix* (Paris, 1785). The word "probabilité" in this title is best translated not by its English cognate but by a phrase, "degree of correctness" or "likelihood of correctness."

[36] *Esquisse d'un Tableau historique des Progrès de l'Esprit humain* (1795), in *Oeuvres de Condorcet,* Vol. VI, p. 236.

theless could provide the same advantage in government that the gambler who knows how to calculate his moves enjoys over the one who plays only by instinct and habit.[37]

When still a girl, Madame de Staël had imbibed these heady ideas. In 1785, at nineteen, she read Condorcet's main work, which had just appeared: "He subjects all moral ideas to algebraic calculations," she wrote, spellbound. "Triangles and angles are the poetic figures with which I shall henceforth embellish my speech."[38] She confused algebra with geometry, but she understood the implications of the theory of probability. In her own first important work, *On the Influence of the Passions,* published in 1796, the year after the publication of two of Condorcet's posthumous essays touching on this subject, Madame de Staël embraced the idea that a science of human affairs could achieve "geometric proof."[39] In her work on *Literature,* published in 1800, she developed her views (in Part Two, Chapter VI) on the place of probability. Citing Condorcet, she observed: "Applied to a large number of cases, the calculus of probability yields a virtually infallible result. Gamblers use it as a guide, however much their goal may seem to be subject to the whims of chance. It may likewise be applicable to the multitude of events making up the political sciences." Statistical information on all countries would enable governors to determine the kind of regime appropriate in each case. But she would not go too far in such reasoning. The study of human behavior must be based, she cautioned, not only on probability but also on morality. Moreover, she added, "whenever the calculation does not

[37] "Tableau général de la science, qui a pour objet l'application du calcul aux sciences politiques et morales," in *Oeuvres de Condorcet,* Vol. I, p. 541.

[38] J. C. Herold, *Germaine Necker de Staël* (Paris, 1962), p. 212.

[39] *Oeuvres Complètes,* Vol. I, pp. 108b, 171a.

agree with morality, the calculation is false, however incontestable its exactitude may appear at first glance." Any calculation that omitted the individual, that ignored suffering and sentiment, was false and barbaric. Politics as a science takes men as a mass, but morality respects the individual. "Morality," she concluded, "must guide our calculations, and our calculations must guide politics." Doubting that the social theorist can trace his steps back from his abstractions to the concrete truths of human affairs, Madame de Staël refused to yield all to mathematics. And this is to be expected of one who could write, as she did in *On Germany:* "The universe resembles a poem more than a machine."

Social scientists today are interested again in probability theory, but many are unaware of the work of these pioneers who charmed Madame de Staël. There are two prominent exceptions. One, Gilles-Gaston Granger, has written an authoritative account of *La Mathématique Sociale du Marquis de Condorcet* (Paris, 1956), in which he shows that pioneer's relevance today also for welfare economics, game theory, and operations research. Another Frenchman, Bertrand de Jouvenel has gone back to Condorcet for valuable insights into the process of decision-making today. In 1961 he established in Paris an organization, Futuribles, to promote the scientific study of the future.[40]

In this review of Madame de Staël's thought I have frequently found it useful to refer to those thinkers who in-

[40] M. de Jouvenel has written an unpublished analysis of Condorcet's *Essay on the Application of the Calculus,* entitled "A Note on Decision-Making," for the Center for the Study of Democratic Institutions, Santa Barbara, California, 1960. In 1962 the Congress for Cultural Freedom sponsored a conference in Geneva on the study of the probable future, which he described briefly in *Preuves-Informations* (published by the magazine *Preuves,* Paris), No. 197, 31 July 1962.

spired her. The tracing of ideas into previous generations, however, is often overdone and, as often, of doubtful value intellectually. If Tocqueville could, as he says in his foreword to *The Old Regime and the French Revolution,* write that book to show that the revolutionaries drew upon ideas developed in the society they sought to overthrow, then it may be that social ideas and institutions flow back and forth through generations and social systems in such a way as to defy attempts to trace origins very exactly. Certainly Madame de Staël drew upon the work of the eighteenth-century Encyclopedists. But the French historian of ideas, Paul Hazard, remarks in the preface to *The European Mind* that the leading ideas of the eighteenth century "were already current as early as 1680." And what of the leading ideas of 1680? Ideas may be traced back infinitely because they emerge out of previous ones and out of a social condition that has its origins in previous ones too.

How "original," then, was Madame de Staël? Since she was neither a revolutionary in ideas nor a plagiarist, we may platitudinously place her within this wide range. Two things are clear. First, she gave such cogent expression to many of the ideas held by the leading thinkers of her time that it is often unfair to say that this or that notion "comes from" this or that source. Second, though she herself "borrowed" from others, she had a great effect upon intellectual life in the nineteenth century in several countries. The question of her "originality," therefore, ought not to be considered apart from that of her influence.

By her own admission (not always a valid criterion but in this case amply supported by other evidence), Madame de Staël was considerably influenced in the choice of subjects and her views on them by Montesquieu, Rousseau, and Condorcet. She also owed much to the great *Encyclopedia* of Diderot and d'Alembert, and to Marmontel, especially in her use of such concepts as enthusiasm, emulation, melancholy, and admiration, and in her ideas of progress and her conception of literature in relation to social ideas and institutions. What is less often mentioned is that she drew upon earlier writers too, chiefly Charles Perrault (1628–1703) and Bovier de Fontenelle (1657–1757), who were involved in the intellectual battle over the question whether the ancients or the moderns were superior, in the course of which they elaborated many of the ideas on art, learning, and progress that became common in the eighteenth century.[41]

To understand how ideas arise from a hint, are developed and then spread, we may consider Madame de Staël's interesting treatment of the relation between fiction and history. In the latter part of the sixteenth century, more than two hundred years before Madame de Staël wrote, Montaigne suggested this relationship. In his essay, "Of the Power of the Imagination," he insists on the value of fiction for the understanding of human affairs. "So in the study that I am making of our behavior and motives," he says, "fabulous testimonies, provided they are possible, serve like true ones. Whether they have happened or no, in Paris or Rome, to John or Peter, they exemplify, at all events, some human potentiality, and thus their telling imparts useful information to me. . . . And of the different readings that histories often give, I take for

[41] Madame de Staël's intellectual debt to these writers may be seen in their works and in various articles in the *Encyclopedia*. The reader will recognize her ideas and others like them in various intellectual histories of the seventeenth and eighteenth centuries, such as Paul Hazard's *The European Mind (1680–1715)*, tr. by J. Lewis May (New Haven, 1953) and Henry Vyverberg's *Historical Pessimism in the French Enlightenment* (Cambridge, Massachusetts, 1958). A concentrated effort to find quite specific sources appears in an unpublished doctoral thesis by Marie Elizabeth Lein, "Les Sources des Théories Littéraires de Madame de Staël" (University of Chicago, 1948).

my use the one that is most rare and memorable. There are authors whose end is to tell what has happened. Mine, if I could attain it, would be to talk about what can happen."[42]

Madame de Staël knew and admired Montaigne's works but she did not refer to this particular passage in them. As I shall show in detail in a later section, she made a valuable addition to this idea in her *Essay on Fiction* (1795). She pointed out that the novel was free from history's necessity to adhere to events as they actually happened but could give the appearance of truth by telling a story that might well have happened. This meant that the novel, while imitating reality, could rise above it and draw moral lessons which actual events might obscure. In his famous introduction of 1842 to *The Human Comedy*, Balzac said much the same thing. Skeptical observers of human nature, he noted, felt that life itself displayed more evil than good. As a novelist, however, he believed he had painted more virtuous characters than bad ones and had, unlike life, always punished evil. "I have done better than the historian," he proclaimed, "I am freer." History, Balzac said, citing (probably in error) Madame Necker rather than her daughter Madame de Staël, must show how things actually were, whereas fiction could show also how they ought to be.[43]

[42] *The Complete Works of Montaigne*, tr. Donald M. Frame (Stanford, 1957), p. 75; Anchor edition, *The Complete Essays of Montaigne*, Vol. I, p. 102.

[43] *Oeuvres Complètes de Honoré de Balzac* (40 vols., ed. Bouteron and Longnon, Paris, 1912–40), Vol. I, p. XXXIII. Balzac's mention of Madame de Staël's mother was probably a slip. Madame Necker wrote little on this subject but touched on the novel in an essay on Rousseau's *The New Heloise* (*Nouveaux Mélanges extraits des Manuscrits de Mme. Necker*, 2 vols., Paris, 1801; see Vol. II, pp. 99 ff.). Madame de Staël, of course, wrote more on the novel and her work is far better known. In an article of 1831, Balzac was probably referring to her when he wrote: "Literature is the expression of society; this truth, so commonplace today, is the result of the observations of a mind that studied in perspective

Madame de Staël's influence extended beyond the clarification of a specific point for a single writer, however important both may have been. Her three main works influenced entire cultures, eras, and disciplines. *Literature Considered in Its Relation to Social Institutions* has been significant in the development of the sociology of literature and of comparative literature. In the last hundred years or so, however, Madame de Staël's effect in these disciplines has been felt not directly but through those who have absorbed her work through others. *Considerations on the Principal Events of the French Revolution* played a very important part in nineteenth-century French liberal thought and historiography. *On Germany*, her best-known work in England and America (and probably elsewhere), helped to move Europe into the Romantic period, and was highly instrumental in acquainting Americans with a new literature and philosophy.

Madame de Staël's influence on American intellectual life in the early nineteenth century used to be so widely recognized that one scholar has now minimized her role. The usual conception, he says, is that the United States was "ignorant of Germany until the early nineteenth century when, so the legend goes, a group of young Harvard men, suddenly fired by Mme. de Staël's account of the great German universities, journeyed thither and brought back with them the weapons wherewith to effect a Teutonic conquest of American learning, literature, and thought. The story is too pat to be

---

the history of peoples and poetry." (See "Du roman historique," *Oeuvres Complètes. Oeuvres Diverses*, 1935, Vol. I, p. 205.) Another indication that Balzac probably referred to Madame de Staël is the high regard in which he held her. He listed her, with Tacitus, Luther, Calvin, Voltaire, Rousseau, Chateaubriand, and Benjamin Constant, as a writer who was the "spokesman of her age." (See his preface to Part III of *Illusions Perdues*, in the edition by Antoine Adam [pub. by Garnier, Paris, 1961], p. 768.)

credible." He goes on to show that there were earlier German influences than the one through Madame de Staël, but then he asserts, what is only true, that her book inspired or spurred the study of German culture by many prominent writers, including Edward and Alexander H. Everett, George Bancroft, Joseph G. Cogswell, Theodore Parker, Margaret Fuller, Emerson, and Longfellow. Though Madame de Staël, according to this historian, was a reliable guide to many aspects of German life, she could not offer much on philosophy. Her influence, however, appears not to be a legend: "The vogue which the book enjoyed in America was tremendous."[44]

Perhaps the first American to be influenced was George Ticknor. Admitted to the bar in 1813, he was too restless intellectually to remain in a law office. Determined to go to Europe, he read Madame de Staël and decided to study in Germany. He was followed by many others, all of whom returned to prominent positions in the world of literature and learning in America. To be sure, men of such intellect, ambition, and social position would probably have reached high place without having read Madame de Staël or studied in Germany. The fact is, however, that both played an important part in their intellectual development. Through these men, German thought and scholarship helped to shape American higher education, philosophy, and transcendentalism. The leading intellectual journal of the time, the *North American Review*, was published and edited by men who had been affected by Madame de Staël's work; they wrote and published articles about her in that influential medium. By the time Henry James began to write, in the last quarter of the nineteenth century, her name was legendary; in *The Euro-*

[44] Henry A. Pochmann, *German Culture in America* (Madison, Wisconsin, 1957), pp. 19, 57, 162, 552 n. 313, 102.

peans (1878) a main character refers to the conversational style of Madame de Staël.[45]

Madame de Staël was a great intellectual and emotional liberator. In her day she introduced the leading cultures of Europe to each other, including their offspring in North America. The spirit of Europe is a leading idea implicit in her work. In *On Germany* she referred to that "association of thinking men from one end of Europe to the other" and said of them: "Often there is no communication between them; they are often scattered over great distances from one another, but when they meet, a word is enough for them to recognize each other. It is not religion, viewpoint, or field of study that unites them, but the worship of the truth."[46] She examined and clarified national character in order to enlarge and liberalize the national spirit rather than congeal it, and in doing so she transcended nations. In 1819, two years after her death, Byron, who had known her well at Coppet, was in Bologna reading her novel about Italy, *Corinne*. In the margin of the copy he held he jotted this note about the author: "She is sometimes right, and often wrong, about Italy and England; but almost always true in delineating the heart, which is of but one nation, and of no country,—or, rather of all."[47]

[45] The intellectual influence of Madame de Staël on America has been studied only scrappily. See Emma Gertrude Jaeck, *Madame de Staël and the Spread of German Literature* (New York, 1915) and William Girard, *Du Transcendentalisme considerée essentiellement dans sa Définition et ses Origines françaises* (University of California Publications in Modern Philology, 1916, Vol. 4, No. 3, pp. 351–498).

[46] *De l'Allemagne*, Vol. IV, p. 402 (Part Three, Ch. XXI).

[47] Thomas Moore, *The Life of Lord Byron* (London, 1854), p. 407, n. 1.

POLITICAL INSTITUTIONS

Almost everything Madame de Staël wrote had to do with politics, for, as a product of the Enlightenment, she conceived politics not merely as the formal trappings of government but as the entire range of man's deliberate and unintended efforts to direct his life as a social being. Politics, government, and "constitution" meant to her the arrangement of social life in general. The great import she attached to "political institutions" in this broad sense was an affirmation of man's ability to shape his own destiny free from the influence of non-human forces, divine or physical.

"Governments," wrote Madame de Staël in *On Germany*, "are the true instructors of nations." National character itself is shaped by political institutions, by the art of human self-management. Though religion, she conceded,[48] could, as in ancient Egypt, make a nation passive and stagnant, she implied it could do so only through its political role. "But in general," she insisted, "nations improve or deteriorate according to the way they are governed. The climate of Rome has not changed, yet from the Romans down to the Italians of our time one can traverse the whole scale of changes which men experience through a variety of governments. The worth of a people, no doubt, consists in knowing how to give itself a suitable form of government." If some nations are frivolous and others serious, this does not mean that the first must submit to despotic regimes while the second enjoy liberty. Each kind may find liberty in its own way through appropriate institutions. "The French," Madame de Staël pronounced, "are frivolous because they have been condemned to a kind of gov-

[48] *Considérations sur les principaux événements de la Révolution française*, in *Oeuvres Complètes*, Vol. III, pp. 281b, 282a, 283a (Part Six, Ch. I).

ernment that could support itself only by encouraging frivolity."

Madame de Staël thus attributed to political institutions certain practices that others might account for on the basis of "inherent" national traits. She admired the English practice, in war, of telling the truth about their losses as well as their victories. "The Russians," she observed, "cannot yet reach that moral perfection, which is the result of a free constitution."[49] But in speaking of political institutions, she was not referring mainly to majorities and the preponderance of coercive power, but, rather, pointing to the combined power of two elite groups that would be one under ideal conditions: the holders of political power, and the intellectuals and artists who influenced both the rulers and the ruled. Power in the political realm was, to her, not only the weight of force but that of ideas, the influence exerted by intelligence, sensibility, learning. As she often indicated, especially in *Literature Considered in Its Relation to Social Institutions,* nations follow their leading thinkers and moralists; so literature, as she broadly conceived it, was in the very midst of political life. This was true even when writers professed to avoid "politics," for then they merely buttressed social evil either by ignoring it, as physical scientists might, or by celebrating it, as poets did when they praised despots.

Madame de Staël's emphasis upon the great role of political institutions in human affairs does not imply advocacy of government action in preference to "private" action. Rather, she stressed government in the sense I have already suggested, the capacity of human beings for self-management through both legislation by parliaments and the less direct and simple inculcation of public attitudes, values, and practices by the

[49] *Dix années d'exil,* p. 312. She makes the same point later in another context, p. 357.

teachings and example of writers, wise leaders, and moralists. In pointing to the pervasive influence of political institutions, she was insisting upon man's ability to control his own affairs by acting here and refraining from acting there. Whatever influence climate, geography, and other physical traits of this world may have exerted earlier, by the eighteenth century, she believed, man had learned that he need not be limited by them any longer. And though she never ceased to advocate religion as a force for morality, she never held that God put any limitation upon man for good or evil.

It is doubtful, therefore, that Madame de Staël can be put at the service of either contemporary liberalism, with its belief in the "welfare state," or contemporary conservatism, with its belief in "voluntary action," although her work indicates that both of these approaches have their origin in the same eighteenth-century optimistic notion that man has found the principle of human happiness. Some have found this principle in social planning guided by governments, others in the free market place guided by individual preferences, but both locate the principle of human happiness in *human hands* rather than in divine power or physical restraints.

Because of this high conception of the nature of political institutions, Madame de Staël believed, as we saw earlier, that there is no more noble intellectual pursuit than their study. An admirer of John Adams, she would certainly have agreed with the view he expressed in 1780, well before she or Auguste Comte put forth similar views. Adams wrote to his wife from Paris:

> The science of government is my duty to study, more than all other sciences; the arts of legislation and administration and negotiation ought to take the place of, indeed to exclude, in a manner, all other arts. I must study politics and war, that my sons may have liberty to study mathematics and philoso-

phy, geography, natural history and naval architecture, navigation, commerce, and agriculture, in order to give their children a right to study painting, poetry, music, architecture, statuary, tapestry, and porcelain.[50]

In her first full-length book, *On the Influence of the Passions upon the Happiness of Individuals and of Nations*, published in 1796, Madame de Staël combined two of her leading ideas —the possibility of a political science based upon the calculus of probability, and the powerful influence of political institutions in shaping social life—insisting that governments could increase the happiness of nations. Her argument was that the human passions are the main source of the obstacles to the happiness of both individuals and nations. The calculus of probability shows that these passions are uniformly distributed in a large group of people; knowing something of this distribution, governments are in a position to take account of the passions, and, as the science of politics develops, governments will be increasingly able to calculate the degree to which the individual passions may be stirred or calmed in such a way as to promote the group's happiness.[51]

Madame de Staël shared the seventeenth and eighteenth centuries' favorable view of the passions as compared with the fear and distrust of them expressed by earlier and more religious epochs. She was, nevertheless, somewhat ambivalent in her feeling. On the one hand, she liked people with enthusiasm and strong feelings, and believed that one of France's great troubles was excessive curbing of natural sentiment. The passionless man may live a life satisfactory to himself, but it must be a monotonous existence depending entirely upon fate

[50] Undated letter of 1780 in *Familiar Letters of John Adams and His Wife Abigail Adams, During the Revolution*, ed. Charles Francis Adams (Boston, 1875), p. 381.

[51] *De l'influence des passions*, in *Oeuvres Complètes*, Vol. I, pp. 107–09, 115.

and external circumstances. Impassioned people try to shape their lives, and so their lives depend in part upon their own natures. But such people, unwilling to be passive receivers of outside influences, cause governments a certain amount of trouble. Society needs their energy but is also endangered by it in some degree. Hence the need to base policy upon a calculus of the probable distribution of the passions in a given nation.

As a woman of many passions, Madame de Staël was concerned in her book not merely with the effect of her kind upon government but also with the happiness of the passionate individuals. Such conspicuous persons, she implied, are marked for pain. Intent upon shaping their lives, they must encounter frustration, and so they need a philosophy to reduce their suffering. Madame de Staël offered little hope that individual happiness could be attained, though she believed governments could go further in achieving happiness as that term could be applied to the group. Happiness for both individuals and nations she defined as the reconciliation or joining of opposites. For the individual it is hope without fear, love without infidelity—in short, the advantages of all conditions and talents and pleasures without the misfortunes or ills that seem to accompany them. For nations, happiness means the reconciliation of other opposites: the liberty of republics with the tranquillity of monarchies, rivalry to produce high quality but not to the point of encouraging factionalism, a martial spirit abroad but willingness to accept the rule of law at home.

Her object was to find the means to increase both individual and national happiness, and she ended up more optimistic about the group because governments could base policy upon probability, whereas the individual could find no such principle to follow. She stated her objective in a soul-searing manner that suggests that actually she sought chiefly the answer to individual happiness. "My only purpose," she lamented, "has been to combat misery in all its guises; to study the thoughts, sentiments, and institutions that cause pain to mankind, in order to seek out the idea, the impulse, the arrangement, that might reduce somewhat the intensity of the soul's suffering: the image of misfortune haunts me and crushes me."

As dangerous as she thought the passions could become to the individual and the state, Madame de Staël never advocated their absolute restraint in the name of order, happiness, or anything else. "The cure for popular passions," she warned, "lies not in despotism but in the rule of law." But it was her fate to become a victim of Napoleon's despotic regime. Her political sensitivity and her desire—as one of those impassioned people marked for suffering—to alter things made her especially aware of Napoleon's ambition and a special target of his impatience with opposition. Madame de Staël correctly said of herself: "I sensed more quickly than others —and I pride myself on it—Bonaparte's tyrannical character and intentions. The true friends of liberty are in this respect guided by an instinct that does not deceive them." All of which, of course, only increased her pain.

Madame de Staël wrote about Napoleon and the "art of tyranny" in *Considerations on the Principal Events of the French Revolution* and in her fragmentary autobiography, *Ten Years of Exile*. Both were published after her death. The autobiography is on the whole the earlier of the two works and was written while Napoleon was still living and holding her in exile; it is, therefore, largely a record of his persecution of her, her family, and her friends. In the *Considerations*, which she completed after Napoleon's fall, she dealt largely with his political role and brilliantly analyzed his rise to power, his exercise of it, and his conduct in decline.

Though she was his enemy, Madame de Staël did not begrudge Napoleon his greatness; she merely saw his failings as well. But what impressed her most about him was that he slipped through or was too large for the categories into which ordinary men and even other geniuses could be fitted. "He was neither good, nor fierce, nor gentle, nor cruel, like others we know. Such a being, having no equals, could neither feel nor arouse any sympathy: he was more than a human being or less than one."

Napoleon's technique in rising to power, according to Madame de Staël, was to paralyze his opposition by pointing to the extreme consequences of denying him his way. "Do you want me to hand you over to the Jacobins?" he demanded. And no one, she complained, was "bold enough" to reply: "We shall be able to fight the Jacobins and you." "Preferred" rather than wanted for his own sake, Napoleon "almost always presented himself in competition with another cause for alarm, in order to make his power acceptable as a lesser evil." In power, he had a "detestable arsenal" of weapons: special commissions, deportation, exile, suppression of freedom. He employed an "artillery of phrases" to defend his steady progress to absolute power—emergencies, reasons of state, the need of the times, the maintenance of order and calm. All these techniques he exercised in the name of liberty, while the rule of law was always postponed. "This is a vicious circle," Madame de Staël warned, "for the public spirit that is awaited in order to permit liberty can come only from liberty itself."

To her credit, Madame de Staël did not allow her belief in stages of history to lead her to the position, so familiar in our own times, first regarding the Soviet Union and then the authoritarian regimes in some newly independent countries of Asia and Africa, that we can reach freedom through coercion. "It was often repeated during the Revolution in France," she said in *Literature Considered in Its Relation to Social Institutions,* "that a certain amount of despotism was necessary to establish liberty. This is a contradiction in terms that has been made into a maxim . . . Institutions based upon force may simulate everything about liberty, except its genuine workings . . ." It was the fact that Napoleon's enemies appealed to liberty, she argued, that sent the opponents of the Revolution scurrying to his support. People no longer thought as individuals, for Napoleon successfully applied the familiar despotic method of turning his supporters into abject dependents and his enemies into a fearful mass. "All individual existence," Madame de Staël wrote, "was annihilated by ten years of disorder . . . No one in France could consider his position secure. Men of all classes, ruined or enriched, banished or rewarded, found themselves one by one equally, so to speak, in the hands of power." Nor did Madame de Staël make another error familiar in our own day, that of associating coercive regimes with order and good government. "When one does not know how to convince," she pointed out in *Literature Considered in Its Relation to Social Institutions,* "one oppresses; in all power relations among governors and governed, as ability declines, usurpation increases."

In passing final judgment on Napoleon and despotism, Madame de Staël was skeptical of either one's efforts to look like something else. After his first fall and return to power, Napoleon made the mistake of trying to appear to be a constitutional monarch. "A man who detested abstract ideas and legal restraints," she pointed out, "instead of being made to talk about constitutions for hours on end, should have been on the field of battle four days after his arrival in Paris . . ." His only weapon was military Jacobinism, not sweet reason and moderation, for such words from such a man could mean only deceit or weakness. "When he uttered the words law and liberty, Europe was reassured: it sensed that this was no longer its old and terrible adversary." Madame de Staël sought to instruct her generation and those to follow that Napoleon was not the carrier of the noble ideas of the Enlightenment and the Revolution. "I believe I have shown," she said, "that there is no counter-revolution so fatal to liberty as the one he made." And her words triumphed over Napoleon's deeds, for, in the nineteenth century, French liberalism, struggling against his legacy, drew steadily upon Madame de Staël's interpretation of the Revolution and what became known as Bonapartism.

Reason and moderation were admirable traits to Madame de Staël, and she would concede them only to those who genuinely believed in constitutional regimes and in liberty. Her ideological affiliation to eighteenth-century reason combined with her painful experiences under despotism to make her a passionate advocate of political moderation and legitimacy. Recognizing the genius in all sorts of individuals and nations, and seeing the need for liberty to encourage these talents to come forward, she saw human society as a delicately arranged set of relationships any of whose junctures could be easily upset by extremism. "The social order," she observed, "is in itself a curious structure" that requires compromises which disturb the noble-minded and stir either discontent or ambition in most men. Religious fanaticism, she felt, had receded only to be replaced by political fanaticism of the sort most fearfully displayed in the Terror. The different mixture of similar elements in these two kinds of extremism fascinated Madame de Staël. "Worldly desires," she commented, "have always been a part of religious fanaticism, while often, on the other hand, true fidelity to some abstract ideas feeds political fanaticism." Religious fanaticism has attracted people by offering an "infinite future," but political fanaticism has attracted those to whom worldly pleasures appear equally without limit because they have never tasted them.

Both types of fanaticism have continuously sought to expand, warned Madame de Staël. The extremes are the bearers of peril, for, as she put it, those at the "top of the wheel" want to continue to rule at any cost while those at the bottom are eager to "make it turn." So for centuries humanity has "exhausted itself in useless efforts to compel men to one creed." She was not in favor of keeping the wheel of power turning rapidly in response to pushes from below or of locking it into one position by resistance from above. Rather, she favored a steady turning according to established principles. "Will it be necessary," she asked in anguish, "always to govern three hundred years behind the times? . . . No, it will be said, there are things that ought to change, but government ought to be immutable. There could be no better way to put revolutions on a regular basis."

To put orderly change and progress, rather than revolution, on a regular basis, Madame de Staël favored legitimacy tempered by democracy. She opposed legitimacy of rule based upon divine right, for it was sacrilegious to involve God in the affairs of men, and divine right only encouraged usurpations. She admired the English system of "heredity sanctioned by representative government." Heredity was necessary to insure tranquillity; election, on the other hand, opened the field to personal ambition and faction. But heredity is contrary to reason, so the power of those who reach high place by the accident of birth must be limited by a constitution worked out by the best minds in the society. Madame de Staël preferred a hereditary ruler, who, if not wise, would at least be less likely to be ambitious for power, to an elected ruler who might be more able but also more ambitious. After seeing Europe under Napoleon, she was perhaps too willing to settle for mediocre rulers controlled through superior constitutions. "Princes of old families," she cautioned, "are much better suited to the welfare of the state than self-made princes. Usually their talents are less outstanding but their disposition is more peaceful; they have more prejudices but less ambition . . ."

In her desire to advance the cause of moderation, Madame de Staël may have too readily believed that the parties in Revolutionary France were closer than they themselves realized. In an early work, she insisted that the constitutionalists and the republicans were one in principle and goal. "It is necessary," she said, "that the one should sacrifice the principle of the monarchy to the certainty of liberty, and the other, democracy to the security of public order."[52]

Public opinion, to Madame de Staël, was a powerful force on the side of moderation even though it gave enough evidence of extremism in her time. It played a tranquillizing role, she felt, because most people stand between the warring parties rather than in the camp of either one. The mass, seeking only its own comfort and uninterested in ideologies, lies squarely in the political middle range. Enlightened somewhat, it no longer cares about the monarchy, yet it is not attracted by a republic that disturbs its tranquillity. It does not care to defend the nobility, nor does it hate privilege enough to want to persecute it. This passivity of public opinion, Madame de Staël felt, could be put to good political use, but it was not anything to admire. In *Ten Years of Exile* she made the mournful pronouncement: "If tyranny had on its side only its

[52] *Réflexions sur la paix intérieure* (1795) in *Oeuvres Complètes*, Vol. I, p. 58b.

fully convinced advocates, it could never maintain itself. The astonishing thing, which more than anything else reveals human wretchedness, is that most ordinary men are at the service of success."

To make clearer the non-ideological interests of the public, Madame de Staël drew a distinction between ancient and modern liberty. The ancients, she said, took an active role in politics because everything that governments did affected them directly and intimately; to them, liberty meant the right to exercise power, to demand things of the government in exchange for their participation in it. But in a large modern state like France, the development of agriculture and industry had given people a livelihood independent of politics; a large class, therefore, could live apart from participation in or concern with government—they could live, that is to say, both comfortably and obscurely.[53] A modern republic must take account of these differences and not expect large numbers of people to sacrifice their convenient privacy to public responsibility. Among the ancients public opinion was swayed by calls to action and even by disorders, whereas in modern times the national spirit demands tranquillity. The ancients thus enjoyed "political liberty"—the right to control their government directly, to act with and through it. The moderns enjoy "civil liberty" and "individual liberty"—the right of each person to be free *from* the actions of government, free to influence government through his representatives as he pursues his own interests outside the narrow political realm. And where, as in large modern republics, only a few can actually operate the government and influence it directly and steadily,

[53] It is this middle class, Madame de Staël showed in her *Essay on Fiction* and in *Literature Considered in Its Relation to Social Institutions*, whose lives, emotions, and morality created and were chronicled in the earliest novels.

where, that is, "political" liberty can not be guaranteed to everyone, it is especially important that "civil" and "individual" liberty be perfectly respected.

An important aspect of Madame de Staël's view of ideal government in the republican era was balance. She meant by this term more than a balance of social classes or governmental powers. She meant balance in political participation itself. Too much popular concern for politics, she felt, tended to produce extremism, but too little concern on the part of the best minds eased the way for tyranny. So she did not argue for mass participation in government; people satisfied with the pursuit of private interests ought to be allowed to go their way, for their uninformed participation in politics might not be beneficial to liberty and order. She did, however, insist that the governing elite and the thinkers in a society fully exercise their influence in government to insure enlightened, liberal, moderate rule. Balance, moreover, meant to Madame de Staël that liberty and order, for example, could be secured only at a certain expense to each other, but the sacrifice must not be too high. Here we must recall, too, her conception of the happiness of individuals and nations as the reconciliation of opposites: hope without fear, love without infidelity, rivalry without factionalism, and so on—that is, the achievement of favorable conditions in such a measure and balance that it is possible to avoid the unfavorable conditions that seem to accompany them.

Madame de Staël did not underestimate the difficulty of holding fast to moderation. In an early essay, written in 1791 and entitled "How Can We Determine What Is the Opinion of the Majority of the Nation?", she set forth the moderate position with characteristic passion. "It is understandable," she remarked, "that the two extreme parties should agree in attacking this common enemy." But she saw no reason to call the middle position "weak and indecisive." Rather, the moderate party more than any other, especially during a revolution, needs "courage of soul and breadth of mind." For it must wage two battles, fight two enemies, avoid two dangers. If it must face such difficulties, moderation can at least console itself that the majority is waiting only for direction from moderate leaders in the midst of rash tendencies that reduce everything to simple extremes in the wrong belief that these are preferred. Perhaps aware that moderation did not appear to be in character for her, Madame de Staël conceded, "Opinions do exist which we must adopt without modification." "But," she quickly added, "are we to allow every lunatic who discovers a new madness to erect a new barrier to truth?" The middle position, she insisted, need not be put in the shade by the extremes or defined merely in their terms. It must be possible to stake out a middle position "that would be stronger, more distinct, and more vigorous than the two opposed extremes." And Madame de Staël devoted her political activity, her thought, and her writing to this task.

LITERATURE AND SOCIETY

Madame de Staël's most general work is *Literature Considered in Its Relation to Social Institutions.* In the first three paragraphs of her introduction she set forth the subjects of her lifelong interests and her approach to them. She really never wrote about anything else; all her work was a brilliant elaboration of these themes.

Having found plenty of works on writing as an art and on matters of literary taste, Madame de Staël resolved to go beyond these eighteenth-century genteel pursuits: she wanted to examine nothing less than the influences that shaped literature. These influences she identified as religion, social institutions, and the political-legal order governing a community. Literature she took to mean "everything that involves the exercise of thought in writing" except the physical sciences; so it included both "philosophical" and "imaginative" writing, or what we today would call history and the social sciences as well as fiction, drama and poetry—in short, everything that deals with human behavior as perceived or imagined by man himself.

Madame de Staël believed, as part of her faith in progress, that literature conceived in this way had steadily improved human faculties. Her conception of human progress was that (1) human institutions improved steadily but not without setbacks, (2) the human mind made slow but uninterrupted progress in "philosophy," or the scientific inquiry into the nature of human affairs, and (3) the arts made "rapid but interrupted progress." She was also interested in the differences between the literature of one European country and another, and these national distinctions she attributed not to innate talents but to differences in social institutions. Finally, she never ceased trying to understand and to direct the great social cataclysm of her time, the French Revolution. "I have thought it important," she remarked, "to know the influence it has exerted upon learning and what effects it can one day produce if order and liberty, republican morality and independence, are wisely and prudently combined."

Because her interest in literature was not only esthetic, Madame de Staël was not really a belle-lettrist or a literary critic, nor even a literary historian. Today, as I have said, we should call her a social scientist, since she sought to find in social institutions the influences that shaped the ideas and forms of literary expression. But she was far from being a detached, clinical observer of art, manners, and politics. Living in an age of great intellectual and social change, she was led to study the nature of human behavior in order to lay down principles and specific policies to preserve and enhance the legacy of progress: civility, freedom, morality, the rule of law and of reason, and the serious arts.

Above all, Madame de Staël was serious. I do not mean that she lacked humor or could not be witty but that she mistrusted levity. She was too ambitious and too bent upon guiding the world to dissipate her energy and influence in merely amusing it. Genevan and Protestant, intellectual and female, she was led by both background and experience to prefer understanding and melancholy to innocence and bliss. "Sadness," she says in praise of the English poets, "leads us to probe much more deeply into the character and destiny of man than does any other disposition of the mind." So she preferred tragedy to comedy, the grave Romans to the witty Greeks. Levity, she feared, distracted a people so much that its rulers were left too free to pursue their own ends. Athens lost its freedom because it abused comedy and indulged its taste for entertainment and witticisms. The Italians of her day, according to Madame de Staël, made jokes about their rulers only for amusement and not to correct abuses; and rulers permit such harmless diversion, she added, because it is only the "ruse of children against their teachers: they obey them on condition that they may make fun of them."

Melancholy, however, did not, to Madame de Staël, imply withdrawal, for she emphasized the need for enthusiasm, energy, activity and she extolled the virtues of rivalry and personal ambition—emulation—directed toward worthy ends. Melancholy was the appropriate disposition for those who govern through the power of the state or through the power of ideas. Referring to England, she sighed, "Happy the country where the writers are gloomy, the merchants satisfied, the rich melancholy, and the masses content." This was the condition she sought for France and Europe as they reached the republican era. Seriousness and morality among the people were not possible without melancholy and virtue in their rulers. Fearing that the great cultural legacy of Europe might be destroyed or confined by the descent into populism and tyranny, Madame de Staël described the nature and the needs of the new republics.

If the Old Regime was guilty of excessive refinement, the danger of the republican era, as she saw it, was that it might push vulgarity and license too far in both manners and literature. The fierce partisanship of the Revolution induced her to call for the cultivation of civility, that form of courtesy somewhere between politeness, which marks the relations among strangers, and intimacy, which marks the relations among friends and family. "Civility alone," she insisted, "can soften the asperities of the partisan spirit. It permits mutual toleration long before affection, and intercourse long before agreement."

Republics, too, Madame de Staël went on, need their appropriate social forms. In a monarchy, ritual and chivalry, for example, compensate for the lack of real merit in the individual. But as an illusion is destroyed, a reality must be created. So a republic must have all the more genuine propriety and morality. If in a monarchy a man's reputation is injured, he may be protected by birth, rank, and other attributes outside himself and irrelevant to his personal worth. But in a republic, she warned, everything depends precisely upon personal worth, and an injured man has nothing left if his name is ruined. Because of this movement from privilege to equality, a republic must encourage emulation and give it greater scope: "Only a small number of men succeed, but all may aspire." In this way, men of talent would rise to political and literary renown. Precisely because equality is sacred in a republic, she pointed out, such a regime must take care to recognize differences rather than to obliterate them—but these differences among men must be only in personal quality and ability.

Turning to the arts, Madame de Staël agreed that a revolution in politics ought to bring about a revolution in literature. Under the Old Regime literature was not in conformity with reason because it had become too precious and too attached to good form. In the republican era, therefore, literature must become more forceful, more serious, and more intellectual. Since republican simplicity of manners would yield fewer opportunities for ridicule, comedy, for example, must in a sense become more serious: "In a monarchy, people like to hold up to ridicule those manners which do not conform to received practices. In a republic, the subject of the shafts of ridicule ought to be the human failings that harm the general welfare." Undoubtedly reaching into her own experience for an illustration, she suggested that republican comedy would arouse scorn not for the deceived woman, as in the Old Regime, but for the deceiving man, the flatterer, and the pretentious moral coward.

Such a comparison of the literature appropriate to monarchies and to republics was but one of Madame de Staël's methods of relating art to the social order. Two others are worth noting here. One was to show how certain literary forms, the drama and the novel, for example, took their shape from the social institutions out of which they emerged. The other was to show how the literature of certain nations developed out of the character and institutions of those nations.

Madame de Staël thought much about the distinction between tragedy and comedy. Tragedy touches upon emotions shared by almost all human beings; success in this form depends, therefore, mainly upon the author's inventiveness. Comedy depends more upon a subtle appreciation of human weaknesses; success in this form is easy to achieve on the popular level, as the Greeks did, by making fun of their leading citizens, but difficult to achieve if the author tries, as Molière did, to maintain good taste. Tragedy draws in the spectator, identifies him with the hero, and so is able to make the audience transcend its own time and place. Comedy keeps the audience slightly aloof emotionally, and depends upon allusions to a particular time, nation, and manner of living. "Tears," Madame de Staël generalized, "derive from our natures, laughter from our customs."

To Madame de Staël, the status of women was always highly relevant to the condition of literature as well as indicative of morality in a community. The Greeks, she asserted, did not permit women to perform their natural function of elevating morals and taste. Moreover, the exclusion of women prevented the discovery of the love story as a means of maintaining the interest of the audience. So the writers of comedy resorted to coarse humor and allusions to events of the day. "Concern with private affairs," Madame de Staël argued, "depends entirely upon the role that women play in a country."

When she came to discuss English character and literature, she pursued the subject of comedy and society. The English had broad humor in the work of Congreve, for example, but neither had nor could appreciate the subtleties of a Molière. For this type of comic talent, "a people must live a great deal in society and attach great importance to social success." The English were absorbed in family life and serious affairs of state and commerce. They did not know the absurdities and vanities of society, that "frivolous area of life" between family and public concerns that gives rise to *finesse* and taste. The

English, she went on, enjoyed a constitutional monarchy in which public opinion ruled; it was not necessary, therefore, as it was in ordinary monarchies, for everyone to acquire that refined understanding of the whims of powerful persons that promotes the sort of comic spirit the French developed. Ties based upon the rule of law rather than the rule of personality tended in England to erase subtle differences and to heighten individuality and eccentricity; this made English humor broad rather than fine.

In turning to the novel as a literary form, Madame de Staël reverted to the place of women in social life. English preeminence in the novel she traced to England's great respect for women's individuality and to the relations of "sensibility and refinement" between the sexes there. "Nowhere so much as in England," she remarked, "have women enjoyed the happiness brought about by domestic affections." This private life, in which women were permitted to become the true partners of men, provided English writers with the material they needed to make novels interesting. They were, indeed, the first authors "who ventured to believe that the representation of private feelings was enough to interest the mind and heart of man, that neither the luster of eminent people, nor magnitude of concerns, nor extraordinary events were necessary in order to captivate the imagination, and that the power of love was enough to provide an endless variety of scenes and situations without exhausting one's interest." Though this reliance upon the details of private life produced many tedious passages, there were two saving graces. First, the novels were created to be read by people just like the ones they portrayed and hence were not so boring to them as to the French. Second, the novel held attention "by a steady succession of accurate and moral comments on life's tender emotions."

Madame de Staël first expressed her ideas on the novel in her *Essay on Fiction,* published in 1795, five years before the appearance of *Literature Considered in Its Relation to Social Institutions.* In the essay she distinguished three kinds of fiction, according to whether the invented story included (1) supernatural or allegorical events, (2) events of history, or (3) "pure fiction"—that is, events that are both invented and based upon human experience, "in which nothing is true but everything is believable." The events in a novel, then, do not actually take place but they are of a *kind* that occur all the time. What advantages, asked Madame de Staël, did the novel have over the writing of history as already practiced?

She saw three advantages in the novel. First, it reached into the lives of ordinary people and touched private sentiments outside the realm of public affairs. Second, unlike history-writing in her time, it permitted a close imitation of life, the "gradual unfoldment of events" that gave the reader the sense of life's reality, and the portrayal of intimate feelings "so natural that the reader often thinks that it is he himself he is reading about under another name." History, on the contrary, Madame de Staël complained, could not sustain this slow pace, this circumstantial detail, and psychological probing. It specialized in the spectacular, as to both events and personalities. Finally, the novel could point the moral of human events better than could the writing of history. Taken in its entirety, history does reveal the superior position of morality, but any given series of events in history does not necessarily do so. As Madame de Staël put it, "History, in a word, cannot make its lesson perfectly clear, whether because we cannot always prove that their inner feelings punished the wicked in the midst of their prosperity and rewarded the virtuous in their misfortune, or because the fate of man is not confined to this life." The novel, however, especially the eighteenth-century English novel Madame de Staël knew, permitted an author to contrive a believable story in which virtue triumphed, and in which he could point the moral not only through the story but by his own observations upon the characters and events he created.

In exemplifying Madame de Staël's method of relating certain literary forms to social life, I have had to touch incidentally upon a second approach she adopted, that of relating a nation's literature to its character and institutions. Although some of her observations in this realm extend into her discussion of national character, her treatment of these two subjects can be reasonably separated for descriptive purposes.

Madame de Staël was fond of contrasting Roman with Greek literature, and English or German literature with French. In a sense, she looked upon the English and Germans, the Northern peoples, as the Romans of her time, and upon the French, a Southern people, as the Greeks.

Greek literature, to Madame de Staël, began in the usual way, with imaginative works, whereas Latin literature was unique in that it began with "philosophy," that is, with the analysis of human behavior, political life, and social institutions. Among the Romans, she wrote, "the art of writing was developed only long after the talent for action," and this produced a literature different in purpose and nature. The Greeks were irreverent and witty, the Romans responsible and solemn. The Greeks had indeed laid the foundations of Roman thought, but the Romans developed the intellectual side at the expense of the imaginative. It was only when the empire began to replace the republic in Rome that poetry developed among the superior minds. Under the republic men of talent were attracted to public life, to "eloquence, history, and philosophy," but "under an autocracy, to the contrary, the fine arts are the only road to renown left to eminent men." Poetry's late arrival in Rome made it superior to Greek poetry. Coming after the growth of knowledge of human affairs, Roman poetry was thereby enriched and ran "its course much more brilliantly." With the onset of tyranny, Roman literature was stifled and taste corrupted by the coarseness of the masters of the realm. The Romans, however, according to Madame de Staël, did not react by "decorating" the tyranny; instead, most of the best minds turned inward toward self-analysis, though a few turned to flattery and affectation.

Madame de Staël found English and French literature similar to Roman and Greek. The English were serious and intellectual, whereas the French, in approaching the analysis of human behavior, gave greater reign to feeling and imagination. The English were utilitarian, moral, commercial, and politically free. What their authors wrote really had an effect upon public affairs. The consequence was a sharp distinction between their prose and poetry. Prose was the medium through which the English sought practical goals in government and economy; it was therefore inelegant and prolix. Poetry was the medium of their imagination, and it was vigorous, warm, and eloquent. "It seems," observed Madame de Staël, "that the English fear to abandon themselves, except to poetic inspiration." But, she complained, "of that mediating style, which unites thought and eloquence, . . . the English have hardly any examples, and their books have but one purpose at a time, utility or pleasure."

The French had the subtlety to combine intellectual content with eloquent expression. Unable to influence events by their writings, French authors, in contrast to English, "aspired only to display cleverness even in the most serious discussions." As a result, they achieved literary perfection: "brevity of style." This talent of the French Madame de Staël characteristically traced to their institutions rather than their instincts. "French wit and elegance," she asserted, "was only the direct effect of the monarchical institutions and customs such as had prevailed in France for several centuries." French royal authority owed much to the nobility: "the king had unlimited power in fact and yet uncertain in law." This was a delicate arrangement which required each side to recognize and tolerate the appearances that masked realities on the other. As the nobles wanted to appear free while being loyal, charm became a "political necessity, for it alone could lend an aspect of choice to obedience." On his side, the king had to appear all-powerful though he was not; so he had to act in such a way that "neither the beginning nor the end of the royal power could be made out." This situation produced subtlety within subtlety, tacit understanding within tacit understanding, acceptance of certain forms and realities so intertwined that only a refined wit and cold perspicacity could distinguish between them and know how to react toward each. And the court set the style for the nation. "Charm and elegance of manners," Madame de Staël concluded, "passed from the customs of the court into the writings of men of letters." The resulting form of levity had its uses. If it made sycophants out of men, it also nurtured hope of advance and so "smoothed social differences without destroying them. It made nobles dream of equality with kings, and poets with nobles." Moreover, this combination of perspicacity and ridicule, though artificial, was at least a form of truth; under cover of charm and wit, one could give rascals their due.

When she came to German literature, Madame de Staël was dealing with something else again. Her full analysis of this subject appears, of course, in *On Germany;* here I want only to indicate her way of relating the German literature of her time to German political institutions. An important political influence upon German literature, according to Madame de Staël, was the disunity of the German states and the consequent absence of a single center of art and learning. Such diversity had the good effect of stimulating emulation but the presence of so many standards in different localities lowered the general level. The Germans were, like the English, systematic in their thought. Unlike the English, however, they could not influence events by their writings; given their philosophic bent, they turned to the speculative study of metaphysics and science. At the same time, their imaginative literature delineated the strongest of human feelings. Both of these tendencies emerged from the new idealist philosophy (to which I shall return in the next section), which stressed the content of ideas rather than their form and gave the widest latitude to speculation and feeling. Though she admired the "kind of inner energy" she saw in German thinkers, she was not blind to the consequences of an excess of feeling in imaginative literature and of abstraction in analytical writing. The apostle of seriousness, even she found the Germans too serious, too ponderous, too ready to dampen an emotional impact with abstractions, elaborations, and definitions. On balance, however, she emerged a great advocate both of German romanticism and of German systematic study of the physical and social order.

What is the current assessment of Madame de Staël's work on the sociology of literature? It should first be noted that not enough attention is given to it even by those writers who make an occasional reference to one or another of her books. Her general contributions are, however, given considerable though brief and occasional praise. Arnold Hauser, the author of an imposing study, observes about the nineteenth century: "The idea emphasized by Mme de Staël, that literature is the expression of society, finds universal recognition and becomes an axiom of French literary criticism."[54] As for her approach to national character as revealed in literature and to comparison of these national literary traditions, Irving Babbitt wrote, in the afterglow of Madame de Staël's brilliant reputation in nineteenth-century America, that she "has perhaps done more than anyone else to help forward the comparative study of literature as we now understand it."[55] When Babbitt wrote this, just before World War I, comparative literature was developing in France as an academic discipline. It was pursued in America too, but only after World War II were graduate programs in comparative literature introduced on a substantial scale in American universities.

Madame de Staël has her detractors. René Wellek finds serious deficiencies in her treatment of Greek, English, and German literature. "Details in Madame de Staël's literary history," he says justifiably, "are often vague, wrong, or simply absent."[56] Yet the broader strokes often illuminate not only individual works but whole eras and literary forms as well. Ian Watt, the author of a recent, highly regarded study, *The Rise of the Novel,*[57] asserts that Madame de Staël's *De la Littérature* was the "first important study of the novel in its larger social background" and that it "anticipated many of the elements" in his own analysis.

These comments on Madame de Staël may suggest that too much credit is given her for empty generalization and too much blame for errors of detail. Her contribution to our understanding of literature was not merely to point out that it

[54] *The Social History of Art* (2 vols., New York, 1951), Vol. II, p. 729.

[55] *The Masters of Modern French Criticism* (New York, 1912), p. 20.

[56] *A History of Modern Criticism, 1750–1950*, Volume II: *The Romantic Age* (New Haven, 1955), p. 221–22.

[57] (Berkeley, 1957), p. 300.

is an "expression" of society; so is everything else that human beings do. Madame de Staël's merit lies in her having *specified* certain relations between art and social life. Her contribution is not the obvious point that literature in a monarchy is different from literature in a republic, but to show precisely *how* they differ; not the general notion that literary forms emerge out of social institutions, but to show precisely, in a given society, the difference between comedy and tragedy, and *how* the novel is related to social life and to history as another form of writing about human affairs; not the highly abstract idea that a nation's literature develops from its character and institutions, but to show how a *given* nation's literature emerges from its experience and its broader intellectual position.

In its general character, the study of the relation between literature and social life does not change much. In 1935 Albert Guérard, for example, framed his task in almost the same terms as Madame de Staël did hers more than a century before: "Literature as one of the elements of a civilization, conditioned if not determined by social life as a whole, reacting upon social life in its turn: such is the problem we propose to study in this book." He wrote a very good book but its value does not lie in a "*proof*" of this relationship but in its *specification*, as, for example, when he discusses the nature of literature in four types of economy: pastoral, agricultural, commercial, and industrial.[58] Rather earlier, in 1904, the French literary historian Gustave Lanson accepted an invitation from the French sociologist Emile Durkheim to discuss the relations between the two disciplines of which they were leading practitioners. He argued that, though the efforts of thinkers like Madame de Staël and Taine to establish the relation be-

[58] *Literature and Society* (Boston, 1935), pp. 8, 60–72.

tween literature and its *milieu* were often weak, they had nevertheless proved to be a valuable stimulus to literary history. What was needed, he said, was not broad generalizations such as, "Literature is the expression of society," but specifications of them in "laws" that are modest, partial, provisional, and firmly grounded in literary history.[59]

The sociology of literature today is of three kinds. First, there are studies of the writer and the audience: their social origins and their relations through the work of art and in the market place. Second, there are studies of literature to determine what it tells us of the social life of the time and place in which it was created. Third, there are efforts to explain literature by showing its relation to the social life from which it has emerged.[60] Madame de Staël, as I have tried to show, did something in each of these domains. She offered exactly the sort of analysis Lanson meant (and mistakenly called "laws") and thereby set forth a large number of specific observations and a mode of analysis that add to our understanding of the relation of literature to social institutions and serve to illustrate how this understanding may be promoted.

NATIONAL CHARACTER

Madame de Staël was always discussing national character.

[59] "L'Histoire Littéraire et la Sociologie," *Revue de Metaphysique et de Morale* (1904), 12:625–26, 634–35.

[60] Examples of these three forms of the sociology of literature are: (1) Robert Escarpit, *Sociologie de la Littérature* (Paris, 1958), and two works by Arthur S. Collins, *Authorship in the Days of Johnson* (London, 1927) and *The Profession of Letters* (London, 1928); (2) in part, Leo Lowenthal, *Literature and the Image of Man* (Boston, 1957), and Victor Ehrenberg, *The People of Aristophanes* (3d edn., New York, 1962); (3) Arnold Hauser, *The Social History of Art* (2 vols., New York, 1951), and Ian Watt, *The Rise of the Novel* (Berkeley, 1957).

Whether she took up literature, philosophy, manners, or politics, and even in her novels, she always tried to relate human behavior to the social institutions of particular nations. The nation was the most meaningful group to her and her times, for the late eighteenth century lies between the healthy growth of European nationhood and its mad descent into nationalism.

In studying men and nations, Madame de Staël looked for their essences. "In a nation, as in a man," she wrote in *Literature Considered in Its Relation to Social Institutions,* "we need to find only the characteristic trait; all the others are the result of a thousand different accidents but that one alone constitutes its being." She believed that national character was determined largely by religious and political institutions, though climate also played a part (for example, by inducing "melancholy" among the Northern peoples). But the political institutions—the relations among people—in the end created the character of nations by shaping the leading social classes, who are the model for the others. People follow the pattern established by their political, spiritual, and intellectual superiors. As she put it in *On Germany,* "Only political institutions can shape the character of a nation." Madame de Staël, as we know by now, was fond of this formulation. The incredible heroine of her novel *Corinne* (much of which is an essay on Italian national character) says the same thing to her English admirer: "It is true that governments shape the character of nations."[61]

Madame de Staël breezed through history, literature, and many countries of Europe seeking out essences and character. Though not always fully prepared for these hunting expeditions from the point of view of scholarship, she bagged enough

[61] *Oeuvres Complètes,* Vol. I, p. 703b.

insights and suggestive generalizations to keep scholars busy for a long time. True to her own essence, she did not tarry over details and was never impeded by humility, modesty, or ridicule. Her search for English character, for example, extended unaccountably to a London men's gymnasium, where the amusing contrast between the old men's stuffiness and their childish exercises struck her as a typically English trait also exemplified in their dead-pan humor.

An eyewitness to Madame de Staël's famous meeting in Berlin with the German philosopher Fichte told her American admirer, George Ticknor, that she asked Fichte for an explanation of his entire system in fifteen minutes. Astonished, he began to answer, but soon Madame de Staël caught on to the complicated philosophy and interrupted him. "Ah!" she said, giving his name a French pronunciation, "that's enough. I understand, I understand you perfectly." His system, she told him before the group, could be explained by a little story about Baron Munchausen which she did not hesitate to tell.[62]

Coppet itself, on traditionally neutral ground in Switzerland, was an inexhaustible source of living material for the study of national character. Madame de Staël learned not only from the way her guests displayed their national heritages but from their analyses of them. Consider her clever delineation, in *On Germany,* of the differences between the German and French languages. "A Frenchman," she remarked, "can speak even when he has no ideas but a German always has in his head a little more than he can express." Or: "In France there are so many commonplaces on every subject that a fool can with their help speak well enough and even seem momentarily to be a man of intelligence." The famous Prussian general and writer on strategy, Karl von Clausewitz,

[62] *Life, Letters, and Journals of George Ticknor,* Vol. I, p. 498.

expressed ideas on these points from which Madame de Staël must certainly have drawn during his visit to Coppet shortly after her return from Germany and Austria in 1807.[63]

Actually she did not spend so much time outside of France and Switzerland as a quick review of her life probably suggests. She spent about a year in Germany and Austria on two trips in 1803–04 and 1807–08. She was in England for five months early in 1793, at the height of the Terror in France, and almost a year in 1813–14 as Napoleon went into military decline. She was in Russia for three months in the summer of 1812, and in Italy for about six in 1804–05.

Madame de Staël's most direct and sustained work on national character is *On Germany*. That country attracted her because she saw its people vigorous in activity, serious in culture, profound in thought, and simple in manners. A Protestant herself, she attributed much of Germany's greatness to the Reformation—freedom, morality, education, and progress in general. Always contrasting the Germans and the French, Madame de Staël made of this book a study of the national character of both.

Good taste and reason, those eighteenth-century ideals that she herself admired, were not, Madame de Staël argued, always the most important values. She insisted upon the need for the virility, boldness, and passion she found in German literature, philosophy, and social thought. All this was in contrast to French excessive refinement under the Old Regime and hypocrisy under Napoleon. Madame de Staël went through the entire range of German life and institutions: manners and morals, literature and the arts, philosophy and

[63] See his *Politische Schriften und Briefe* (Munich, 1922), p. 26, and a letter in Linnebach, (see note 10 above), p. 133. I am indebted to Mr. Peter Paret for bringing these writings of Clausewitz to my attention.

social thought, and religion. In everything—big and little—she contrasted the Germans with the French, "the two extremes of the human chain."

In fundamental outlook, she said, the French "regard external things as the source of all ideas," while the Germans "regard ideas as the source of all impressions." In manners: "The Germans . . . are hardly able to succeed in anything that calls for tact and facility. . . . The French, on the contrary, approach action with the freedom of art, and ideas with the bondage of custom." And in speech: "The Germans make the mistake of often putting into conversation things appropriate only to books, while the French sometimes put into their books things appropriate only to conversation." And so Madame de Staël proceeds from aphorism to concrete observation, approbation, disapproval, and exhortation. She makes a tart comment on the Germans like, "Enthusiasm for the arts and poetry is joined to rather common behavior in social life," but also a maudlin one like, "I had the experience of entering poor homes blackened by tobacco-smoke and of suddenly hearing not only the mistress but also the master of the house improvising on the harpsichord. . . ."

Above all, however, Madame de Staël was interested in institutions, character, and thought. She gave a convincing demonstration of her method in an attempt (Part Three, Chapter IX) to explain the influence of the new idealist philosophy upon literature and the arts. Having tried to show how political and religious institutions shaped German character and thought, she went on to show that the new philosophy stressed an unchanging moral law; this freed the German thinker from the conventions erected by society. In France, on the other hand, where ideas were presumed to come from outside oneself, the rules of propriety were more valued. Less concerned with these rules, the Germans were more interested in the "truth of sentiment" than in "grammatical correctness." The new German philosophy, moreover, stressed ideal forms, and hence German literary theory saw the goal of art as the approximation of ideal beauty rather than (as classical doctrine held) the imitation of nature. Thus German Romanticism, in harmony with German idealist philosophy, encouraged boldness and self-expression, and gave the artist wide latitude.

But the new doctrines had unfavorable results as well. The desire, inspired by the new philosophy, to know oneself profoundly led to obscure thought and writing. Not having abandoned all classical ideals of good form, Madame de Staël could not abide poor expression except in return for something else. "When one deals with thoughts that are boundless," she asserted, "obscurity of style is sometimes an indication of the very reach of the mind, but obscurity in the analysis of the affairs of life only shows that one does not understand them." The new doctrines also inspired all men to reach great heights of thought and feeling; this, she complained, stimulated the genius but made all lesser men seem pretentious. Finally the new doctrines encouraged their own rigidity: people were condemned if they liked a work that did not merit approval according to the doctrine, while works created in conformity with it were praised even if they did not please. Madame de Staël nevertheless considered it better that "poetics be based upon philosophical ideas, even if a bit abstract, than upon simple, superficial rules, for these rules are merely gates to prevent children from falling."

How much of Madame de Staël's serious discourse on the character of various nations was the consequence of her disappointment in France and her desire to make Napoleon look bad? If she complained about the lack of freedom in France, she extolled English character for its guarantee of liberty. If she disliked the effete upper classes in France, she praised the energy and benevolent paternalism of those in Russia. She seemed able to find an infinitude of goodness in Napoleon's enemies and very little in his France. Yet this is not the whole story, for her visits to and contemplation of other nations also brought out for her the greatness (past and potential, not current) of France; nor did she hesitate to criticize other nations even while showing what the world could learn from them.

In one sense, Madame de Staël created an imaginary nation wherever she went in Europe and England, and whenever she wrote about national character. She found in these places all the virtues she missed in France. Heine remarked in his *Confessions,* published four decades after *On Germany,* that her praise of German life was really intended as a criticism of Napoleon. "The good lady," wrote the great German poet in self-imposed exile in Paris, "saw in our country only what she wanted to see; a misty land of spirits, where human beings without bodies, wholly virtuous, wander over snowy meadows and discourse on morals and metaphysics. . . . She sees everywhere German spiritualism; she praises only our honesty, our virtue, our intellectual culture . . . she does not see our barracks, our brothels, our penitentiaries. . . ."[64]

This was only a half-truth. There is plenty of criticism of Germans in Madame de Staël's generally favorable portrait. She saw a certain vulgarity in their social life. They had imagination but lacked understanding. They were slow, awkward. They displayed a great gap between belief and feeling on the one hand, and behavior and inclinations on the other: in them "civilization and nature do not yet seem to be well blended." Their "gentleness of soul does not prevent rudeness in manners," and often "weakness of character reveals itself through

[64] Quoted in Emma Gertrude Jaeck, *Madame de Staël and the Spread of German Literature* (New York, 1915), p. 64.

the rough language and conduct." They were indifferent to political liberty. The weakness of their political institutions produced weakness in character; they preferred, in relations with each other, to follow established rules rather than to have to make their own decisions. In a single statement Madame de Staël severely arraigned the nation: "The mind and character of the Germans appear not to be in touch with each other: the one cannot bear any restriction, the other submits to every yoke."

It was only after *On Germany* became a classic (and therefore seldom read) that it was assumed to be an unrelieved commendation. At the time it appeared, some readers saw the critique as well as the praise. A German living in England wrote an anonymous attack upon the book just after the publication of the second edition in 1814. He complained of Madame de Staël's "peremptory, severe, and unwarrantable strictures on my countrymen" and called her book a "provocation" to every self-respecting German reader.[65] And only a few years ago an American writer criticized various aspects of German life today, citing Madame de Staël's own unfavorable judgments a hundred and fifty years earlier.[66] But today such awareness of her criticism of the Germans is rare.

I have said that Madame de Staël's Germany is in a sense imaginary. So, of course, is any abstraction like national character. The description of national character poses two dangers. First, the closer the writer sticks to the details of one nation in their variety, the more he remains on the level of anecdote and the less he approaches a general formulation that sum-

[65] *A Critical Analysis of Several Striking and Incongruous Passages in Madame de Staël's Work on Germany, with Some Historical Accounts of that Country*, by a German (London, 1814), p. vi.

[66] John McCormick, "The Frozen Country," *The Kenyon Review* (1960), 22:32–59.

marizes traits and tendencies. Second, the more the writer attempts to generalize, the closer he comes, if he is talking about a single nation, to overlooking evidence contrary to his summary, or to including contradictory traits in it, or to describing traits common to other nations as well and therefore missing something about the one whose character he seeks to distill. The choice a writer makes between these two dangers depends upon his purpose and his capacity to observe and generalize. Madame de Staël, I think, did rather well—not only for her time but for ours as well. She has helped us to understand the nations of Europe by describing some of their central features in a way that is still enlightening.

Conclusion

Madame de Staël has a way of captivating her biographers; they are happy to forgive her her faults. Her first biographer, her cousin Albertine Necker de Saussure, observed that although nothing Madame de Staël wrote was as great as she herself was, it is in her works that at least a trace of herself may be found. For everything Madame de Staël uttered, even her most intellectual expression, came straight from her heart. So her works, her cousin said, are the "*mémoires* of her life in abstract form." Madame de Staël herself knew this; she concluded *Literature Considered in Its Relation to Social Institutions:* "I am aware how easy it is to reproach me with thus confounding the emotions of my soul with the general ideas this book ought to have. But I cannot separate my ideas from my feelings."

Passionate and demanding, Madame de Staël was also generous. She sustained others in many ways—financially, intellectually, morally. Meanness was beyond her. Advocating cultural education for the people, not merely training for necessary employment, she remarked in *On Germany:* "There is something revolting about the necessary in every domain when it is meted out by those who enjoy the superfluous." She could understand deprivation because she had both largeness of spirit and her own experience of yearning. She yearned for the love of individuals and the power to influence events to preserve or restore liberty and culture. She was quite aware that these two cravings pushed in different directions. For one interested in politics, she was unusually indifferent to what people in general thought of her, but when she needed someone's love she devoted herself completely to making that man or woman dependent upon her. "The desire to please," she said in *On Germany,* "makes us dependent upon general opinion, the need to be loved frees us from it." It is easy to see which course she herself had to follow.

Madame de Staël's latest biographer feels her influence as much as did her earliest one. Mr. J. Christopher Herold says in the preface to his *Mistress to an Age:* "In my attempt to unravel and understand the life of her passions, I remained a fascinated spectator . . . but in discovering her thought, I found myself an active partner in a conversation . . . in which she often helped me to find my own convictions, for which I had long been groping." Why are her political and social views so relevant for us today? I think because the eighteenth century's ethics and rationalism have not yet been superseded as ideals; its distillation of the accumulated knowledge about social life remains largely valid. Madame de Staël spoke for rationality and also for feeling. She saw European civilization as a whole, not in order to oppose it to other civilizations but to give it its place among them. She did not believe that Europe's energy, integrity, and greatness depended upon injustices like slavery and imperialism, or that the end of these injustices would reduce Europe's cultural potentialities. She was often wrong but never weak. She often failed but was never dispirited for very long or vindictive at all. She saw the defeat of reason many times but never doubted it as an ideal. As she wrote of herself in her book on the French Revolution, "Throughout my life the errors I have made in politics have stemmed from the idea that men could always be moved by the truth if it was presented to them vigorously."

One

POLITICAL POWER AND ITS USES

Section I

Napoleon: The Despot's Way

This Section, bearing my own title, is from Considérations sur les principaux événements de la Révolution française, *completed in 1816 and published posthumously in 1818. I have retained Madame de Staël's division into Parts and Chapters, and her titles of the Chapters.*—Ed.

from Part Three

Chapter XXVI. Treaty of Campo Formio, 1797. General Bonaparte's Arrival in Paris
Chapter XXVII. General Bonaparte's Preparations to Go to Egypt. His Opinion of the Invasion of Switzerland

from Part Four

Chapter III. How the Consular Constitution Was Established
Chapter IV. The Advance of Bonaparte's Absolute Power
Chapter VIII. On Exile
Chapter XIX. Intoxication of Power; Bonaparte's Reverses and Abdication

from Part Five

Chapter VI. The Appearance of France and Paris during the First Occupation
Chapter XIII. Bonaparte's Return
Chapter XIV. Bonaparte's Conduct upon His Return
Chapter XV. Bonaparte's Fall

Part Three

Chapter XXVI. Treaty of Campo Formio, 1797[1]

General Bonaparte's Arrival in Paris

The Directory was not inclined to peace, not because it wished to extend French rule beyond the Rhine and the Alps but because it believed war useful for the propagation of the republican system. Its plan was to surround France with a belt of republics. One of the great faults of the French—a consequence of their social customs—is to imitate each other and to want to be imitated. They take the natural differences in men's or even nations' ways of thinking as a hostile feeling against themselves.

General Bonaparte was certainly less serious and less sincere than the Directory in the love of republican ideas, but he was much more shrewd in estimating a situation. He sensed that peace would become popular in France because passions were subsiding and people were weary of sacrifices; so he signed the Treaty of Campo Formio with Austria.

General Bonaparte distinguished himself as much by his character and mind as by his victories, and the imagination of the French was beginning to attach itself to him strongly. A tone of moderation and nobility prevailed in his style, which contrasted with the revolutionary gruffness of the civil leaders of France. The warrior spoke like a magistrate, while the magistrates expressed themselves with martial violence.

[1] *Napoleon I becomes the central figure of Madame de Staël's* Considerations on the Principal Events of the French Revolution *at the point of his great popularity as he returned to Paris in 1797 following his victories in the Italian campaign. The Directory, then ruling France, encouraged him to carry out his plan to strike at England through Egypt, which he invaded in 1798. The next year he returned to Paris, helped overthrow the Directory and became First Consul. In 1804 he proclaimed himself Emperor.*—Ed.

It was with this feeling, at least, that I saw him for the first time in Paris. I could find no words of reply when he came to me to tell me that he had sought my father at Coppet and that he regretted having passed through Switzerland without having seen him. But when I was somewhat recovered from the confusion of admiration, a very strong sense of fear followed. Bonaparte at that time had no power; he was even believed to be somewhat threatened by the jealous suspicions of the Directory. So the fear he inspired was caused only by the extraordinary effect of his person upon nearly all who approached him. I had seen men worthy of respect, and I had seen fierce men: there was nothing in the impression Bonaparte produced upon me that recalled either the former or the latter. I very quickly saw, in the various occasions I had to meet him during his stay in Paris, that his character could not be defined by the words we ordinarily use; he was neither good, nor fierce, nor gentle, nor cruel, like others we know. Such a being, having no equals, could neither feel nor arouse any sympathy: he was more than a human being or less than one. His appearance, his mind, and his speech were foreign in nature—an added advantage for subjugating the French.

Far from being reassured by seeing Bonaparte more often, I was made increasingly apprehensive. I had a vague feeling that no emotion of the heart could influence him. He considers a human being a fact or a thing, not a fellow man. He does not hate nor does he love. For him, there is nothing but himself; all others are ciphers.

Every time I heard him speak I was struck by his superiority: yet it had no resemblance to that of men educated and cultivated by study or by social intercourse, such as may be found in England or France. But his speech showed a feeling for the situation, like the hunter's for his prey. Sometimes he related the political and military events of his life in a very interesting way; he even had a touch of Italian imagination in the stories that permitted some humor. Nothing, however, could overcome my unconquerable aversion for what I saw in him. I sensed in his soul a cold and sharp sword that froze as it wounded. I sensed in his mind a deep irony that nothing could escape—neither greatness, nor beauty, nor even his own glory. For he despised the nation whose support he wanted, and no spark of enthusiasm could be found in his need to awe the human race.

It was in the interval between Bonaparte's return and his departure for Egypt—that is, toward the end of 1797—that I saw him several times in Paris; and never could I rid myself of the difficulty in breathing that I felt in his presence. One day I was at table between him and the Abbé Siéyès—an extraordinary spot, had I been able to foresee the future![2] I studied his face carefully, but whenever he noticed my searching glances he seemed to erase all expression from his eyes, as if they had turned to marble. His face became blank, except for the faint smile into which he shaped his lips, as a precaution, to confound anyone who might wish to observe the external signs of his thoughts.

His face, at that time lean and pale, was rather pleasant. Since then he has become fat, which ill suits him; we need to believe that such a man is tormented by his own nature, in order to tolerate the fact that this nature makes others suffer so. As he is short, though his body is long, he looks much better on horseback than on foot. In everything, it is war and only war that suits him. His conduct in company is awkward without being shy. He appears somewhat scornful when he controls

[2] *About two years after this event, on the 18th Brumaire, 1799, Napoleon and Siéyès overthrew the Directory and established rule by the Consulate.*—Ed.

himself and somewhat common when relaxed. Scorn suits him better, so he readily adopts it.

The Directory gave General Bonaparte an official reception[3] which, in several respects, should be regarded as an important moment in the history of the Revolution. The courtyard of the Luxembourg Palace was chosen for the ceremony. No room would have been large enough to hold the crowd it attracted; there were spectators at all the windows and on all the roofs. The five Directors, in Roman dress, were seated upon a platform at the end of the courtyard.

Bonaparte came dressed very simply, followed by his *aides-de-camp*, all taller than he but almost stooped by the respect they showed him. The *élite* of France present there covered the victorious general with applause. He was the hope of everyone: republicans, royalists, all saw the present and the future resting in his powerful hand.

Alas! What has happened to those days of glory and peace France anticipated twenty years ago! All these good things were in the hand of one man. What has he done with them?

Chapter XXVII. General Bonaparte's Preparations to Go to Egypt. His Opinion of the Invasion of Switzerland

General Bonaparte, at this same time, the end of 1797, sounded public opinion regarding the Directors; he realized that they were not liked but that republican sentiment made it as yet impossible for a general to take the place of civilian officials. The Directory proposed to him the assault upon England. He went to examine the coasts, and, quickly seeing that this expedition was senseless, returned resolved to attempt the conquest of Egypt.

[3] *At the end of 1799.*—Ed.

Bonaparte has always sought to seize the imagination of men and, in this respect, he knows well how one must govern when one is not born to the throne. An invasion of Africa, the war carried to an almost fabulous country like Egypt, must make an impression upon every mind.

There was no money to transport an army to Egypt, and it was particularly reprehensible of Bonaparte to arouse the Directory to invade Switzerland in order to seize the treasury of Berne, which two hundred years of prudence and economy had accumulated. The pretext for the war was the situation of the Vaud region.[4] But it was not only a matter of the Vaud region in a war that must necessarily jeopardize the independence of all Switzerland. The cause appeared so sacred to me that I did not yet, at that time, believe it entirely impossible to enlist Bonaparte to defend it. Throughout my life the errors I have made in politics have stemmed from the idea that men could always be moved by the truth if it was presented to them vigorously.

I remained almost an hour *tête-à-tête* with Napoleon. He listens well and patiently, for he wants to know if what is said to him can shed light on his own concerns; but Demosthenes and Cicero together could not lead him to the slightest sacrifice of his personal interest.

General Bonaparte, in speaking with me about Switzerland, pointed to the situation in the Vaud region as grounds to send French troops there. He told me that the inhabitants of the region were subject to the aristocrats of Berne and that in these times men could not exist without political rights. I tempered this republican ardor as much as I could by pointing out to him that the Vaudois were completely free in all civil respects and that when liberty exists *de facto* it is unnecessary, in order to

[4] *Coppet, where Madame de Staël retreated in exile to her father's chateau, is located in the Vaud, now a Swiss canton.*—Ed.

obtain it *de jure*, to expose one's self to the greatest of misfortunes, that of seeing foreigners in one's land.

The word *principle* has since then seemed highly suspect to General Bonaparte; but at that time it suited him to use it, and he raised it against me. I insisted again upon the happiness and beauty of Switzerland, upon the tranquillity it had enjoyed for several centuries. "Oh yes, no doubt," Bonaparte interrupted, "but men must have *political rights*. Yes," he repeated, like something learned in school, "yes, *political rights*." And, changing the conversation because he no longer wanted to hear about this subject, he spoke to me of his love for seclusion, for the countryside, for the fine arts, and he took the trouble to reveal himself to me in ways appropriate to the kind of taste he supposed me to have.

Part Four
Chapter III. How the Consular Constitution[5] Was Established

The most potent magic that Bonaparte used to establish his power was the terror the mere name of Jacobinism inspired, though anyone capable of reflection knew perfectly well that this scourge could not reappear in France. People readily pretend to fear defeated parties in order to justify harsh measures. Everyone who wants to promote the establishment of despotism forcefully reminds us of the terrible crimes of demagogy. It is a very simple technique. So Bonaparte paralyzed every form of resistance to his will by the words: *Do you want me to*

[5] *Madame de Staël refers to what became known as the Constitution of the Year VIII, written by Siéyès and Bonaparte after their establishment of the rule of the Consulate. It was adopted in 1800, or the year VIII according to the French Revolutionary calendar.*—Ed.

hand you over to the Jacobins? And France bowed down before him, no man bold enough to reply to him: *We shall be able to fight the Jacobins and you.* In short, even then he was not liked, only preferred. He almost always presented himself in competition with another cause for alarm, in order to make his power acceptable as a lesser evil.

Chapter IV. The Advance of Bonaparte's Absolute Power

We cannot watch too attentively for the first symptoms of tyranny; when it has grown to a certain point, there is no more time to stop it. One man sweeps along the will of many individuals of whom the majority, taken separately, wish to be free but who nevertheless surrender because people fear each other and do not dare to speak their thoughts freely.

Despite differences of time and place, there are points of similarity in the history of all nations that have fallen under the yoke. It is almost always after prolonged civil disturbance that tyranny becomes established, because it offers to all the exhausted and fearful parties the hope of finding shelter in it. Bonaparte has said of himself, with reason, that he could play the instrument of power marvelously. His plan for achieving control over France rested upon three main bases: to gratify men's self-interest at the expense of their virtues, to deprave public opinion with sophisms, and to give the nation the goal of war instead of liberty.

General Bonaparte decreed a constitution[6] in which there were no safeguards. Besides, he took great care to leave in existence the laws announced during the Revolution, in order

[6] *The Constitution of the Year VIII (1800).*—Ed.

to select from this detestable arsenal the weapon that suited him. The special commissions, deportations, exiles, the bondage of the press—these steps unfortunately taken in the name of liberty—were very useful to tyranny. To adopt them, he sometimes advanced reasons of state, sometimes the need of the times, sometimes the acts of his opponents, sometimes the need to maintain tranquillity. Such is the artillery of phrases that supports absolute power, for "emergencies" never end, and the more one seeks to repress by illegal measures the more one creates disaffected people who justify new injustices. The establishment of the rule of law is always put off till tomorrow. This is a vicious circle from which one cannot break out, for the public spirit that is awaited in order to permit liberty can come only from liberty itself.

Bonaparte took the Tuileries as his residence; this choice was a stroke of victory. The king of France used to be seen there and royal practices were still present to the eye. The walls alone could, so to speak, revive everything. Toward the final days of the last century I saw the First Consul enter the palace built by the kings. Though Bonaparte was still very far from the magnificence he later displayed, one could already see in all who surrounded him an eagerness to become obsequious courtiers in the Oriental manner, which must have convinced him that to govern the earth was a very easy thing.

It was particularly advantageous to Bonaparte's power that he had to manage only a mass. All individual existence was annihilated by ten years of disorder, and nothing sways people like military success; it takes great power of reason to combat this tendency instead of profiting from it. No one in France could consider his position secure. Men of all classes, ruined or enriched, banished or rewarded, found themselves one by one equally, so to speak, in the hands of power. Bonaparte, who always moved between two opposed interests, took very good care not to put an end to these anxieties by fixed laws that might let everyone know his rights. To one man he returned his property, while another he stripped of his forever. The First Consul reserved to himself the power of determining, under any pretext, the fate of everything and everyone.

Those Frenchmen who sought to resist the ever-increasing power of the First Consul had to invoke liberty to struggle against him successfully. But at this word the aristocrats and the enemies of the Revolution cried "Jacobinism," thus supporting the tyranny for which they later sought to blame their adversaries.

The many newspapers in France were soon subjected to the most rigorous but cleverly devised censorship. For it was not a question of commanding silence from a nation given to meaningless loquacity, as the Romans had needed circuses. So Bonaparte established that prattling tyranny from which he later derived so much benefit. All the press repeated the same thing each day, without any one being allowed to contradict them. Just as regular troops are a greater threat than militias to the independence of nations, so hired writers make public opinion much more depraved than it would be if people communicated only by speech and thus based their judgments only upon facts.

Great power cannot be achieved except by taking advantage of the tendency of the age. So Bonaparte studied well the spirit of his. There had been, among the leading men of the eighteenth century in France, a superb enthusiasm for the principles that support the happiness and dignity of mankind, but under the shelter of this great oak grew poisonous plants, selfishness and irony; and Bonaparte could cleverly use these baneful inclinations. He held up all beautiful things to ridicule.

Chapter VIII. On Exile

Among all the prerogatives of authority, one of the most favorable to tyranny is the power to exile without trial. The *lettres de cachet* of the Old Regime have been justly advanced as one of the most urgent grounds for making a revolution in France. But it was Bonaparte, the people's choice, who, trampling under foot all the principles for which the people had risen up, arrogated the power to exile anyone who displeased him a little and to imprison, without any meddling from the courts, anyone who displeased him more. I can understand, I admit, how most of the former courtiers rallied to Bonaparte's political system. They needed to make only one concession to it: to change masters. But the republicans, who must have been shocked by every word, every act, every decree, of Napoleon's regime—how could they lend themselves to his tyranny?

To banish a man or a woman from Paris, to send them—as it was then put—to breathe the country air, was to prescribe a severe punishment in such mild terms that all the flatterers of power easily turned it to ridicule. Yet the fear of such an exile was enough to bend to slavery all the inhabitants of the leading city of the Empire. The scaffolds may finally arouse courage, but the domestic worries of all sorts resulting from banishment weaken resistance and arouse only dread of the disfavor of the ruler who can inflict such a wretched existence upon one. A man may voluntarily spend his life outside his country. But when he is forced to do so he constantly imagines that his loved ones may be ill, while he is not allowed to be near them and perhaps may never see them again. What he most loves—often even his family, his social life, his material interests—is imperiled. What is even more cruel, all his ties are loosened and he ends up a stranger to his own land.

During the twelve years of exile to which Napoleon condemned me, I often reflected that he could not feel the misfortune of being barred from France. He did not have a single memory of France in his heart. Only the rocks of Corsica recalled to him the days of his childhood, but the daughter of M. Necker was more French than he.

I sensed more quickly than others—and I pride myself on it—Bonaparte's tyrannical character and intentions. The true friends of liberty are in this respect guided by an instinct that does not deceive them. But my position, at the outset of the Consulate, was made more painful by the fact that respectable society in France thought it saw in Bonaparte the man who had saved them from anarchy or Jacobinism. They therefore vigorously condemned the spirit of opposition I displayed toward him.

I still remember one of the drawing-room tortures, if I may put it this way, that French aristocrats can, when it suits them, so expertly inflict upon those who do not share their opinions. A large part of the old nobility came around to supporting Bonaparte—some, as has since been seen, in order to return to their practices as courtiers, and others hoping that the First Consul would restore the former dynasty. People knew that I strongly opposed the form of government Napoleon was following and preparing, and the advocates of arbitrary power, according to their custom, described as anti-social those opinions that tended to raise the dignity of people. If some *emigrés* who returned under Bonaparte's rule were reminded of the fury with which they then blamed the friends of liberty, who consistently supported but one system, they might learn tolerance in looking back upon their errors.

I was the first woman Bonaparte exiled, but he soon banished many others of various opinions. Since women, on the one hand, could in no way further his political schemes, and since, on the other hand, they were less susceptible than men to the fears and hopes that power dispensed, they irritated him like so many rebels, and he took pleasure in saying offensive and vulgar things to them. He hated the spirit of chivalry as much as he sought pomp—a bad choice among the old customs. He retained, also, from his early ways during the Revolution, a certain Jacobin antipathy for the brilliant society of Paris, over which women exerted much influence. He feared their wit, which, it must be admitted, is particularly characteristic of Frenchwomen.

Bonaparte wanted me to praise him in my writings, not, certainly, that an additional eulogy would have been noticed in the fumes of incense surrounding him, but it annoyed him that I was the only writer the French knew who had published under his rule without making any mention of his majestic existence. And he ended by suppressing my book on Germany with incredible fury. Until then my misfortune had consisted only in my removal from Paris, but after that I was forbidden all travel, and I was threatened with prison for the rest of my days. The contagious nature of exile, an invention worthy of the Roman emperors, was the most bitter aggravation of this penalty. Those who came to see the exiles exposed themselves to exile in turn. Most of the Frenchmen I knew avoided me like the plague. This seemed comic to me when I did not suffer too much from it. Like travelers in quarantine who maliciously throw their handkerchiefs at passers-by to make them share the annoyance of confinement, when I happened to run into a man from Bonaparte's court in the streets of Geneva I was tempted to terrify him with my courtesies.

Chapter XIX. Intoxication of Power; Bonaparte's Reverses and Abdication

From the moment the Allies passed the Rhine and entered France[7] it seemed to me that the prayers of the friends of France must undergo a complete change. I was then in London, and one of the English Cabinet Ministers asked me what I wished for. I ventured to reply that my desire was to see Bonaparte victorious and slain. The English had enough greatness of soul to make it unnecessary for me to conceal this French sentiment from them. Yet I was to learn, in the midst of the transports of joy with which the city of the conquerors reverberated, that Paris was in the power of the Allies. At that moment I felt there was no longer a France: I believed Burke's prediction[8] realized and that where France had existed we should see only an abyss. The Emperor Alexander, the Allies, and the constitutional principles adopted through the wisdom of Louis XVIII banished this gloomy presentiment.

There was, nevertheless, something of grandeur in Napo-

[7] *In December 1813. The Allies took Paris the following March and Madame de Staël arrived there from England in May.*—Ed.

[8] *Edmund Burke frequently said that revolutionary France was ruined or was heading toward ruin, tyranny, and anarchy. The specific "prediction" Madame de Staël referred to may be his remark in the "Speech on the Army Estimates, 1790"* (The Works of Edmund Burke, *5th edn., 12 vols., Boston, 1877, Vol. III, pp. 214–15) that France was destroyed as a political power in Europe and that it was "not easy to determine" whether the country could ever regain its position. In 1793 he opposed those who favored the utter reduction of France and he advocated a strong France as the best guarantee of Europe's freedom—but a properly governed France, of course. He pointed out that Britain and Austria, leading the coalition against France, aimed "totally to destroy" it as a European power. ("Remarks on the Policy of the Allies with Respect to France,"* ibid., *pp. 454–55).*—Ed.

leon's farewell to his troops and to their eagles,[9] so long victorious. His last campaign had been long and skillful: in short, the fatal magic that bound France's military glory to him was not yet destroyed. Thus the conference at Paris must be blamed for having made his return possible.[10] The representatives of Europe ought to admit this error frankly; it is unfair to blame the French nation for it. It was certainly with no evil intention that the ministers of the foreign kingdoms permitted a danger that threatened all of Europe to hover above the throne of Louis XVIII. But why do not those who suspended this sword admit their responsibility for the evil it caused?

Many people like to argue that Bonaparte would still be emperor if he had not attempted the expeditions against Spain or Russia. This opinion pleases the supporters of despotism, who insist that so fine a government could not be overthrown by the very nature of things but only by an accident. I have already said, what observation of France will confirm, that Bonaparte needed war to establish and maintain absolute power. A great nation would not have supported the dull and degrading burden of despotism if military glory had not ceaselessly moved or exalted the public spirit. He was a man destined to the virtues of Washington or the conquests of Attila. But it was easier to reach the ends of the civilized world than to stop the progress of human reason, and French public opinion would soon have accomplished what Allied arms brought about.

In the various remarks I have just put together on Bona-

[9] *Napoleon's troops carried the symbol of an eagle on their flagstaffs. When he bade his men farewell before going into exile, he called for a standard and embraced it.*—Ed.

[10] *This was the Allies' meeting in Paris in April 1814, at which they offered Napoleon generous terms of surrender.*—Ed.

parte, I have avoided his private life, with which I am not acquainted and which is irrelevant to the interests of France. I have not offered a single shady detail of his past, for the slanders showered upon him seem to me even more vile than the adulations. I trust I have evaluated him as all public men should be—in accordance with what they have done for the prosperity, enlightenment, and morality of nations. The persecutions Bonaparte made me undergo have not, I can honestly state, affected my opinion of him. On the contrary, it was necessary for me rather to resist the sort of trepidation caused by a man of extraordinary talent and ominous destiny. I should even have rather willingly let myself be tempted by the satisfaction that courageous people find in defending the underdog and by the pleasure in thus taking a stand in greater contrast to the writers and orators who, yesterday prostrate before him, now ceaselessly abuse him—while, I suppose, carefully checking the height of the rocks that confine him. But one cannot be silent on Bonaparte even in his misfortune, because his political doctrine still rules in the minds of his enemies as well as his partisans. For, of the entire heritage of his terrible power there remains to mankind nothing but the baneful knowledge of a few more secrets in the art of tyranny.

Part Five
Chapter VI. The Appearance of France and Paris during the First Occupation

It would be a great mistake to be surprised at the sorrow the French felt upon seeing their famous capital overrun in 1814 by foreign armies. The sovereigns who made themselves masters of it behaved at that time with the most perfect fairness. But it is a bitter blow for a nation even to have to praise foreigners, since that is proof that its fate depends upon them. The French armies, it is true, had several times entered almost all the capitals of Europe, but none of those cities was so important to its country as Paris was to France. The monuments of the fine arts, the memories of men of genius, the brilliance of society all contributed to make Paris the center of Continental civilization. For the first time since Paris had held such a position in the world, the flags of the foreigner were waving upon its ramparts.

After ten years of exile[11] I landed at Calais, and I was looking forward to great happiness upon again seeing beautiful France, which I had missed so—my feelings were entirely different from what I was expecting. The first men I saw on shore wore the Prussian uniform. They were the masters of the city by right of conquest. O France! O France! Only a foreign tyrant could have reduced you to such a state. A French sovereign, no matter who he was, would have loved you too much ever to expose you to it.

I continued on my way, my heart always in pain from the same thought. Approaching Paris, I saw Germans, Russians, Cossacks, Bashkirs, on all sides. They were camped around the Church of St. Denis, where the ashes of the kings of France rest. The discipline imposed by their leaders kept these soldiers from doing any harm to anyone—any harm but the despondency it was impossible not to feel. At last I entered the city where I spent the happiest and brightest days of my life—as though in a painful dream. Was I in Germany or Russia? Had

[11] *In Part Four, Chapter VIII, "On Exile," Madame de Staël refers to her twelve years of exile by Napoleon. She entitled her manuscript of memoirs, published after her death,* Ten Years of Exile. *This discrepancy seems to be the result of the fact that she was writing at different times. Actually she was first threatened with exile by Napoleon in 1802 and exiled the following year; she returned to Paris in 1814 after his first defeat by the Allied powers.*—Ed.

the streets and squares of the capital of France been copied in order to recall their memory when they no longer existed? I was completely confused, for despite the acuteness of my pain I respected the foreigners for having shaken off the yoke. I admired them unreservedly at that moment, but to see Paris occupied by them—the Tuileries, the Louvre, guarded by troops from the farthest reaches of Asia to whom our language, history, and great men were all less familiar than the least important Tartar khan—was an unbearable pain.

Chapter XIII. Bonaparte's Return

I shall never forget the moment when I learned, from one of my friends the morning of March 6, 1815, that Bonaparte had landed on the French coast. I had the misfortune to foresee at once the consequences of that event—as they have since taken place—and I thought the earth was about to open under me. I said, "There will be no liberty if Bonaparte wins and no national independence if he loses." Events, it seems to me, have borne out this sad prediction only too well.

I shall not indulge, as has only too often been done, in all kinds of tirades against Napoleon. In trying to regain the throne he had lost, he did what was only natural. But what are we to say of the enlightened men who did not see the misfortune to France and to the world in the possibility of his return? The nations were more vehement than the kings in the war against Bonaparte, and France, in taking him back as leader, necessarily incurred the hatred of both governments and peoples.

The ministers of foreign countries have called the French army perjured, but this word is not justified. The French soldiers, most of them under forty years old, did not know the

Bourbons and had fought for twenty years under Bonaparte's orders. Could they fire on their General? And from the moment they did not fire, were they not necessarily swept into following him? But, the accusers of our country will still say, if the army may be pardoned, what shall one think of the peasants and the townspeople who welcomed Bonaparte? I shall make the same distinction in the nation as in the army. Enlightened men could see in Bonaparte nothing but a despot, but by a rather fatal conjunction of circumstances this despot was presented to the nation as the defender of its rights. All the benefits achieved by the Revolution, which France will never willingly give up, were threatened by the endless rashness of the party that wants to repeat the conquest of Frenchmen, as if they were still Gauls. And that part of the nation that most feared the return of the Old Regime thought they saw in Bonaparte a way to save themselves from it. The most fatal association that could overwhelm the friends of liberty was that a despot should join their ranks—should, so to speak, place himself at their head—and that the enemies of every liberal idea should have a pretext for confusing popular violence with the evils of despotism and thus make tyranny appear to be the result of liberty itself. The consequence of this fatal association has been that the French have been hated by the sovereigns for seeking to be free and by the nations for not knowing how to be free.

Chapter XIV. Bonaparte's Conduct upon His Return

If it was criminal to recall Bonaparte, it was silly to try to disguise such a man as a constitutional monarch. As he was taken back, a military dictatorship should have been handed to him, conscription re-established, and the nation called to arms—in short, no one should have bothered about liberty when independence was in danger. In being made to adopt language quite contrary to what had been his own for fifteen years, Bonaparte's reputation necessarily suffered. Clearly, it was only because he was forced by circumstances that he could proclaim principles so different from those he had followed when he was all-powerful.

Now what is such a man when he allows himself to be coerced? The terror he used to inspire, the power that came from that terror, no longer existed; he was a muzzled bear who could still be heard to grumble but whose masters made dance as they pleased. A man who detested abstract ideas and legal restraints, instead of being made to talk about constitutions for hours on end, should have been on the field of battle four days after his arrival in Paris, before the preparations of the Allies were completed and especially while the shock caused by his return still stunned the imagination. He should have aroused the passions of the Italians and the Poles, promised the Spaniards to expiate his errors by giving them back their parliament—in short, liberty should have been regarded as a weapon and not an obstacle.

Indeed, how could Bonaparte have put up with the constitution he was made to proclaim? When the responsible ministers resisted his will, what would he have done with them?

Military Jacobinism, one of the world's greatest scourges, was, if still possible, Bonaparte's only resort. When he uttered the words law and liberty, Europe was reassured: it sensed that this was no longer its old and terrible adversary.

Chapter XV. Bonaparte's Fall

Whether Napoleon lives or perishes, whether or not he reappears on the continent of Europe, only one reason moves me to speak of him: the ardent wish that the friends of liberty in France completely separate their cause from his and beware of confusing the principles of the Revolution with those of the Imperial *régime.* I believe I have shown that there is no counter-revolution so fatal to liberty as the one he made.

Section II

The Requirements of Tolerance and Stability

This Section, bearing my own title, is from Considérations sur les principaux événements de la Révolution française, *completed in 1816 and published posthumously in 1818. I have retained Madame de Staël's division into Parts and Chapters, and her titles of Chapters.*—Ed.

from Part One
Chapter I. General Remarks

from Part Three
Chapter XV. Political Fanaticism

from Part Five
Chapter I. What Constitutes Legitimate Monarchy

Part One
Chapter I. General Remarks

The French Revolution is one of the great occurrences of the social order. Those who consider it an accidental event have looked to neither the past nor the future. They have taken the actors for the play, and passionate wishful thinking has led them to attribute to men of the moment what it took centuries to prepare.

One need only cast a glance upon the principal turning points of history to become convinced that they were all inevitable whenever they were connected in any way with the development of ideas, and that after a struggle and more or less prolonged misfortunes the triumph of enlightenment has always been favorable to the greatness and improvement of mankind.

I would like to speak of the time in which we have lived as if it were already remote from us.

I shall limit myself, in this chapter, to some general remarks on the political progress of European civilization, but only in its relation to the French Revolution.

The two ancient peoples whose literature and history still comprise our main intellectual treasure owed their amazing superiority to nothing but the possession of a free country. But slavery existed among them, and consequently the privileges of and grounds for emulation that ought to have been common to all men were shared exclusively by a few citizens. The Greek and Roman nations disappeared from the world as a result of the barbarous—that is to say, unjust—features of their institutions. The vast regions of Asia are lost in despotism and for the past several centuries such civilization as remained to them has been stagnant. So the great historical change whose results are apparent in the present condition of the modern nations dates from the invasions by the Northern peoples; for the public law of most European states today still rests upon the law of conquest.

It seems to me that we may direct our attention to four eras in which changes, already foreshadowed, became strikingly clear.

The first political era is the one in which the nobles, that is, the conquerors, considered themselves partners in the royal power of their chief, while the nation was divided among the various lords who disposed of it as they pleased. There was at that time neither education, nor industry, nor commerce; landed property was virtually the only known kind. Everything indicates that in this period the great lords were very independent of the kings. They upheld liberty for themselves—if one who imposes servitude on others can himself be free.

The feudal *régime* was much better for the nobles than the status of courtiers to which royal despotism has condemned them. It is now a purely metaphysical question whether the human species would gain more from the independence of one whole class or from oppression exerted mildly but equally over all. The point is simply that the nobles, during their glorious era, enjoyed a kind of political liberty, and that the absolute power of kings was established against them with the support of the populace.

In the second political era, that of partial emancipation, the middle classes of the cities claimed certain rights; for when men unite they thereby gain at least as much wisdom as strength. The German and Italian republics and the municipal privileges of the rest of Europe date from this period. Yet the institutions of these republics reflected the period in which they were established; the rights of individual liberty, assuring the exercise and development of the faculties of all men, were not guaranteed. The period of partial emancipation, as I have just shown it, is no longer clearly noticeable except in the free cities and republics that have subsisted down to our times. Thus, in the history of large modern states we should acknowledge only three entirely distinct eras: feudalism, despotism, and representative government.

For about five centuries independence and enlightenment have been influencing events in all ways and almost by chance, yet royal power has steadily grown from various causes and through various means. Kings, often having reason to fear the arrogance of nobles, sought an alliance with the populace against them. The regular army made the assistance of the nobles less necessary, while the need for taxes forced the sovereigns to have recourse to the third estate. And to obtain direct taxes from it, the sovereigns had to disengage it, more or less, from the control of the nobles. The Renaissance, the invention of printing, the Reformation, the discovery of the New World, and the advance of commerce taught men that there could be a force other than military; and they have realized since then that military force is not the exclusive province of gentlemen.

In the Middle Ages only the clergy had any learning. They rendered great service during the Dark Ages. But when the clergy found themselves attacked by the Reformation, they combated the progress of the human mind instead of helping it. The middle class of society monopolized the sciences, literature, the study of law, and commerce; and thus its importance grew daily. On the other hand, the states became increasingly centralized and governmental resources became greater; and the kings, by using the third estate against the barons and the higher clergy, set up their own despotism, that is, the combination of executive and legislative power in the same hands.

England is the only great European empire that has

achieved the final stage of perfection of the social order known to us. The third estate, or rather the nation, as elsewhere, aided the royal power under Henry VIII to curb the nobility and the clergy, and expanded at their expense. But the British nobility were early on more liberal than in any other country, and from the time of the Magna Carta we see the barons making demands in favor of the liberties of the people.

The same impulses among men produced the English revolution, and that of France in 1789. Both belong to the third era of the progress of the social order, to the establishment of representative government, toward which the human spirit is advancing from all sides.

Let us now examine the circumstances peculiar to France, where we have seen the colossal events that in our times have aroused so many hopes and so many fears.

Part Three

Chapter XV. Political Fanaticism

The events we have reviewed up till now are merely the sort of history that may be found anywhere. But an abyss is now about to open in our path. We shall pass as quickly as we can over this ghastly crisis, in which there is no man or event worthy of our regard. Everything is the same but extraordinary, monotonous but horrible. One is almost ashamed to be able to examine these gross atrocities closely enough to describe them in detail. Let us examine only the main principle of these monstrous phenomena, political fanaticism.

Worldly desires have always been a part of religious fanaticism, while, on the other hand, true fidelity to abstract ideas often feeds political fanaticism. The mixture occurs everywhere, but it is its proportion that determines good and evil.

The social order is in itself a curious structure, yet it cannot be conceived other than it is. But the compromises into which we must sink so that it may endure rack the noble-minded with pity, satisfy the vanity of some people and arouse the discontent and ambition of most. It is to this state of things, more or less accentuated or tempered by custom and education, that we must attribute the political fanaticism of which we have been the witnesses in France. A kind of fury possessed the poor in the presence of the rich. The honors of the nobility adding to the envy property inspires, the populace took pride in its numbers, and everything that went to make up the power and splendor of the minority seemed to it nothing but a usurpation. The germs of this sentiment have existed at all times, but until the era of the Terror in France human society had not trembled to its foundations. One should not be surprised if this abominable scourge has left deep traces upon us. The only reflection one can make, which the remainder of this book will, I hope, confirm, is that the cure for popular passions lies not in despotism but in the rule of law.

Religious fanaticism offers the kind of infinite future that raises all the hopes of the imagination. But the pleasures of this life appear equally unlimited to those who have not tasted them; men often expose themselves to death in order to live better. As to the wealthy, vanity increases as it defends its advantages; it appears less guilty than those who attack it because even injustices, when they have existed for a long time, come to be regarded as a property right. The two elements of religious fanaticism and political fanaticism still persist: in those who are at the top of the wheel, the desire to rule; in those at the bottom, the eagerness to make it turn. Such is the basis of all violence: the pretext changes but not the cause, and the mutual fanaticism remains the same.

Massacres no less horrible than those of the Terror have been committed in the name of religion; the human race has for several centuries exhausted itself in useless efforts to compel men to one creed. Such a goal could not be achieved, and the simplest idea, tolerance, such as William Penn professed, has banished forever from North America the fanaticism of which the South[1] has been the dreadful scene. It is the same with political fanaticism; liberty alone can abate it. After a certain time, some truths will no longer be disputed and people will regard obsolete institutions as they do old ideas of physics that have been completely obliterated by factual evidence.

Part Five

Chapter I. What Constitutes Legitimate Monarchy

In evaluating monarchy in its relation to the happiness and dignity of nations—as all institutions should be judged—I shall assert in general, while acknowledging the exceptions, that princes of old families are much better suited to the welfare of the state than self-made princes. Usually their talents are less outstanding, but their disposition is more peaceful; they have more prejudices but less ambition, are less awed by power because from infancy they have been told that they were destined for it, and they do not fear its loss so much, which makes them less suspicious and less apprehensive. When a man—the first in his family—is suddenly raised to the highest office, he must have the magic of glory to dissolve the contrast between royal pomp and his previous status as a commoner.

Moreover, the principle of heredity in a monarchy is indispensable to the tranquillity, even, I will say, to the morality

[1] *Madame de Staël seems to have meant South America.*—Ed.

and progress, of the human mind. Elective monarchy opens a vast field to ambition. The factions arising from it invariably end by corrupting the heart and diverting thought from every pursuit that does not have an immediate interest as its goal. But the privileges accorded to birth, whether for creating a nobility or for establishing succession to the throne within a single family, need to be confirmed by the passage of time. They differ in this respect from natural rights, which do not depend upon any authority or agreement. The principle of heredity is thus better established in old dynasties. But in order that this principle not become contrary to reason and to the general welfare for which it has been adopted, it must be indissolubly tied to the rule of law. If millions of men must be ruled by one man in accordance with his wishes or whims, then it would be better if he were a man of talent; and that is more likely when we resort to election than when we adhere to the accident of birth.

Nowhere has heredity been more solidly established than in England, though the English people have rejected legitimacy based upon divine right in favor of heredity sanctioned by representative government. Everyone with common sense understands well how, by virtue of laws made by the representatives of the people and accepted by the king, it suits nations—which are also hereditary and even legitimate in character—to recognize a dynasty called to the throne by the right of primogeniture. If, on the other hand, royal power is based upon the doctrine that all power comes from God, then nothing could be more favorable to usurpation. For it is not power that usurpers usually lack. Their whole theory amounts to nothing more than saying that force is force and that they are its high priests. We want a different creed and different priests, and we believe that only then will monarchy be stable.

On the one hand, representative government inspires more

respect for the sovereign among those who do not want to see the affairs of this world transformed into religious dogma, for fear of taking the name of God in vain; and, on the other, the conscientious sovereign need not fear that the entire welfare of the state rests upon his head only.

Legitimacy, as it has been recently set forth, is thus absolutely inseparable from constitutional limitations. It matters little whether the limits that formerly existed in France were an inadequate barrier to the abuse of power or whether they were violated and obliterated gradually. These limits should be applied now, even if their antiquity cannot be proved.

It is humiliating to go back to the evidence of history to prove that something as absurd as it is unjust ought to be neither adopted nor maintained. The four thousand years slavery has lasted has never been advanced in its defense. The serfdom that succeeded it has not seemed the more equitable for having endured more than ten centuries. The Negro slave trade has never been defended as a venerable institution of our forefathers. It would be interesting to know which generation among our ancestors was granted infallibility. Which is the past era that ought to be a model for the present and from whose course we cannot deviate without falling into pernicious innovations? If every change is to be condemned only because it is change, and no matter what its influence upon the general welfare and the progress of mankind, it will be easy to oppose to the old order of things that you invoke another still older order of things which it replaced. In short, what human being endowed with common sense can pretend that a change in customs and ideas should not lead to a change in political institutions? Will it be necessary always to govern three hundred years behind the times? Or shall a new Joshua command the sun to stand still? No, it will be said, there are things that ought to change, but government ought to be immutable.

There could be no better way to put revolutions on a regular basis. For if the government of a country does not want to participate in the progress of things and men, it will necessarily be shattered by it. I think I have proved that in Europe, as in France, it is liberty that is old and despotism that is modern, and that those defenders of the rights of nations whom it pleases some to represent as innovators, have never ceased to invoke the past. Even if this truth were not evident, the only consequence would be a more urgent duty to inaugurate the rule of justice that might not yet have been put into effect. But the principles of liberty are so engraved in the heart of man that, if the history of all governments presents a picture of the efforts of power to trespass, it also presents a picture of popular struggle against these efforts.

Section III

Public Opinion: Its Power and Inertia

Madame de Staël's own title for this essay was "Of Public Opinion." It is Chapter III of Part One of Des circonstances actuelles qui peuvent terminer la Révolution et des principes qui doivent fonder la République en France, *a book written in 1799 but not published until 1906.*—Ed.

In a realm where two opposed parties furiously battle one another, there is hardly a public opinion. All opinions are intensified by difference. The slightest objection to their plans inspires the fanatical parties with so much hatred that every man is compelled to rely upon a certain number of like-minded men, and, as in places infested with brigands, people travel only in a caravan. In countries where hatreds are unleashed, people join a party to have protectors. There are some honest and courageous men who expose themselves to all the furies by adopting none of them. They quietly lay the basis for historical accounts and, if they can, make themselves the contemporaries of posterity through their observations—but they do not influence opinion. There is nevertheless a mass within the nation, always indifferent and unmoved, which in times of disorder has no other concern than to discover the stronger party in order to join it. This mass, which it is so tempting to oppress because it is so tractable, nevertheless in the long run exerts pressure in a single direction and, as soon as there is tranquillity and all danger is past, gently whispers a kind of public opinion.

I have not pictured this influence upon governments as something very formidable. It takes no part in the war between the two parties. Yet the victor absolutely must win its support; for the vanquished, always thinking they can reconquer the mass, will renew their efforts in the hope of arousing it.

Here are the opinions of this mass. It has been sufficiently enlightened by writers and by the Revolution not to care anything for the monarchy, but it is not so enthusiastic about having the Republic at the price of its tranquillity. It does not care for the privileged castes because it is not part of them and they have never done it any good, yet it does not hate the privileged castes enough to want them persecuted. For the mass knows well that persecution disturbs the peace of even those who are neither persecutors nor persecuted, and it wants tranquillity above all. Agriculture, commerce, the public debt, taxes, peace and war—all these concern the mass because it has but one desire: material comfort and tranquillity.

The individuals in this mass will not fight for tranquillity because peaceful men are incapable of the kind of calculation that would lead them to abandon their immediate comfort out of fear of the future. But if they have no assurance of lasting tranquillity, they will be anxious and dissatisfied, and though no hostile evidence will show it, a traveler passing through the country will feel that its government is not firm, nothing is stable, no one can count on the future, there is no consent between the rulers and the ruled, and that the parties are free to speculate on the nation's future without any interference from it. The government will, so to speak, be frightened at not meeting any resistance, as one who walks in the dark is afraid of feeling the emptiness. It would like to see some resistance as a sign of life, to have an opposition declare its numerical strength and put some kind of purpose in motion. This is indeed a fatal attitude in a republic. It is unpardonable in the ruled, and the rulers must combine all their efforts to overcome it.

The royalist will cry out: "The nation does not want the Republic, does not want liberty." The nation never wants anything but results and does not care about the means. At one moment it is the Republic, at another the monarchy, that it thinks more favorable to its tranquillity. The party spirit exists only in individuals cast outside the circle of domestic life, and two thirds of the population of France and of all the countries of Europe are concerned only with money. All the affections and interests of the ancients were wrapped up in the fate of their country. Their earth was ravaged if the enemy won a battle on it; such a defeat for the community might condemn them to slavery. They had no means of transporting their wealth to any other country. The citizens of a small state, all of them individually known, were continually subject to the will of a nation that deliberated in the public square. As in our day, fame was dangerous but there was no guarantee of obscurity, and personal calculations could never be withheld from others.

Thus there was not, as in our large states, a mass of complacent men concerned only with their personal affairs, scornful of those rash people who get themselves talked about, and quite able, with the help of all individual resources and of the present organization of commerce and property, to create their future apart from public events.

This possibility of existing apart from public affairs is for most men, I believe, a great blessing. This calm, unknown to the ancients, is an advantage of large associations of men and offers an added opportunity for happiness to the variety of human natures. But in such a country the governors must take account of this fact so as not to depend upon the kind of patriotism that moved the ancient republics. Sparta, Athens, and Rome never placed public tranquillity among the chief assets. The goal of their institutions was not stability, or immobility, so to speak, in public affairs. People complained of the lack of this or that advantage and loudly demanded action by the leaders of the state. In France people will always believe that things will go better if the government does not act. Far from calling for its assistance, people regard it as an obstacle. The social order being much better organized than in the past, agriculture and commerce being easier to manage, the government—that is, the common power—is no longer necessary to each person. Since private life easily provides many pleasures, the government is no longer called upon to serve people's personal concerns. One must start from this great difference, in order to base the Republic in France upon a very small number of personal sacrifices. It must also be borne in mind that the political unit among the ancients was very small; practically all men taking part in public affairs felt compensated for their trouble by rewards or the hope of rewards. But in France, where seven hundred men out of twenty-five million are called upon to deal with public affairs, the odds against ambition are too great to make it worth the bother. Such a government, though free and derived from the principle of popular sovereignty, must, like monarchies, be careful not to disturb the tranquillity of the mass of citizens. Civil liberty and individual liberty must be highly respected in a country where all men cannot be granted the effective and varying exercise of political liberty.

To win over public opinion, then, the ancients had to move the soul, to stir up patriotism through conquests, triumphs, and dissension and even disorders, which brought all the emotions into play. In France we must no doubt shape a national spirit to the extent that we can. But we must not lose sight of the fact that public opinion will be based upon the love of tranquillity, the desire to acquire wealth, and the need to preserve it; that people will always be more concerned with administrative concepts than political questions because they bear more directly upon private life; and that, while keeping in mind the lofty goal of elevating the French nation to the level of all philosophical ideas and all republican institutions, every individual's private sphere must always be respected.

Rome's well-being embraced the well-being of all Roman citizens, and invariably generated enthusiasm by proposing the sacrifice of personal interests to the common good—not that the Romans were more generous than we are, but because the contribution of each individual was outweighed by the benefit he derived from the common weal. But in France, where the situation is reversed, the only thing that can make people prefer the Republic is respect for private life and private wealth. In the present era liberty means everything that protects citizens' independence of the government. The liberty of ancient times means everything that ensured citizens the largest share in the exercise of power. These two great differences make it necessary that the Republic in France not demand things of or exert pressure upon the people, that it be guided by a preventive ethic rather than a doctrine of sacrifice that becomes brutal when it ceases to be voluntary—in short, we must remember that progress in the technique of social organization, having made private welfare easier to achieve, has alienated citizens all the more from sacrificing for the common good. For public opinion, so placid, so submissive to the slightest demonstration of force, is at the same time the only invincible power. It cannot be conquered, for it does not fight. Its influence cannot be destroyed, for it is the influence of each and of all. It cannot be made to change its mind, for it wants only its well-being. So long as there is war its existence may be ignored, but since it is the true national power, as soon as we want to base government upon realities we must rally public opinion to the Republic—or the government will not firmly establish itself.[1]

[1] *The ideas in the last three paragraphs were written in 1799 but not published until 1906. In two well-known works of 1814 and 1819, Benjamin Constant, Madame de Staël's lover and political and intellectual collaborator, extended them. It is very likely that they had earlier worked them out together.* (*See Constant,* De l'Esprit de conquête et de l'Usurpation, *1814, Part Two, Ch. VI, and the speech of 1819, "De la liberté des anciens comparée à celle des modernes," in* Cours de Politique Constitutionelle (*4 vols., Paris, 1820*), *Vol. IV, pp. 238–74.*—Ed.

Section IV

The Superiority of Moderation over Extremism

Madame de Staël wrote this essay in 1791 and called it, "How Can We Determine What Is the Opinion of the Majority of the Nation?" Her aim was to strengthen the position of the "majority," the moderates who accepted the Revolution insofar as it had ended abuses but wanted to retain the monarchy as a unifying institution. The constitution she refers to was that of 1791, which the revolutionaries imposed on King Louis XVI. But the Revolution continued. In 1792, a few months after this article appeared, the monarchy was overthrown, a republic established, the King tried and executed. Shortly before the Reign of Terror fell in full force, Madame de Staël herself managed to flee France. The following translation omits a brief section of the original which is mainly a eulogy of Mirabeau.—Ed.

In a tranquil era this question would be easy to settle, but in the very midst of revolt, which seems to reveal a dominant opinion most vigorously, we must concentrate all our mental powers to distinguish what is momentary from what is enduring, and what fear inspires from what reason prompts, and above all what is born of hatred for the old form of government from what is born of attachment to the new.

The more odious the old government, the more agreement there was to overthrow it, and the more difficult it is to distinguish among the various opinions separating those who, united for destruction, are divided in rebuilding.

The right wing of the Assembly, known as *Aristocrats,* claims that fear stifles the voice of the majority. A section of the left wing, known as the *Jacobins,* blames all opposition it encounters upon an attachment to the old abuses. The two parties agree in professing to submit to the general will. But both wrongly rest (the one with logic completely contrary to the facts and the other with facts completely contrary to logic) upon the existence of a majority that never appears or upon one that is always in rebellion.

In human as in physical nature, there are two all-powerful forces: the tendency to cherish repose and the impulse to seek liberty. Each prevails in turn, but the abiding general will results from both in combination. It is when this problem of combination is solved that we can look for and be sure to find the abiding general will.

During a revolution the party that holds moderate opinions needs, more than any other, courage of soul and breadth of mind. It has two struggles to carry on, two kinds of argument to refute, two dangers to avoid. If leaders in such a party are rare, nothing is more numerous than the army awaiting their direction to learn where to find the common welfare it desires. This large group of people is neither oppressors nor oppressed. If they had been allied with the enemies of the Revolution, it would have died long ago; if they were for the Jacobins, we would not see that party acting in so many ways to prolong anxiety and persecution in order to retain the effective power of fear and hatred.

Some people heap ridicule upon opinions that are removed equally from two conflicting extremes. It is understandable that the two extreme parties should agree in attacking this common enemy. But it is by no means understandable that anyone should dare to call this way of thinking weak and indecisive. Nor is it understandable that it should be impossible to establish a party somewhere between the aristocratic and the democratic positions that would be stronger, more distinct, and more vigorous than the two opposed extremes. People have the knack of reducing everything to extremes in the belief that these are certain to be preferred. Opinions do exist that we must adopt without modification. But are we to allow every lunatic who discovers a new madness to erect a new barrier to truth?

If it is true that the nation does not agree with any of the excesses of the Jacobins, and that it distinguishes clearly between private interests and public welfare, between the establishment of the Constitution and the ambition of those who are associated in managing it, then, one may argue, why does it not give evidence of this? Because, favoring the Revolution, the people do not yet know if its enemies are sufficiently weakened for them to dare to make a choice among its friends; because the horror the people conceived for the Old Regime makes them still cling strongly to this feeling (as a kind of shield) which, though it has perhaps been retained too long, had at first to be regarded as sacred. Finally both the enemies of the Revolution and those whom they appear to detest seem to agree in making fears endure and to compete in perpetuating threats (on the part of the former) and useless terrors (on the part of the latter); so the people, in doubt, do not dare to feel at ease and still allow to act those radicals who know nothing of liberty but its conquest and who devastate the land they have seized.

I would say to the partisans of the Old Regime, to the Aristocrats (if we may dare still to use a word that so often serves to make inquiry—and even more often ability—unnecessary): Do not regard as secret allies of your party those enlightened men who are dissatisfied with some sections of the Constitution nor those good souls who are rightly indignant at the crimes of the Revolution; the unbridgeable gap that separates you comes from the bottom of their hearts, and if one day you were to be victorious you would realize that it is so.

And you, too, present-day enemies of the common good, you who desecrate all words merely by using them and who, always hiding your deeds with speech, calling one to aid the other in order to deceive men—you do not have as allies all those who are proud to call themselves friends of the Constitution, a title that has nourished your hatred of these individuals much more than your love of the common good. If in disturbed times men and opinions merge, they are separated when peace returns; the more that faith in liberty becomes universal, the more will it be proper not to regard its mere profession as its guarantee and to inquire what kind of conduct is joined to this faith. In such a subject a host of comparisons drawn from religion come to mind. For fanaticism and hypocrisy accompany all the causes by which people have been stirred: the fanaticism theirs, the hypocrisy their leaders'.

By examining the character of the Puritans in the history of England and by observing what is happening in our own time, we can see that a lasting and awesome power over the people can never be gained except by those who appear to have all the virtues. Their very morality makes people a prey to hypocrisy. The earliest successes of hypocrisy are always with people who are at a distance from it; its only enemies are the enlightened men who see it up close. But it is they who, sooner or later, determine reputations in all domains. Public recognition must radiate from the enlightened center, and the kind that originates on the periphery is lost on the way.

So I believe that the majority of the nation wants and will always want equality and liberty, but also that it wants order and holds that the legal authority and the legitimate power of a king are necessary to maintain that order.

The Revolution made more rapid progress possible. Each day yielded a benefit by destroying an abuse. A constitution, however, is a more complicated process, the outcome of so many ideas and intentions that judgments of it must differ. One must seek support with righteousness of mind and heart, which for a long time to come will not be unanimous. This great question must be debated by only two parties. The partisans of the Old Regime, who assert that their status as gentlemen exempts them from thinking, must no longer be regarded as French citizens. We must waste neither time nor precious energy in attacking this futile ghost. There are only two parties, the Royalists and the Republicans: why should not both dare to state their names? What feelings doom the Republicans to hypocrisy and the Royalists to silence? Why does this bizarre contrast persist? Why do they not learn from one another? Why do the Republicans fear the Royalists, who dare not even avow their views, and the Royalists the Republicans, who think they are forced to profess a contrary view? Can not both of these political positions be upheld? Is there sacrilege in the one and servitude in the other? Is not the time when royalty was made a religion gone forever? Have we not reached the point where we can regard royalty as a political idea whose advantages and disadvantages ought to be weighed like those of every other social institution? Why do all Republicans not dare to attack it? Why do the Royalists not dare to defend it? It is treated as a prejudice, when it ought to be analyzed as a principle; the first yields to words, the second entails consequences.

When this great question is cleared up, two parties may stand forth. People will perhaps attack each other, but they will no longer deceive each other or attack with sophisms that are insults the people must not forget. Let these two parties created to divide the Kingdom and the Assembly raise themselves to that level of truth. The one preferring the monarchy is not slavish, and the one preferring the republic is not seditious. Slaves and the seditious are to be found only among hypocrites. Whoever says what he believes has the entire nation as witness and judge. But it is high time that those who are firmly convinced that the only republic possible in a large state is a federative one and that the unity of the realm can exist only with a king spoke out clearly for their views in the National Assembly. Far from rallying to itself feeble and timid souls, this party needs more than any other the courage that braves all kinds of distrust and danger. It must impress by the boldness of its character those whom it heartens by the wisdom of its opinions. It must be itself and not some absurd mixture or an irrelevant alternative to opposed extremes. It must combat them instead of becoming a compromise between them. It must in short demonstrate to all that reason is not a shade of meaning between extremes, but the primary color given off by the purest rays of the sun.

Two

LITERATURE

Section V

Literature Considered in Its Relation to Social Institutions

This Section retains the titles Madame de Staël gave to the entire book, De la Littérature *(1800), and to its individual Parts and Chapters.*—Ed.

Introduction

from Part One. Literature among the Ancients and the Moderns

Chapter I. The First Age of Greek Literature
Chapter II. Greek Tragedy
Chapter III. Greek Comedy
Chapter IV. The Philosophy and Eloquence of the Greeks
Chapter V. Latin Literature under the Roman Republic
Chapter VI. Latin Literature in the Reign of Augustus
Chapter VII. Latin Literature from the Death of Augustus to the Reign of the Antonines
Chapter VIII. The Invasions of the People of the North, the Establishment of the Christian Religion, and the Renaissance of Letters
Chapter IX. The General Spirit of Modern Literature
Chapter X. Italian and Spanish Literature
Chapter XI. Literature of the North
Chapter XII. The Main Fault for Which Northern Literature Is Criticized in France
Chapter XIII. Shakespeare's Tragedies
Chapter XIV. English Joking
Chapter XV. English Imagination in Poetry and the Novel
Chapter XVI. The Philosophy and Eloquence of the English

Introduction

My purpose is to examine the influence of religion, custom, and law upon literature, and the influence of literature upon religion, custom, and law. There are treatises in French on the art of writing and the principles of taste that leave nothing to be desired, but it seems to me that the social and political influences that affect the nature of literature have not been frequently analyzed. I think it has not yet been considered how the human faculties were gradually expanded by the illustrious works in every *genre* that have been created from the time of Homer down to our own day.

I have tried to explain the slow but continual march of the human mind in philosophy and its rapid but interrupted progress in the arts. Ancient and modern works on ethics, politics, or science clearly prove the cumulative progress of thought from the time we know its history. This is not the case with poetic values, which concern only the imagination. Also, I have believed it possible to demonstrate that political and religious institutions had a great share in producing the invariable and characteristic differences in the writings of the Italians, the English, the Germans, and the French. Finally, in contemplating both the ruins and the hopes the French Revolution has, so to speak, mingled, I have thought it important to know the influence it has exerted upon learning and what effects it may one day produce if order and liberty, republican morality and independence, are wisely and prudently combined.

Before presenting a more detailed outline of this work, it is necessary to recall the importance of literature considered in its widest meaning, that is, including works of philosophical writings and works of the imagination—in short, everything that involves the exercise of thought in writing, the physical sciences excepted.

I shall examine literature first in a general way in its relation to virtue, renown, freedom, and happiness.

How I wish I could call back all enlightened minds to the enjoyment of philosophical thinking! Those who live in revolutionary times often lose all interest in the search for truth. So many issues settled by force, crimes absolved by success, virtues stained by vilification, misfortunes mocked by power, generous feelings become the object of ridicule, base calculations taken with sham seriousness—all this exhausts the hope of men most faithful to the creed of reason.

THE IMPORTANCE OF LITERATURE IN ITS RELATION TO VIRTUE

Perfect virtue is, in the intellectual realm, perfect beauty. There are connections between the impression that perfect virtue makes upon us and the feeling aroused by all that is sublime, whether in the fine arts or physical nature. The regular proportions of ancient statues, the calm and pure expression of certain paintings, the harmony of music, the appearance of a beautiful vista in fertile open country carry us away with an enthusiasm not unlike the admiration the sight of honorable behavior inspires. Oddities, produced by man or nature, may momentarily stun the imagination, but the intellect requires peace based upon order.

Literature can derive its enduring beauty only from the most perfect morality. Men may surrender their deeds to vice, but never their judgment. No poet, whatever his talent, can create a tragic effect from a situation that admits immorality as a guiding principle. Judgment, so vacillating concerning the events of real life, assumes a fixed character when called upon to evaluate works of the imagination. Literary criticism is thus very often a treatise on ethics. The great writers, by giving themselves up only to the impulse of their talent, may reveal what is most heroic in devotion and most moving in sacrifice. To study the art of stirring men is to probe the secrets of virtue.

The masterpieces of literature, apart from the models they present, produce a kind of intellectual and physical shock, a quiver of admiration that inspires us to generous deeds. The Greek legislators attached great importance to the effect that martial or sensuous music could produce. Eloquence, poetry, dramatic situations, and melancholy thoughts, though they appeal to reflection, also affect our senses. Virtue thus becomes an involuntary impulse, a movement that courses through one's blood, and sweeps one along irresistibly like the most powerful passions. It is regrettable that the writings that appear in our day do not arouse this exalted enthusiasm more often. Our taste is undoubtedly formed by reading all the already known masterpieces in our literature; but familiarity from infancy makes us impervious to them, and each of us is struck by their beauty at different stages of life and receives individually the impression they produce. If we were to attend in a group the first performance of a tragedy worthy of Racine; if we were to read Rousseau together; if we were to listen to Cicero making himself heard for the first time among us, then the interest that comes with surprise and novelty would fix our attention upon neglected truths, and genius, ruling every mind, would repay morality something of what it has received from morality —it would restore that faith to which it owes its inspiration.

There is a relationship among all the faculties of man such that even in improving one's taste in literature one acts to elevate one's character: one feels within one's self a certain impression of the language one uses, for the images it recalls to us modify our inclinations. Each time that he is called upon to choose among different expressions, the writer or speaker decides upon the one that summons up the most refined idea; his mind chooses among expressions in the way his soul ought to decide in the actions of life, and the former practise can lead to the latter.

It has been frequently repeated that historians and comic authors, in short all those who have studied men in order to portray them, become indifferent to good and evil. A certain knowledge of men can produce such an effect; a more profound knowledge leads to the opposite result. He who portrays men as does Saint-Simon or Duclos[1] only adds to the triviality of their opinions and their morals, but whoever might judge them as Tacitus does would necessarily be useful to his time. The art of observing human nature, of explaining its motives and bringing out its subtlety, gives so great a power over opinion that wherever freedom of the press is established no public figure can withstand the contempt inflicted by genius. Descriptions of vice leave an indelible impression when they are the work of a writer who observes profoundly.

I must now deal with the objections against works of genius that describe immorality. Undoubtedly such works might injure morals if they could produce a deep impression; but they always leave only a superficial trace which genuine feelings easily remove. Light or indelicate works are generally a simple relaxation of the mind, which retains very little of them. Human nature is serious, and in the silence of thought one seeks only works of reason or sensitivity. It is in this *genre* alone that literary renown has been won and in which its true influence can be recognized.

[1] *Louis de Rouvroy, duc de Saint-Simon (1675–1755), not to be confused with the later social philosopher and reformer, Claude Henri de Rouvroy, comte de Saint-Simon (1760–1825); and Charles Pinot Duclos (1704–72), who wrote gossipy accounts of court life.*—Ed.

LITERATURE IN ITS RELATION TO RENOWN

If literature can serve morality, it must also have a powerful influence upon renown, for there can be no enduring honor in a country where there is no public morality. If a nation did not adopt certain invariable principles as the basis of its beliefs, if each individual were not fortified in his own beliefs by the certainty that they had universal assent, then brilliant reputations would be only a succession of accidents. The splendor of certain actions might be impressive; but as to sentiment, there must be a progression in order to reach the most sublime of all, admiration. One cannot judge except by comparing. Esteem, approbation, and respect are necessary steps toward enthusiasm. Morality lays the foundation upon which renown rises; and literature, independent of its support of morality, contributes in a more direct way to the existence of renown, which is the most noble incentive to all public virtues.

Love of one's country is a purely social attachment. Man, created by nature for family relations, would not carry his ambition beyond them except in response to the irresistible attraction of general esteem; and it is upon that esteem, formed by public opinion, that literary talent has the greatest influence. In Athens and Rome, in the ruling cities of the world, it was by speaking in the public squares that one directed the will of the people and the fate of all; in our day it is by reading that great events are prepared and minds enlightened.

The dissemination of ideas and knowledge which the destruction of slavery and the discovery of printing produced among Europeans must lead to unlimited progress or to the complete degradation of society. If analytical inquiry goes back to the basis of institutions, it will fortify the truths it may have already secured; but superficial analysis that decomposes only the first layer of ideas presented, without examining the whole matter, inevitably weakens the mainspring of fruitful thought. In an irresolute and *blasé* nation, profound admiration would be impossible; and even military successes could not bring an immortal reputation if literary and philosophical ideas did not make men capable of feeling and consecrating the glory of heroes.

It is not true that a great man is more brilliant standing alone than when surrounded by other famous names among which he is the first. It has been said in politics that a king could not subsist without a nobility or a peerage; at the court of opinion, too, it is necessary that gradations of rank guarantee supremacy.

LITERATURE IN ITS RELATION TO LIBERTY

Liberty, virtue, honor, knowledge: an imposing procession of man in his natural dignity—these related ideas of the same origin could not exist separately. The fulfillment of each lies in the union of all.

The advancement of literature, that is to say, the perfection of the art of thinking and of expressing one's self, is essential to the establishment and preservation of freedom. It is obvious that knowledge becomes the more indispensable in a country as all its citizens have a direct part in the conduct of government. And it is equally true that political equality, the principle inherent in every structure based upon reason, cannot endure unless degree of education as the criterion for classifying people is followed with even more care than feudalism exercised in its arbitrary distinctions. Purity of language and nobility of expression—manifestations of the elevation of the soul—are necessary above all in a state founded upon a democratic basis. In others, artificial barriers make the external signs of good education irrelevant; but when power rests only on the supposition of personal worth, what care ought not to be taken to maintain for such merit all of its external signs?

In a democratic state there is always the fear that the desire for popularity may lead to imitation of vulgar taste; before long one could be persuaded that it is useless, and all but harmful, to have too marked a superiority to the crowd one wants to master. The people would accustom themselves to choosing ignorant and stupid rulers, these rulers would extinguish all enlightenment, and by an inevitable route the loss of enlightenment would bring back the enslavement of the people.

In a free state it is impossible for public authority to do without the genuine consent of the citizens it governs. Reason and eloquence are the natural ties of a republican society. What power can one have over the free will of men without this force, this sincerity, of language that reaches people and inspires them with its message? When one does not know how to convince, one oppresses; in all power relations among governors and governed, as ability declines, usurpation increases.

New institutions must create a new spirit in countries that people want to make free. But how can anything be based upon public opinion without the help of distinguished writers? The desire to obey rather than to command obedience must be aroused; and even though a government rightly wishes the establishment of such institutions it must be solicitous enough of public opinion to seem to be only granting its wish. Only sound writings can in the long run direct and change certain national habits. In the privacy of his thought, man has an asylum of liberty that violence cannot penetrate; indeed, conquerors have often taken over the customs of the conquered: conviction alone has changed long-standing customs. It is through the advancement of literature that we can successfully combat old prejudices. Governments in countries that have just become free must, in order to destroy old errors, use ridicule, which will set the youth against these errors, and conviction, which will alienate the mature. Such governments must, in order to lay the foundation of new institutions, arouse interest, hope, enthusiasm, in short those creative sentiments that give birth to everything that exists, to everything that endures; and it is in the art of the spoken and written word that we find the only means to inspire such sentiments.

Among the various achievements of the human mind, it is philosophical literature—eloquence and reason—that I regard as the true guarantee of liberty. The sciences and the arts are a very important part of intellectual activity; but their discoveries, their successes, exercise no direct influence upon that public opinion that decides the destiny of nations. Geometricians, physicists, painters, and poets may well receive encouragement under the reign of almighty kings, whereas to such masters political and religious inquiry may appear to be the most dangerous kind of rebellion.

Those who devote themselves to the study of the exact sciences, never running into the emotions of men, become accustomed to considering only what is susceptible to mathematical proof. These scholars almost always classify as an illusion whatever they cannot submit to the logic of calculation. They assess first the strength of the government, whatever its form; and as they have no other wish than to devote themselves quietly to their work, they are inclined to obedience to the ruling authority. The profound thought required by abstraction in the exact sciences diverts the scholars from concerning themselves with the affairs of life; and nothing pleases absolute monarchs more than men so deeply occupied with the physical laws of the world that they leave the human realm to whoever is determined to take it. Undoubtedly the discoveries of science must in the long run give a new strength to that higher philosophy* that judges of nations and kings; but so remote a future does not in the least intimidate tyrants; we have seen many of them patronizing the sciences and arts, but all of them fear those natural enemies of patronage itself, the thinkers and the philosophers.

Poetry, of all the arts, is the one that is closest to reason. Yet poetry does not allow the kind of analysis or inquiry that is useful in the discovery and propagation of knowledge of philosophical ideas. Anyone who would like to enunciate a new and bold truth would prefer to write in language that conveys thought exactly and precisely; he would seek to persuade by reasoning rather than to carry away by imagination. Poetry has more often been dedicated to the praise of despotic power than to its censure. The fine arts in general can sometimes contribute, by their very pleasures, to molding subjects as tyrants wish them. The arts can, by the amusements of each day, di-

* I have been asked how I would define the word *philosophy,* which I have used many times in the course of this work. Before answering this question, let me quote here a note from Rousseau, in the second book of his *Emile:* "I have a hundred times reflected while writing that it is impossible in a long work to give always the same meanings to the same words. I believe that one can achieve clarity . . . by seeing to it that whenever one uses a word, the meaning given to it will be adequately fixed by the ideas referred to, and that each phrase in which the word occurs will serve, so to speak, as a definition." After having cited this opinion of a great master against definitions, I shall state that I never give to the word *philosophy,* in the course of this book, the meaning that its detractors have preferred to give it nowadays, whether in opposing philosophy to religious ideas or in calling purely sophistical systems philosophical. I understand by philosophy the general knowledge of cause and effect in the human realm or in physical nature, the freedom of the mind, the exercise of thought—in short, in literature those works that result from reflection or analysis and that are not merely the product of the imagination, the emotions, or the feelings.

vert the mind from any grand and commanding conception; they lead men back to their feelings, and they instill in the mind a sensuous outlook, a deliberate indifference, a passion for the present and a neglect of the future, all highly favorable to tyranny. In a curious contrast, the arts, which enable us to enjoy life, make us rather indifferent to death. Only deep emotions, creating a passionate will to reach their objective, bind us firmly to life; but a life devoted to pleasures amuses without persuading; it prepares us for intoxication, sleep, and death. During eras famous for their sanguinary repressions, the Romans and the French devoted themselves to public amusements with the greatest eagerness, whereas in contented republics, family attachments, sober pursuits, the love of fame and reputation, often turn people away from even the delights of the fine arts. The only literary force that can make unjust rulers tremble is noble expression, independent inquiry, which judges in the court of reason all the institutions and all the beliefs of mankind.

It was often said during the Revolution in France that a certain amount of despotism was necessary to establish liberty. This is a contradiction in terms that has been made into a maxim, but it changes nothing in the reality of things. Institutions based upon force may simulate everything about liberty, except its genuine workings; they may be so much like their models in form as to startle you by the resemblance: you will recognize everything in them—except life.

LITERATURE IN ITS RELATION TO HAPPINESS

The idea of happiness has been almost entirely lost sight of in the midst of efforts that seemed at first to seek it; selfishness, by depriving each person of the help of others, has greatly reduced the degree of happiness that the social order promised to all. In vain would sensitive people nowadays try to practice expansive good will; insurmountable difficulties would obstruct this generous intention: public opinion itself would condemn it, for it censures those who seek to escape the circle of selfishness everyone wants to preserve as his inviolable asylum. One is forced, therefore, to stand alone, since relieving misery is forbidden and love can no longer be found. One must stand alone to preserve in one's mind the idea of all that is great and beautiful, to protect within one's bosom the sacred fire of true inspiration and the image of virtue.

Those writings that are the guardians of ideas and virtuous love at least protect us from the arid sorrow born of loneliness, the icy hand that misery lays heavily upon us, when we believe we cannot arouse even the slightest compassion. Such writings can draw tears from people in any situation; they elevate the soul to more general contemplation, which diverts the mind from personal pain; they create for us a community, a relationship, with the writers of the past and those still living, with men who share our love for literature. In the desolation of exile, the depths of dungeons, and on the verge of death, a particular page of a sensitive author may well have revived a prostrate soul: and I who read that page, I who am touched by it, believe I still find there the trace of tears, and by feeling similar emotions I enter into some sort of communion with those whose fate I so deeply grieve.

OUTLINE OF THE WORK

Having brought together a few general ideas showing the influence that literature can exert upon the destiny of man, I shall illustrate them by a chronological examination of the principal renowned eras in the history of letters. The first part of this work will include a social and philosophical examination of Greek and Latin literature; some reflections on the consequences, for the human mind, of the invasions of the Northern peoples, the establishment of the Christian religion, and of the *Renaissance* of letters; a quick sketch of the distinctive features of modern literature, and some more detailed observations on the masterpieces of Italian, English, German, and French literature treated in accordance with the general aim of this work; that is, according to the relations between the political status of a country and the predominant spirit of its literature. I shall try to show the character that this or that form of government gives to eloquence; the moral ideas that this or that religious faith develops in the human mind; the workings of the imagination produced by what different nations are willing to believe; poetic qualities that depend upon climate; the level of civilization most favorable to the vigor or perfection of literature; the various changes introduced in writings, as in customs generally, by the status of women both before and after the establishment of the Christian religion—in short, the universal progress of enlightenment resulting simply from the succession of eras: such is the subject of the first part.

In the second I shall examine the state of knowledge and literature in France since the Revolution; and I shall venture a few conjectures on what they ought to be and what they will be if one day we enjoy republican morality and liberty. Basing my conjectures upon my observations, I shall recall what I shall have said in the first part on the influence of religion, government, and custom, and I shall draw certain inferences for the future I am predicating. This second part will show both our present degradation and our possible improvement. This subject must sometimes involve the political situation in France in the last decade; but I shall consider it only in its relation to literature and the study of human society without indulging myself in anything foreign to my purpose.

As I scan the great changes in the world and the succession of ages, I never divert my attention from one prime notion: the perfectibility of the human species. I do not believe that this ideal of human nature has ever been abandoned; in enlightened and in benighted eras the gradual progress of the human mind has never been interrupted.

This order of things has become odious to some persons because of the terrible inferences drawn from it during some disastrous moments of the Revolution; but nothing is less connected with such inferences than this noble order of things. Nature sometimes makes partial evils serve the general welfare; thus, some ignorant barbarians considered themselves supreme lawgivers in pouring down on mankind innumerable misfortunes whose effects they thought they could control but which have led to nothing but unhappiness and destruction. Philosophy may sometimes regard past sufferings as useful lessons, corrective devices in the hand of time; but this notion does not justify in the slightest anyone's deviation in any circumstance from the true principles of justice. So in this work I have reverted constantly to everything that demonstrates the perfectibility of mankind. I am impelled to do so not by an empty theory but by the observation of facts. We must guard against a metaphysics that has no support from experience; but we must not forget that in corrupted times everything that is not so narrow as selfishness or so exact as the schemes of personal interest is called metaphysical.

Part One. Literature among the Ancients and the Moderns
Chapter I. The First Age of Greek Literature

The extraordinary success of the Greeks in literature, and especially in poetry, could be urged as an objection to the notion of the perfectibility of the human mind. The first writers we know, one might argue, and particularly the first poet, have not been surpassed for almost three thousand years, and often those who came after the Greeks remained quite inferior to them; but this objection falls if the scheme of perfectibility is applied only to the progress of ideas and not to the masterpieces of the imagination.

It is possible to set a limit to the progress of the arts, but not to the discoveries of the intellect. For in the intellectual domain, as soon as a limit appears, the road leading to it is quickly covered. But the pace must always seem slow on a boundless journey. The fine arts are not infinitely perfectible; so the very first creations of the imagination, which gave birth to the fine arts, are far more brilliant than even their happiest successors.

Modern poetry consists of images and feelings. In the first respect, it is a depiction of nature, in the second an expression of emotion. It is in the first *genre,* by the vivid description of external things, that the Greeks excelled in the earliest era of their literature. In expressing one's experiences, one may adopt a poetic style, resorting to images to intensify the impressions; but poetry proper is the art of painting in words everything that strikes our eyes. To connect the emotions with sensations is already a first step toward understanding human behavior. But here we are concerned with poetry considered only as an imitation of physical nature. In that sense it is not susceptible of unlimited perfection. The description of spring, a storm, the night, beauty, battles, may be varied in its details; but the most powerful impression must have been created by the first poet who described them. The elements may be combined anew but not increased.

Introduced into poetry for the first time, the contrasts of nature, the wonderful impressions that strike every eye, offer the imagination the sharpest images, the starkest antitheses. The ideas added to poetry are a happy extension of its beauty but that is not poetry itself, which Aristotle was the first to call an art of imitation. The power of reason unfolds itself gradually and daily extends itself to new things. In this realm the centuries are the heirs of the centuries; each generation begins where the preceding one left off and thinkers forge a chain of ideas across the ages that even death cannot break. It is not so with poetry; with the very first impetus it can reach a certain kind of beauty that cannot be surpassed. Whereas in the cumulative sciences the latest stage is the most wonderful of all, the power of the imagination is the keener as its exercise is fresher.

An examination of the three separate eras of the literature of the Greeks clearly reveals the natural progress of the human mind. At the very beginning, in the remotest period of their known history, the Greeks were made famous by their poets. It is Homer who stamps the special character of the first era of Greek literature. During the age of Pericles, there was rapid progress in the drama, eloquence, and ethics, and there were the beginnings of philosophy. In the time of Alexander, a more profound study of the analytical sciences became the main pursuit of the superior literary minds. Doubtlessly, a certain level of development of the human mind is required to reach the loftiness of poetry; but this branch of literature must lose some of its effects as the advance of civilization and of the sciences corrects all the errors of the imagination.

It has been frequently said that the fine arts and poetry flourish particularly in corrupt eras; this merely means that most free nations have concerned themselves only with the preservation of their morality and their liberty, whereas kings and despots have willingly encouraged diversions and amusements. But the origin of poetry, the poem most remarkable for its imagination, Homer's, belongs to an era noted for the simplicity of its customs. It is neither virtue nor depravity that promotes or retards poetry; it owes much, rather, to the freshness of nature, to the beginnings of civilization. The youth of the poet cannot entirely take the place of the youth of mankind.

The deeds, predispositions, superstitions, and customs of heroic times were especially appropriate to poetic imagery. Homer, however great he may be, is neither superior to all other men nor unique in his time or in the several eras preceding his. The rarest genius shines always in proportion to the enlightenment of his contemporaries, and at least a rough estimate ought to be made of how far any man's thought can exceed the state of knowledge of his time. Homer collected the traditions of his day; and the story of all these happenings was itself highly poetic. The less easy the communication among different regions the more was the narration of events exaggerated by the imagination. The brigands and ferocious animals that infested the land made the exploits of warriors necessary to the individual safety of their fellow citizens. Public affairs having thus a direct influence on everyone's destiny, gratitude and fear kindled enthusiasm. Heroes and gods were mingled because help was sought from both; and the lofty deeds of battle made a great impression upon frightened spirits. Miracles were thus mingled with the world of man as well as the world of nature. Philosophy, that is to say, the knowledge of cause and effect, arouses the admiration of all thinkers for the totality of the great work of the Creation; but each separate aspect of it is given an ordinary explanation. In acquiring the capacity to foresee, mankind loses much of the capacity to be surprised; and enthusiasm, like fear, often depends upon surprise.

The paganism of the Greeks was one of the main causes of the perfection of their taste in the arts; their gods, always close to men and yet always superior to them, sanctified elegance and beauty of form in all *genres*. Religion was also a great help to the varied masterpieces of literature. The priests and legislators turned men's propensity to belief toward purely poetical conceptions; and thus the mysteries, oracles, hell, everything in Greek mythology, seemed to be the creation of a free imagination. It seemed as though the painters and poets took advantage of popular belief in order to place in the heavens the springs and secrets of their art. The ordinary activities of life were ennobled by religious practices. The agricultural, hunting, and pastoral occupations of the most famous heroes of antiquity also promoted poetry by bringing together the most important political acts and natural images.

All men have undoubtedly known mental anguish, and its forceful description in Homer is acknowledged. But the power to love seems to have grown with other advances of the human mind and, above all, through the new customs that summoned women to share life with men. Shameless prostitutes, slaves degraded by their fate, women secluded in their homes and unknown to the rest of the world, strangers to the concerns of their husbands, reared to have neither ideas nor feelings—this is all the Greeks knew of the ties of love. Even sons hardly respected their mothers. Telemachus orders Penelope to be silent and she leaves imbued with admiration for his wisdom. The Greeks neither expressed nor experienced the prime sentiment of human nature, affection in love. Love, as they described it, is a disease, a spell cast by the gods, a kind of delirium, that presupposes no qualities of mind in its object. What the Greeks understood by affection prevailed among men; but they did not realize, and their customs forbade them even to imagine, that they might find woman their intellectual equal and, under the influence of love, a life-companion happy to devote her capacities, her entire time, her feelings, to make another's life complete. The Greeks honored the dead; their religious doctrines expressly ordered them to carry out funeral ceremonies. But sorrow, tender and lasting grief, was not in their nature; it is in the hearts of women that enduring memories dwell. I shall often have the occasion to note the changes wrought in literature since the time women began to share the intellectual and emotional life of men.

I must now examine how the form of government and the national character of Athens affected the rapid development of all *genres* of literature. It cannot be denied that the legislation of a country has an all-powerful influence upon taste, talent, and customs, since Sparta existed alongside Athens in the same era and climate, with virtually the same religious doctrines, yet with such different customs.

Every Athenian institution stirred emulation. The Athenians were not always free but the spirit of incentive always exercised the greatest influence among them. No nation ever showed itself more responsive to all distinguished talents. This penchant for admiration created the masterpieces that merited it. Greece, and Attica within it, was a small civilized country in the midst of a still barbarian world. The Greeks were few in number but the whole world looked up to them. They combined the double advantage of small states and large scenes: that emulation that comes from the certainty of becoming known in their own *milieu,* and that offers the possibility of renown without limit. What they said among themselves echoed throughout the world.

It would be better for mankind if enlightenment were more widely distributed. But the passion for honor among those who are enlightened is greatest when enlightenment is concentrated. The life of celebrated men was more glorious in ancient times whereas that of humble men is happier in modern times.

Among the Greeks approval was expressed more warmly

than the calculated endorsements of moderns. A nation that encouraged distinguished talents in so many ways must have stimulated great rivalries; but these rivalries served the advancement of the arts. Their most glorious laurel stirred up less hatred than is created by the limited tokens of grudging esteem obtainable in our day. Genius and virtue were allowed to put themselves forward, and anyone who thought himself worthy of some degree of renown could without fear announce himself a candidate for glory. The nation was gratified to see such eagerness for its esteem.

Today an all-powerful mediocrity obliges superior persons to appear colorless. One must sneak into fame, one must steal men's admiration from behind their backs. It is not only important to reassure them through modesty, it is even necessary to affect indifference to commendation if one wants it. Such restraint embitters some spirits and stifles in others the talents that need release and scope. Pride may persist, but true genius is often discouraged. Among the Greeks there was sometimes envy between rivals, but it has now passed to the spectators. By a strange aberration, the mass of men are suspicious of efforts to add to their pleasures or to warrant their approval.

Chapter II. Greek Tragedy

In works of the theatre especially, the customs, religion, and laws of the country in which they are written and successfully enacted may be clearly seen. To be appreciated in the theatre, an author must have, apart from literary qualities, the ability to evaluate political actions—a knowledge of men, their habits, and their preconceptions.

Suffering and death are the main elements of tragedy; and

religion always considerably mitigates the effect of suffering and the fear of death. Let us see, then, what dramatic effects in tragedy the religious beliefs of the Greeks made possible, and what effects they made impossible.

Their religion attributed to the gods great power to inflict remorse upon the guilty. It painted the torments of criminals in the most terrifying colors. Transposed to the stage in varied forms, this conception always produced an unconquerable fear in the theatre. It was also by means of this terror that the legislators exerted great power and the principles of morality were maintained among men. The picture of death produced a less gloomy effect upon the Greeks than upon people today. Pagan faith considerably mitigated the fear of death. The ancients clothed the future life in the most glittering colors; they made the hereafter real by descriptions of all kinds, and the abyss that nature has placed between life and death was, so to speak, filled by their mythology. These beliefs had their political uses too; but since the idea of death today produces a stronger and more painful feeling, its effect upon us is much more tragic.

The Greeks were much less sensitive to misfortune than any other nation of antiquity—there are fewer cases of suicide among them than among the Romans. Their political institutions and national character disposed them more to pleasure and happiness. The alleviation of the intensity of suffering among the ancients must, as a rule, be attributed to the superstitions of paganism. Their dreams, presentiments, oracles, everything that injects the extraordinary and the unexpected into life, precludes belief in irrevocable misfortune.

Basing most of their plays upon the constant exercise of the whims of the gods, Greek writers of tragedy were exempt from a certain kind of verisimilitude, that is, the slow processes of natural events; they brought forth great effects without having led up to them gradually. The minds of the Greeks being always prepared for fear by religion and for the extraordinary by faith, they were not bound by the greatest difficulties of the dramatic art. They did not delineate their characters with the more exact truth demanded by modern times. The contrast of vices and virtues, the inner struggles, the mixture and opposition of feelings, which must be portrayed in order to arouse the concern of men—all this was scarcely developed. For the Greeks an oracle from the gods was enough to explain everything.

To the Greeks love, like all the other violent passions, was only an accident of fate. In their tragedies as well as in their poems one is constantly struck by what is lacking in their conception of love when women were not encouraged to feel and to judge.

Greek tragedies were, therefore, I believe, very much inferior to our own modern tragedies, because dramatic ability consists not only of the art of poetry but also of a profound knowledge of the emotions; and in this respect tragedy has had to keep up with the progress of the human mind.

The three Greek writers of tragedies[2] all wrote about the same subjects. They invented no new ones—the audience did not want any, and the writers did not think about them and probably could not have succeeded if they had. The successful invention of extraordinary incidents is more the creation of folklore than of the poets. In philosophical inquiry, discoveries are made through a chain of reasoning, but invention in poetry is almost always a matter of luck. History, customs, and even popular tales help the imagination of writers. Sophocles could not make up a play about Tancred, nor did Voltaire create the story of Oedipus. New fables cannot be invented when popular beliefs are no longer suited to them.

[2] *Aeschylus, Sophocles, and Euripides.*—Ed.

The importance given to the chorus, supposed to represent the people, is almost the only trace of a republican spirit that can be noticed in Greek tragedy. The comedies often suggested the political character of the nation, but the tragedies always portrayed the misfortunes of kings; it was their fate that aroused concern. The appearances of royalty thus remained among the Greeks, though they were contented with their republican government. The Greeks did not seem to feel the degree of enthusiasm for liberty that characterized the Romans; they had had much less difficulty in gaining it. They did not have to dethrone, as the Romans did, a race of cruel tyrants who could well inspire a horror of everything that summoned up their memory. The love of liberty was for the Greeks a matter of habit, a way of life, and not a controlling passion whose expression they had to rediscover everywhere.

The Athenians loved their institutions and their country but this was not, as among the Romans, an overriding sentiment. There is only one feature peculiar to a democracy in their tragedies: the reflections, which their main characters and the choruses repeat incessantly, upon the rapidity of reversals of fortune and the fickleness of fate. The sudden and frequent overthrow of popular governments often leads to this kind of thinking. Racine did not imitate the Greeks in this respect. Under the rule of a monarch like Louis XIV, the ruler's will takes the place of fate and no one would dare to suppose him capricious. But in a country where the people rule, what strikes people most are the overturns of fortune, the rapid and dreadful fall from the pinnacle of greatness to the abyss of misfortune.

The authors of tragedies always seek to revive those sentiments that are familiar to their audience. Indeed, memories are always an important element of tender feelings. In intellectual matters it is new associations that win attention. But when one wants to make the tears flow, one must summon up the familiar.

Chapter III. Greek Comedy

Tragedy (except for a few masterpieces) requires less understanding of human nature than does comedy; to depict suffering and pain, which are normal occurrences, inventiveness suffices. But it took ages to bring the human mind to that refinement of taste, the superior understanding of human nature, that Molière displayed in his comedies.

One wonders, in reading the comedies of Aristophanes, how it was possible that such plays could be applauded in the age of Pericles, how it was possible that the Greeks could show so much taste in the fine arts and so repulsive a coarseness in their humor. They had good taste in what concerned the imagination but not in what springs from morality. Beautiful form in every *genre* pleased them but they lacked refinement in the expression of their judgments.

Gradual and subtle processes hardly suit democratic ways. Since it was the populace whose understanding and approval were always sought, to amuse them one had to indulge in exaggerated contrasts that struck everyone readily.

Tragedy was less affected by this desire to please the multitude; it was a part, as I have already said, of religious celebrations. Moreover, to move people to pity, it is not necessary to appeal to their taste or knowledge; pity reaches all hearts by the same route. Tragedy is addressed to what is human in all men, but to attain popular success in comedy one must be familiar with a particular period, nation, and mode of life. Tears derive from our natures, laughter from our customs.

Moral principles generally serve as rules of taste for the lower classes of society, and these principles often suffice to guide them even in literature. The Athenian populace did not have the morality that can compensate for the lack of refinement. They indulged in religious superstitions but they had no firm ideas on virtue and recognized no rule, no limit, no modesty in their amusements.

The exclusion of women also prevented the Greeks from improving themselves in comedy. As authors had no reason to check, conceal, or merely imply anything, their humor was necessarily lacking in charm and subtlety.

Most of the comedies of Aristophanes concerned the events of his own time. Maintenance of interest by a love story had not yet been invented; concern with private affairs depends entirely upon the role that women play in a country. The art of comedy, as it was in the time of the Greeks, could not do without references to affairs of the day; they had not probed the secret passions of the heart thoroughly enough to arouse interest by portraying them only, but it was very easy to please the people by holding their leaders up to ridicule.

The *comédie de circonstance* succeeds so easily that it cannot bring a lasting reputation. These portraits of living men, these witticisms about contemporary affairs, are family jokes, successes for a day which can only bore other nations and times; the value of such works can evaporate even from one year to the next.

In tragedy, the audience enters completely into the illusion; it is so much interested in the hero of the play that it can even understand foreign customs and transport itself to entirely new places. Emotion permits it to accept and to visualize everything. But in comedy the imagination of the audience is inactive, it does not lend help to the author.

The republic of Athens itself owed its subjection to its abuse of the comic *genre* and its inordinate taste for witticisms, which constantly stimulated the need for entertainment. The comedy *The Clouds*[3] prepared people for the accusation against Socrates. Demosthenes, in the following century, could not wrench the Athenians from their entertainments and frivolous pursuits in order to turn their attention to Philip.[4]

Having sacrificed their honor to preserve their pleasures, the Athenians were deprived of their independence and with it of those very pleasures that they preferred to the defense of their liberty.

Chapter IV. The Philosophy and Eloquence of the Greeks

Philosophy and eloquence were often united by the Athenians. Plato's metaphysical and political systems have contributed much less to his reputation than the beauty of his language and the nobility of his style. Most of the Greek philosophers talked eloquently about abstract ideas. But I must first consider the philosophy of the Greeks separately from their eloquence, for my purpose is to observe the progress of the human mind, which only philosophy can show with certitude.

The powerful effect produced by their works has contributed to the imposing image we have of the ancients; but it is not according to this standard that they must be judged. The small number of enlightened men whom the Greeks presented for the admiration of the rest of the world, the difficulty of travel, the state of ignorance concerning most of the information that the writers collected, the rarity of their manuscripts

[3] *In this play Aristophanes held Socrates up to ridicule.*—Ed.
[4] *Philip of Macedon* (382–336 B.C.), *conqueror of Athens.*—Ed.

—all this conduced to inspire the liveliest interest in these famous works. The ancient philosophers achieved, in their time, a much more brilliant reputation than the moderns; but it is no less true that the moderns, in metaphysics, ethics, and the sciences, are infinitely superior to the ancients.

The ancients were stronger in ethics than in metaphysics. In order to progress beyond metaphysics it is necessary to study the exact sciences, whereas nature has already placed in man everything capable of leading him to virtue. Yet nothing is less fixed and unified than the moral code of the ancients. Pythagoras seemed to attach the same importance to proverbs and folk wisdom as to the precepts of virtue. Some of the Greeks likewise confused the various grades of morality; they placed the love of learning on the same level as the fulfillment of the most fundamental obligations. Their enthusiasm for the faculties of the mind prevailed over their esteem for anything else; they spurred men to seek admiration but they did not inspire an anxious or searching glance into the inner sorrows of the soul.

I do not think that the word happiness, in its modern meaning, is mentioned even once in the writings of the Greeks. They did not attribute great importance to private qualities. For them, politics was a branch of ethics; they thought of man in society, almost always in his relation to his fellow citizens. And since free states generally had small populations, in whose life women had no part, man's entire existence consisted of his relations with other men. And it was to the perfection of this public life that the studies of the philosophers were exclusively devoted. Monarchy and the large size of modern states have detached men from a concern with public affairs; they are wrapped up in their families—and they have been just as happy for it. But everything stirred the ancients to follow a public career and the main aim of their ethics was to encourage this.

The Greek philosophers were very few in number and the works previous to their age offered them no help; they had to cover everything in their studies. Thus they could not go very far in any particular *genre;* they lacked the method that only the exact sciences can supply, that is, the power of generalization.

Aristotle, who lived in the third Greek era, which was necessarily intellectually superior to the two preceding ones, substituted the spirit of observation for the spirit of preconceived doctrines, and this distinction was enough to assure his renown. What he wrote in literature, physics, and metaphysics is a summary of the ideas of his time. Historian of the progress of knowledge in that era, he set it all down and arranged it as he conceived it. He is an admirable man for his time. But to seek in antiquity all philosophical truth is to want to force men to go backwards, to apply the spirit of discovery to the past instead of the present. The ancients, and Aristotle above all, were almost as able as the moderns in certain aspects of politics; but this exception to the law of progress is entirely owing to the republican liberty that the Greeks enjoyed and that the moderns have not known.

Aristotle was in total ignorance on every general question that the history of his own time did not clarify.

Among the Greeks, the eloquence of the philosophers nearly equaled the eloquence of the orators. Socrates and Plato liked speaking better than writing because they felt, without precisely understanding their own talent, that their ideas depended more upon inspiration than upon analysis. They needed to resort to the impulse and stimulation produced by the lively speech of conversation. They sought for whatever could stir the imagination with as much care as the scientific metaphysicians and the rigorous analysts of human behavior[5] in our day guard themselves against any poetic adornment.

The love of reputation was the source of every action of the Greeks. They sought knowledge and did not flinch in pain, in order to be admired; they adopted opinions, in order to have disciples; they defended their country, in order to govern it. But they did not have that deep-seated feeling, that deliberate will-power, that national spirit, that patriotic devotion that distinguished the Romans. The Greeks gave the impulse to literature and the fine arts. The Romans stamped the world with the imprint of their genius.

Chapter V. Latin Literature under the Roman Republic

We must distinguish in all literatures the indigenous from the imitative. The Roman Empire having succeeded the rule of Athens, Latin literature followed the route that Greek literature had marked, first because it was the superior one in many respects and to want to deviate from it in everything would be to renounce good taste and truth; and perhaps also because only necessity prompts invention and people adopt rather than create when they find a model in accord with their customary ideas.

It is important to note the differences between Greek and Latin literature, and the progress of the human mind, in the three eras of the literary history of the Romans: that which preceded the reign of Augustus, that which bears the name of that emperor, and that which may be reckoned from his death down to the reign of the Antonines. Chronologically, the first two overlap somewhat, but their spirit is extremely dif-

[5] *The "moralistes" like Montaigne, La Rochefoucauld, and La Bruyère.* –Ed.

ferent. Though Cicero died under the Triumvirate of Octavius, his spirit belongs entirely to the Republic; and although Ovid, Virgil, and Horace were born while the Republic still lived, their writings bear the character of monarchical influence. In the reign of Augustus himself, some writers, Titus Livy above all, often displayed a republican spirit in their manner of writing history. But in order to analyze accurately the distinctive styles of these three eras we must consider their general features and not the individual exceptions.

Roman character did not fully display itself except during the Republic. A nation has no character unless it is free. Roman aristocracy had some of the assets of an enlightened aristocracy. Though it may justly be reproached for its purely hereditary appointment of senators, still the government of Rome, within the precincts of its own walls, was free and paternal. But its conquests gave the rulers immense power, and the leading Romans, the *élite* of the city which was the queen of the universe, considered themselves the patricians of the whole world. From this feeling of aristocracy among the nobility, and of absolute superiority among the inhabitants of the city, arose the eminent character of Roman writings, speech, customs, habits, and their dignity.

The Romans never displayed great excitement, no matter what the circumstances; and when they wanted to stir people by eloquence it was even more important to them to maintain the calm dignity of a strong mind, to avoid compromising the feeling of respect that was the basis of all their political institutions as well as of their social relations. There was in their speech an authority of expression, a depth of tone, a regularity of periods hardly suited to the halting accents of a troubled mind and to the quick sallies of wit.

The Romans at first scorned the fine arts, especially literature, until the philosophers, orators, and historians made the talent of writing useful in commerce and public morality. When the first members of the profession took up literature, their works had the advantage, over those of the Greeks, that comes from a practical knowledge of men and administration; but they were written, necessarily, with more circumspection. Cicero ventured to attack the received ideas of Rome only with timidity. The nation's views could not be defied by anyone who sought its support for the leading posts in the Republic; the writer always aspired to maintain the reputation of a statesman.

Latin literature is the only one that began with philosophy; in all the others, and above all in Greek literature, the first efforts of the human mind were of the imagination. Utility is the creative principle of Latin literature. The patricians initiated, in condescension to the populace, entertainments, songs, and festivals; but since lasting power was concentrated in the Senate, that body necessarily guided the public spirit.

The Roman people were a celebrated nation, wisely governed and vigorously constituted, even before there was a single writer in the Latin language. Literature began when the mind of the Romans had already been shaped by several centuries in which the principles of philosophy had been put into practice. The art of writing was developed long after the talent for action; literature among the Romans thus had an entirely different character, an entirely different goal, from those countries where imagination was the first to stir.

A more serious taste than that of the Greeks necessarily resulted, in Rome, from class distinctions. The lower classes, seeking always to rise, were not slow to notice that nobility of conduct and refinement of breeding made the distance between ranks more palpable than all the legal distinctions. The Romans would never have suffered, on their stage, the coarse jokes of Aristophanes; they would never have allowed contemporary affairs and public personalities to be thus committed to exhibition. They allowed the showing of certain conventionally theatrical customs which bore no relation to their own qualities—pantomimes or coarse farces, with Greek slaves taking the leading roles in these Greek works, but nothing that could have the slightest analogy to Roman customs. The ideas and feelings expressed in these comedies were for the Roman audience just another invention in a work of the imagination; yet Terence maintained in these foreign themes the kind of decency and moderation that human dignity demands even when there are no women in the audience.

Women had a greater place among the Romans than among the Greeks; but it was in the family that they obtained great influence, not yet in general social relations. Roman taste and urbanity had a masculine quality that borrowed nothing from feminine refinement and maintained itself solely by habitual austerity.

Democracy inspires a lively and almost universal spirit of emulation, whereas aristocracy stimulates rather the perfection of what is undertaken. As he composes, the writer always has his judges in mind, and all works of art are the combined result of the talent of the author and the level of the audience he chooses as his judges.

The Greeks were much more experienced than the Romans in the quick, cutting repartee that assures popularity among a witty, free-and-easy people; but the Romans had more real intellect—that is to say, they saw a greater number of relations among ideas and examined more thoroughly all kinds of thought. Their progress in philosophical ideas is highly apparent from Cicero to Tacitus. Imaginative literature proceeds at an uneven rate; but the knowledge of the human heart and of its morality always improves steadily. The main foundations of the philosophical views of the Romans were borrowed from the Greeks; but since the Romans adopted in the conduct of their life the principles the Greeks developed merely in their books, the practice of virtue made them superior to the Greeks in the analysis of everything relating to morality.

Chapter VI. Latin Literature in the Reign of Augustus

Republican customs continued for several years into the reign of Augustus; several historians retain some. But among the poets everything suggests the influence of courts. Most of them, desiring to please Augustus, and living off him, gave literature the character it must have under the rule of a monarch who wants to charm public opinion without yielding any of his power.

Philosophy, in Rome, preceded poetry. This is a reversal of the usual order and is perhaps the main reason for the perfection of the Latin poets.

Before the reign of Augustus, the spirit of emulation was not inclined toward poetry. The exercise of power and political advantage was almost invariably considered better than purely literary success. When the form of government summons superior talents to the exercise of public functions, it is toward eloquence, history, and philosophy—toward the realm of literature that more directly concerns the understanding of men and affairs—that efforts are made. But under an autocracy the fine arts are the only road to renown left to eminent men; and when the tyranny is mild, the poets often make the mistake of glorifying the autocrat's reign in their masterpieces.

Nevertheless, Virgil, Horace, and Ovid, despite the flatteries they lavished upon Augustus, proved in their writings to be much better philosophers and thinkers than any of the Greek poets. They owe this superiority in part to the profound intellect of the writers who preceded them. Every literature has its poetic era. Certain beauties of imagery and harmony have been successively carried over into most new and improved languages; but when, as in Rome, the poetic genius of a nation develops during an enlightened age, it is enriched by the knowledge of that age. The imagination, in some respects, has only one era in which to develop in every country, and it usually precedes philosophical ideas; when that era finds such ideas already understood and developed, it runs its course much more brilliantly.

In the reign of Augustus, almost every poet adopted the Epicurean doctrine in his writings. It is, first, very favorable to poetry, and, moreover, it seems to lend a certain respectability to *insouciance,* a certain principle to sensuousness, a certain dignity even to slavery. This doctrine is immoral but not servile. It forsakes liberty as it does all other things that may require effort, but it does not reduce despotism to a principle or obedience to fanaticism, as the sycophants of Louis XIV were willing to do.

The love of the countryside, which has inspired so much beautiful poetry, takes among the Romans a character different from that among the Greeks. These two nations take equal pleasure in the imagery suited to similar climates. They invoke and summon up with delight the bloom of nature to escape their consuming sun. But the Romans also ask of the countryside a shelter against tyranny. It was in order to rest from painful feelings, to leave behind a degrading yoke, that they withdrew far from the crowded cities. Moral reflections were mingled with their descriptive poetry. We can discern regret and remembrance in all that the poets wrote at this time, and it is doubtless for this reason that they arouse in us, more than did the Greeks, a sympathetic impression. The

Greeks lived in the future, but the Romans, like us, already liked to cast their eyes upon the past.

So long as the Republic lasted, there was a refinement in the feeling Romans had for women. Women had not as yet the independent existence that modern laws assure them. But relegated to the household along with the Penates, women, like these domestic divinities, inspired some religious feeling. Since the writers who lived under the Republic never allowed themselves to express the affections they experienced, it is in the brief transition from the strictest morals to the most appalling depravity that the Latin poets displayed a more tender sensibility than can be found in any Greek work. Republican austerity was still remembered in the reign of Augustus, and the portrayal of love owed some of its charms to these memories of virtue. Nevertheless, the true language of a profound and passionate sensibility is extremely rare even among the Romans of the age of Augustus. The Epicurean doctrine, the dogma of fatalism, the customs of antiquity before the establishment of the Christian religion, almost completely perverted everything relating to the feelings of the heart.

One wonders why the ancients, especially the Romans, had historians so faultless that they have never been equalled by the moderns, and particularly why the French do not have a perfect example to offer in this *genre*. This superiority is not in conflict with the continual progress of thought.

There are types of history properly called philosophical, and there are other types whose worth lies in the truth of the portrayals, the excitement of the story, and the beauty of the language. It is in this latter *genre* that the Greek and Latin historians won renown.

One must have a much more profound understanding of mankind to be a great analyst of human behavior than to become a good historian. Titus Livy, Sallust, the historians of an inferior order, Florus, Cornelius Nepos, etc., enchant us by the grandeur and the simplicity of their stories, by the eloquence of the speeches they ascribe to their great men, by the dramatic interest they know how to give to their portrayals. But these historians were concerned, so to speak, with only the exterior of life. This means man as he appears, as he shows himself; this means strong colorings, the striking contrast of vice and virtue. But there is in the history of the ancients neither philosophical analysis of human feelings, nor careful observation of character, nor the hidden signs of the soul's emotions. Montaigne's intellectual range of vision goes very much further than that of any writer of antiquity. But this kind of superiority, it is true, is not at all desirable in history, where human nature must be portrayed only as a whole, and heroes must remain great so that they may appear that way through the ages. The analysts of human behavior reveal the weaknesses, that is, the hidden resemblances among men; the historian must emphasize their differences. The ancients, who delighted in admiration, who sought neither to diminish the odiousness of vice nor the worth of virtue, had a quality almost as essential to the interests of truth as to those of fiction: they were as faithful to enthusiasm as to abhorrence, and often, indeed, their descriptions of character were better sustained in their historical portrayals than in their works of the imagination.

Chapter VII. Latin Literature from the Death of Augustus to the Reign of the Antonines

The reign of Augustus had degraded men; a repose without dignity had almost obliterated even the memory of the spirited virtues to which Rome owed its greatness. Horace was not ashamed to proclaim in his poetry that he had fled the day of battle. Cicero and Ovid both bore with difficulty the misfortune of exile. But what a difference in the expression of their regrets! Ovid's *Tristia* are filled with the evidence of weak and hopeless dejection, with the basest flattery of his persecutor; while Cicero, even in the intimacy of his correspondence with Atticus, controlled and ennobled in a thousand ways the suffering that his unjust banishment caused him. Such differences must be attributed not only to the diversity in personalities but to that of the times. Prevailing opinion is a core with which individuals always maintain some relations; and if the general spirit of the age does not alter individual character, it does modify the forms chosen to express it.

After the flourishing reign of Augustus, there arose the most savage and raw tyrannies of antiquity. Excessive misfortune tempered men's souls anew. The comfortable yoke enervated superior minds as well as the multitude. The ragings of cruelty, endured for a long time, debased the majority of the nation even more; but a few enlightened men raised themselves from this general dejection and felt more than ever the need for Stoic philosophy.

When tyrants threaten death, philosophers, forced to endure nature's greatest horrors and the most atrocious of crimes, and unable to act openly, examine more closely the workings of the soul. The writers of the third era of Latin literature had not yet attained complete knowledge, the analytical observation of human traits, such as one finds in Montaigne and La Bruyère. But they did understand more about their own character; oppression confined their genius to their own selves.

Tyranny, like all great public misfortunes, can aid the development of philosophy, but it gives a deathblow to literature by stifling emulation and corrupting taste.

It has been asserted that the decline of the arts, letters, and empires is inevitable after a certain degree of splendor. This idea lacks precision. The arts have a limit, I believe, beyond which they do not rise, but they can maintain the eminence they have reached; whereas in all learning susceptible of continual advancement, the human mind tends steadily to improve itself.

Writers in the days of the emperors, despite the terrible circumstances against which they had to struggle, are superior, as philosophers, to the writers of the Augustan age. But the style of the Latin authors of the third era of their literature has less elegance and purity: refinement of taste could not be maintained under such coarse and fierce masters.

Under the tyranny of the emperors it was neither permitted nor possible to stir the people by eloquence; philosophical and literary works had no influence on public affairs. One does not find, therefore, in the writings of that period, the character that always marks the hope of being useful, that sense of proportion whose aim is to bring about action, to lead by the power of speech to a genuine result. It is necessary to provide amusement for the spirit in order to be read by men separated from one another, whose ambitions have nothing to do with thought and who expect nothing from it. It is possible, in such a situation, for writers to fall into affectation because it is very important to them to make the elements of their style stimulating. Seneca and Pliny the Younger, especially, are not free of this fault.

To the honor of the Roman people, the arts of the imagination failed almost completely during the tyranny of the emperors. Men of letters did not decorate the tyranny; and the only pursuit they devoted themselves to under these detestable masters was the study of philosophy and eloquence—they drilled with the weapons that could help overthrow the oppression itself.

Flattery has tainted the writings of some philosophers of this era; and their very reticence was likewise shameful. Yet that era's ignorance of printing was in some respects favorable to the freedom to write, for books were less closely inspected by despotism when the means of publicity were extremely limited. Polemical writings, those that ought to influence opinions and events of the day, could be of no avail or influence before the employment of the press. They could never be diffused widely enough to produce an effect upon the populace; the tribune alone could reach that goal. So books were written only about general ideas or previous occurrences suitable for the instruction of posterity. Tyrants at that time were thus much less concerned than tyrants in our day about the freedom to write. Posterity, however, not being in their domain, they rather willingly allowed the philosophers to take refuge in it.

We wonder why, in this era, the exact sciences did not make more progress, why it happened that practically no Roman devoted himself to them. Under a tyranny, apolitical researches have often engaged men who wanted neither to rebel nor to debase themselves. Perhaps the dangers that then threatened all distinguished men were too imminent to allow them the leisure necessary for such works; or perhaps the Romans retained too much republican indignation to allow their attention to be distracted from the destiny of their country. Philosophical thoughts are linked to all the sentiments of the soul, but the sciences carry one away to an entirely different system of ideas. In short, in that era, since the true method to follow in the study of physical nature had not been discovered, the stimulus of emulation did not exist in a domain where great successes had not yet been obtained.

One of the causes of the destruction of empires in antiquity is the ignorance of a few important discoveries in the sciences which established greater equality among nations as well as among men. The decline of empires is no more in the natural order of things than is the decline of letters or of knowledge. But before all of Europe was civilized, before the political and military order and the employment of artillery had created a balance of forces, and finally before printing was invented, national spirit and national luminaries must have been the easy prey of barbarians always more inured to war than other men. Had the printing press existed, with public opinion and enlightenment gaining more strength daily, the character of the Romans would have been preserved and with it the nation and the Republic.

If it were demonstrated to be a social necessity that renowned nations should disappear from the world after having enlightened it for a time, then the human spirit, and especially patriotic emulation, would be completely discouraged. The succession of dethroned nations is not absolutely inevitable. From a study of the sublime reflections of Montesquieu on the causes of the decline of the Romans, it is clear that most of these causes no longer exist in our day.

The half of Europe that was not yet civilized must ultimately overrun the other. The advantages of society had to become universal, for everything in nature tends toward equality. Indeed, the pleasures of private life, the diffusion of knowledge, and the establishing of greater equality of possessions will gradually mitigate international rivalry through trade.

Chapter VIII. The Invasions of the People of the North, the Establishment of the Christian Religion, and the Renaissance of Letters

It is rather generally believed that for more than six centuries of history the human mind retrogressed. If during such a considerable length of time the great work of perfectibility had retreated, that would be a strong argument against the theory of the progress of knowledge. But this argument, which I would consider all-powerful if it were well grounded, can be easily refuted. I do not believe that the human species retrogressed during that epoch. I believe, to the contrary, that huge strides were made in the course of these six centuries, both in the propagation of learning and in the development of the intellectual faculties.

It seems to me that by studying history we become convinced that all the most significant events lead to the same end, the civilizing of the world. In every century we see that new peoples have been admitted to the benefits of social order and that war, despite all its disasters, has often spread the rule of enlightenment. The Romans civilized the people they subdued. At first, light had to come from a brilliant speck, from a small country like Greece; not many centuries later, a nation of warriors had to put a portion of the world under one rule in order to civilize while conquering it. The nations of the North, in eradicating for a time the literature and arts that reigned in the South, nevertheless acquired some of the knowledge of the vanquished; and the inhabitants of more than half of Europe, until then strangers to civilized society, shared its advantages. Thus does time reveal to us a design in the course of events that seem to be only the simple result of chance, and we see an intent, always the same, emerging out of the welter of deeds and ages.

The barbarians' invasion was undoubtedly a great misfortune for the nations contemporary with this upheaval, yet knowledge was spread by this very event. The enervated people of the South, mingling with the men of the North, took from them a certain energy and gave them a certain flexibility that was to help them perfect their intellectual faculties. War among equally enlightened nations for purely political interests is the most deadly scourge that human passions have produced; but war and the striking lesson of actual events can sometimes cause the adoption of certain ideas through the authority of power.

Some writers have put forward the idea that the Christian religion was the cause of the decline of letters and of philosophy, but I am convinced that the Christian religion, in the era of its establishment, was absolutely indispensable to the process of civilization and to the blending of the spirit of the North with the customs of the South. I believe further that the religious meditation induced by Christianity, applied to other subjects, developed the mental faculties for the sciences, metaphysics, and morality.

The peoples of the North attached no value to life. This attitude made them courageous among themselves but cruel to others. They had imagination, melancholy, and an inclination to mysticism but also a profound contempt for learning as weakening the martial spirit. The women were more learned than the men because they had more leisure. The men loved them, were faithful to them, worshiped them. They could thus experience at least some feeling, through love. Strength, loyalty in war, and truth as an attribute of strength were their only idea of virtue. Man was born to immolate man. Age was scorned, study depreciated, humanity unknown. The mental faculties had only one use among these men, which was to increase physical power. War was their single goal.

It was from such elements that morality of conduct, tenderness of feeling, and a taste for literature had to be made to emerge.

The task of influencing the peoples of the South was not less difficult. The Roman character, that miracle of national pride and political institutions, no longer existed. The inhabitants of Italy were disgusted with every conception of glory; they no longer believed in anything but sensual pleasure. If some innate taste for literature, the arts, and philosophy still existed in the South, it was directed largely toward metaphysical subtleties. The sophistical mentality cast doubt upon the truths of reason, and *insouciance* upon the affections of the heart.

The Christian religion was the bond between the peoples of the North and South; it so to speak amalgamated opposite principles of conduct into one way of thinking. In bringing together enemies, it made nations in which vigorous men fortified the character of enlightened men while the enlightened men developed the minds of the vigorous men.

In the corrupted centuries of the Roman Empire, the most unbridled licentiousness rescued women from servitude but only by degrading them; but it is Christianity that, at least in moral and religious relations, granted them equality. By making marriage a sacred institution, Christianity has strengthened conjugal love and all the feelings deriving from it. The doctrine of hell and paradise promise the same punishments and rewards to both sexes.

Women have not written any truly superior works. But they have nonetheless eminently served the progress of literature by the host of thoughts that constant relations with these volatile and sensitive beings has inspired in men.

If the [early] Renaissance were considered only with respect to works of pleasure and the imagination, we should undoubtedly feel that sixteen hundred years have been lost, and that from Virgil to the Catholic mysteries performed in the Paris theatre the human mind, in the arts, has done nothing but retreat to the most absurd barbarities. But it is not the same with works of philosophy. Bacon, Machiavelli, Montaigne, Galileo, all four virtual contemporaries in different countries, suddenly emerge from these obscure times and show themselves to be several centuries ahead of the latest writers of ancient literature and especially of the latest philosophers of antiquity.

If the human mind had not advanced even during those centuries in which we can hardly follow its history, should we have seen in the Renaissance men who, in morality, politics, and the sciences, far surpassed the greatest geniuses among the ancients? If there is an infinite distance between the last celebrated men of antiquity and the first among the moderns who won renown in the pursuit of the sciences and letters; if Bacon, Machiavelli, and Montaigne have ideas and knowledge infinitely superior to those of Pliny, of Marcus Aurelius, etc., is it not clear that human reason has made progress during the interval which separated the lives of these great men? For we must not forget the principle I set down at the beginning of this work, that the most distinguished genius rises only a few degrees above the other luminaries of his era.

A main cause of the keen emulation that literature stimulated in the Renaissance was the extraordinary splendor that the reputation of a good writer conferred. One is staggered by the innumerable tributes to Petrarch, by the unparalleled importance attached to the publication of his sonnets. Wearied of the absurd military prejudices that sought to degrade literature, people leaped to the opposite extreme. Perhaps, also, the full display of these public rewards was necessary in order to promote, three centuries ago, the difficult labors required by the perfection of modern languages, the rebirth of the philosophical spirit, and the creation of a new method in metaphysics and the exact sciences.

Chapter IX. The General Spirit of Modern Literature

Novels, those diverse productions of the mind of moderns, are a *genre* almost entirely unknown to the ancients. They did write some pastorals in the style of novels, which date from the time when the Greeks sought to fill the spare time left them by servitude; but before women had created an interest in private life, love hardly engaged the interest of men—they were absorbed in public pursuits.

Women discovered in human nature a host of *nuances,* which the need to dominate or the fear of being dominated made them perceive. These *nuances* provided dramatists with new means to move people. Every feeling women are permitted to indulge in—the fear of death, the regrets of life, boundless devotion, unrestrained indignation—enriched literature with new expression. Not being responsible for themselves, so to speak, women go in their speech just as far as the feelings of their souls lead them.

A vague and profound sensibility is one of the greatest beauties of some modern works. And women, knowing nothing of life but the capacity to love, have transmitted their tenderness to the style of some writers. In reading books written since the Renaissance, one may identify on every page those ideas that were lacking before women were granted a sort of civil equality.

In works of the imagination, the only advantage of recent

writers over the ancients is the talent, owing to knowledge of mankind, for expressing a more delicate sensibility and for giving greater variety to situation and characters. But the philosophers of our day are infinitely superior in the sciences —in method and analysis, in generalization, and in linking the results. They have a thread of which they can daily unroll more, without ever becoming confused.

Mathematical reasoning is like the two great ideas of higher metaphysics, space and eternity. Thousands upon thousands of miles may be added and the centuries may be multiplied, yet each calculation is precise and unlimited. The greatest advance the human mind made is the abandonment of the uncertainty of preconceived dogmas and the adoption of the method of proof, for the only real achievements for the general good are those truths that have actually been proved.

I do not believe that any book or orator among the ancients was the equal, in the sublime art of moving men, of Bossuet or Rousseau, or of the English in some of their poetry or the Germans in some of their language. It is to the spirituality of Christian ideas, to the melancholy truth of philosophical ideas, that we must attribute this skill in introducing, even into the discussion of a personal matter, universal and moving thoughts that take hold of all people, awaken memories, and restore men completely to a concern for man.

The knowledge of ethics necessarily improved with the progress of human reason. We must not compare the virtues of modern men with those of the ancients, as public men, for it is only in free countries that there are tolerant relations and established obligations between citizen and fatherland. It is in the private attributes, therefore, in philanthropic feelings and in certain superior writings, that we must examine the progress of ethics.

The ancients asked of others only to refrain from harming them; they simply wanted others to stand away from their bit of sunlight in order to leave them to themselves and to nature. A more mellow feeling gives moderns the need for that positive help, support, and solicitude that they can inspire. They have made a virtue of everything that can serve mutual happiness and comforting relations among themselves. Family ties are cemented by a reasonable amount of freedom: man no longer has a legal arbitrary right over his fellow man.

Chapter X. Italian and Spanish Literature

The patronage of the princes of Italy contributed much to the Renaissance but it necessarily hindered philosophy. This hindrance would have persisted even if religious superstition had not in several ways adulterated the search for truth.

We must recall here once more the meaning that I have consistently attached to the word philosophy in the course of this work. I call philosophy the investigation of the source of all political and religious institutions, the analysis of the personalities and events of history—in short, the study of man and of the natural rights of man. Philosophy in this sense presupposes freedom or must lead to it.

The men of letters of Italy, needing the money and the approval of the princes to recover the ancient manuscripts that were to serve them as a guide, were further than those of any other country from that sort of independence necessary to philosophy of such a kind. There was a host of academies and universities in the large cities of Italy. These associations were singularly fitted for the scholarly labors that were to bring so many masterpieces out of oblivion. But public establishments are by their very nature completely obedient to governments. Public bodies, like Estates, social classes, and religious sects, are extremely useful for some specific purposes but are much less favorable than individual efforts and talent to the continuous advancement of philosophical learning.

We should add to these general considerations that the long and patient research required to examine and analyze ancient manuscripts particularly suited the monastic life; and it was indeed the monks who were the most actively engaged in literary studies. Thus the very causes of the rebirth of literature in Italy set themselves against the development of natural reason. The Italians cleared the first passage in the road along which the human mind has since made such great progress, but they themselves were fated never to advance on the path they had opened.

Poetry and the fine arts, by their unique charms, intoxicate the imagination, but the writers in prose are, in general, neither moralists nor philosophers and their attempts at eloquence produce only exaggeration. Nevertheless, as it is the nature of the human mind always to go forward, the Italians, to whom philosophy was forbidden and who could not in poetry go beyond perfection—the limit of all the arts—were renowned for the remarkable progress they steadily made in the sciences. After the age of Leo X, after Ariosto and Tasso, their poetry declined; but they had Galileo, Cassini, and others; and even recently many useful discoveries in physics have associated them with the intellectual improvement of the human species.

Superstition indeed tried to persecute Galileo, but several princes of Italy itself came to his help. Religious fanaticism is the enemy of the sciences and arts as well as of philosophy, but absolute monarchy or feudal aristocracy often protects the sciences and the arts while detesting independence only in philosophy.

Let us examine in each branch of human understanding, in philosophy, eloquence, and poetry, the causes of the successes and faults of Italian literature.

The subdivision of states within the same country is ordinarily favorable to philosophy: I shall have the occasion to develop this point in speaking of German literature. But in Italy this subdivision has not produced its natural effect; the despotism of priests, pressing heavily on all parts of the country, destroyed most of the happy results a federal government or separate small states ought to enjoy. It would perhaps have been better if the whole nation had been united under a single government. The nation's memories of ancient times would thus have been aroused sooner, and the awareness of its power would have revived the awareness of its virtue.

It would seem that eloquence of the pulpit ought to have existed in Italy more than elsewhere, since it is the country most consigned to the control of a religion that closely regulates life. Yet this country offers nothing of value in this *genre*, in which France can boast the greatest and most beautiful talents. The Italians, except for a certain class of enlightened men, are in religion as in love and in liberty: they like exaggeration in everything and can feel the true measure of nothing. They are vindictive yet servile. They are slaves to women yet strangers to profound and lasting feelings of the heart. They are wretchedly superstitious in their observances of Catholicism, but they do not believe in the indissoluble union of morality and religion.

Such is the effect that must be produced upon a people by fanatical prejudices, by various governments that do not combine defense and love of the same fatherland, and by a burning sun that stirs up all the sensations and must induce voluptuousness if this consequence is not combated, as among the Romans, by the force of political passions.

After having stated, perhaps harshly, all that is lacking in the literature of the Italians, we must return to the delightful charm of their brilliant imagination.

It is a noteworthy literary era that discovered the secret of arousing interest by the invention and narration of love affairs. The novel as a *genre* was introduced by two distinct influences in the North and in the South. In the North the spirit of chivalry often gave rise to extraordinary incidents; and in order to interest the warriors it was necessary to relate to them exploits similar to their own. To dedicate literature to the relating or invention of chivalrous deeds was the only way to overcome the repugnance that men who were still barbarous felt for letters.

The Spanish ought to have had a more noteworthy literature than that of the Italians. They should have united the imagination of the North with that of the South, the grandeur of chivalry with Oriental grandeur, the martial spirit continuous wars glorified with the poetry the beauty of the sun and climate inspired. But the royal power, supporting superstition, smothered these happy germs of all kinds of glory. The subdivision of states, which prevented Italy from becoming one nation, gave it at least enough freedom for the sciences and arts. But the unity of Spanish despotism, supporting the effective power of the Inquisition, left no living space to thought in any field, no means of escaping the yoke. We should, nevertheless, judge from some scattered essays that can still be collected what Spanish literature might have been.

The Moors who settled in Spain borrowed from chivalry the worship of women expressed in their romances; this devotion did not exist in the national customs of the Orient. The Arabs who remained in Africa did not resemble, in this aspect, the Arabs who settled in Spain. The Moors gave the Spanish their spirit of splendor; the Spanish inspired in the Moors their chivalrous love and honor. No mixture could have been more favorable to works of the imagination, if literature had been able to develop in Spain.

No element of philosophy could develop in Spain; the invasions from the North brought only the martial spirit, and the Arabs were the enemies of philosophy.[6]

Spain, just as foreign as Italy to philosophical works, was diverted from all literary competition by the dark and oppressive tyranny of the Inquisition; she did not profit from the inexhaustible sources of poetic invention the Arabs brought with them. Italy had ancient monuments and close relations with the Greeks of Constantinople; she took from Spain the Oriental style that the Moors had brought there and that the Spanish neglected.

Europe, and especially France, nearly lost all the advantages of natural genius by imitating the Italian writers. The beauties that make the Italian poets immortal depend upon language, climate, imagination, upon circumstances of all kinds that cannot spread elsewhere; whereas their faults are highly contagious.

They have no novels, as the English and the French do, because love as they conceive it, not being a passion of the soul, cannot be minutely analyzed. Their habits are too licentious to be able to build up any interest in this *genre.*

Their comedies have much of the buffoonish merriment that depends upon exaggeration of vice and folly, but we do not find in them, except for some plays of Goldoni, the striking and true portrayal of human failings, as in the French comedies. So the Italian comedies are a caricature of life rather than a portrait of it.

In their stories, and often even upon their stages, the Italians ridicule the priests, to whom they are in fact entirely subservient. But it is not from a philosophical point of view that

[6] *Like her contemporaries, Madame de Staël held curious and largely incorrect ideas about Arab intellectual life and the relation of Arabic to European literature.*—Ed.

they attack the abuses of religion. Unlike some of our writers, they do not aim to correct the defects they joke about; they want merely to amuse themselves, the more as the subject is more serious. Their beliefs are fundamentally opposed to all the forms of authority to which they are subject, but this spirit of opposition only makes them contemptuous of those who command them. It is the ruse of children against their teachers: they obey them on condition that they may make fun of them.

Melancholy, that fertile sentiment in works of genius, seems to belong almost exclusively to Northern climates.

The Orientals, whom the Italians have often imitated, did indeed have a kind of melancholy. One finds it in some Arabic poems and especially in the psalms of the Hebrews; but it has a character distinct from that melancholy we shall speak of in analyzing the literature of the North.

In the Orient, practical religious ideas, among the Mohammedans as well as the Jews, sustained and guided the sentiments of the soul. Such ideas do not display that awesome vagueness that produces a more philosophical and more melancholy impression upon the soul. The melancholy of Orientals is that of men happy in the enjoyment of nature; they reflected with regret only upon the rapid passing of prosperity, the brevity of life. The melancholy of the peoples of the North is the kind that arises out of the suffering of the soul, the emptiness that sensibility causes one to find in life, the meditation that constantly leads the mind from thoughts of the weariness of life to the mystery of death.

Chapter XI. Literature of the North

There are, it seems to me, two entirely distinct literatures, that coming up from the South and that coming down from the North, that of which Homer is the main source and that of which Ossian is the origin.[7] The Greeks, Latins, Italians, Spanish, and the French of the age of Louis XIV belong to that *genre* of literature that I shall call the literature of the South. English works, German works, and some Danish and Swedish writings should be classed in the literature of the North, which began with the Scottish bards, the Icelandic fables, and Scandinavian poetry. Before characterizing the English and German writers, it seems to me necessary to consider in a general way the main differences between these two hemispheres of literature.

The English poets, it may be said, are noteworthy for their philosophic spirit—it is displayed in all their works—whereas Ossian has almost no serious ideas: he narrates a succession of incidents and impressions. I answer to this objection that the most common images and ideas in Ossian are those that call to mind the brevity of life, respect for the dead and the celebration of their memory, and the devotion of those who remain to those who are departed. If the poet has not combined with these sentiments any moral maxims or philosophical reflections, it is because in that era the human mind was not yet capable of the abstraction necessary for the drawing of conclusions. But the shock to the imagination caused by the songs of Ossian dispose the mind to the most profound meditations.

Melancholy poetry is the type of poetry that is most in accord with philosophy. Sadness leads us to probe much more deeply into the character and destiny of man than does any

[7] *Ossian is a legendary third-century poet to whom various exploits are attributed in Gaelic poetry. He was mistakenly regarded by Madame de Staël and others as a real poet and author of what are now known as several cycles of Ossian poetry, the best known of which were by James Macpherson* (1736–96).—Ed.

other disposition of the mind. The English poets who have followed the Scottish bards have added to their descriptions the thoughts and ideas these descriptions necessarily evoked.

We cannot in general decide between the two types of poetry of which we may consider Homer and Ossian the first models. All my feelings and all my ideas lead me to prefer the literature of the North. But what matters now is to examine its distinctive characteristics.

Climate is certainly one of the main causes of the differences between the images the North found congenial and those that people in the South preferred to summon up. The poets of the South continually mingle the representation of coolness, dense woods, and limpid streams with all their impressions of life. They cannot describe even the pleasures of the heart without combining with them the idea of the benevolent shade that protects them from the burning heat of the sun. The vigorous nature that surrounds them arouses in them impulse rather than thought. I think it is wrong to say that the passions are more violent in the South than in the North. The South has a greater variety of concerns but less depth in any single one. And it is intensity that produces the miracles resulting from passion and will.

The peoples of the North are less occupied with pleasures than with suffering, and their imagination is all the more fertile for it. The spectacle of nature powerfully affects them; and it makes them exactly like their climate: always dark and moody. Of course, the changing circumstances of life can change this disposition to melancholy, but it alone bears the imprint of the national character. In a nation, as in a man, we need to find only the characteristic trait; all the others are the result of a thousand different accidents, but that one alone constitutes its being.

Northern poetry is much more suitable than Southern to the

spirit of a free people. The first known creators of the literature of the South, the Athenians, were more jealous of their independence than any other nation. But it was easier to reduce the Greeks to slavery than the men of the North. Independence was the main and unique good fortune of the Northern peoples. A certain pride of spirit, an indifference to life, generated by both the harshness of the soil and the gloom of the sky, were to make slavery unbearable. And long before England knew either the theory of constitutional government or the advantage of representative government, the martial spirit that Irish and Scandinavian poetry sang with such enthusiasm gave man an extraordinary conception of his individual strength and the power of his will. Independence existed for each one before liberty was established for all.

At the time of the Renaissance, philosophy began with the Northern nations, among whose religious customs reason had to struggle against fewer prejudices than among the Southern peoples.

The Northern peoples, judging by traditions left to us and by Teutonic customs, had at all periods a respect for women that was unknown among the peoples of the South. In the North women enjoyed independence, whereas elsewhere they were condemned to slavery. This is another of the main causes of the sensibility that characterizes the literature of the North.

The history of love in all countries may be considered from a philosophical point of view. It would seem that the portrayal of this sentiment should depend solely upon the feelings of the writer who expresses it. Yet such is the influence of custom upon writers that they surrender to it even the expression of the most private feelings. It is possible that Petrarch was in his life more in love than the author of *Werther* or many English poets such as Pope, Thomson, and Otway. Yet might we not think, upon reading the writers of the North, that they are of another nature, with other bonds, in another world? The perfection of some of this poetry indeed proves the genius of its authors, but it is no less certain that in Italy the same men would not have written the same things even had they felt the same emotions. So true is it that in literary works seeking a wide audience there are usually fewer traces of the personal character of the writer than of the general spirit of his nation and his time.

Finally, the Protestant religion, which almost all of the modern peoples of the North adopted, gave them a more philosophical spirit than those of the South had. The Reformation was the historical period that most effectively advanced the perfectibility of the human species. The Protestant religion harbors no active germ of superstition, yet lends virtue all the support that it can extract from sensibility. In the countries where the Protestant religion is professed, it does not retard philosophical inquiry at all and effectively upholds morality.

Chapter XII. The Main Fault for Which Northern Literature Is Criticized in France

In France the literature of the North is reproached for its lack of taste. The writers of the North reply that "taste" is a purely arbitrary establishment of rules which often deprive feeling and thought of their most original beauties. I believe there is a happy medium between these two positions. The rules of taste are not entirely arbitrary; we must not confuse the principal bases upon which universal truths are founded with the modifications caused by local circumstances.

The obligations of virtue—that code of moral principles supported by the unanimous consent of all peoples—are to some extent changed by the manners and customs of the various nations; and though the fundamental relations among them remain the same, the place of this or that virtue may vary according to custom and form of government. Taste, if we may compare it to man's most noble sentiments, is likewise fixed in its general principles. National taste should be judged upon these principles; the closer it approaches them, the nearer it is to truth.

It is often asked: Must genius be sacrificed to taste? Of course not. But taste never requires the sacrifice of genius. You often find ludicrous scenes alongside great beauties in the literature of the North. What is good taste in such writings are the great beauties, and what should have been omitted is what good taste condemns.

To the question which is worth more, a work with great beauties and great faults or a mediocre and proper work, I would reply without hesitation that we ought to prefer the work with however slight the trace of genius.

Pleasant impressions are what men seek in masterpieces of the imagination. So taste is nothing but the art of understanding and anticipating what can lead to such impressions. If you summon up disgusting things, you stimulate an unpleasant impression, which people would take pains to avoid in real life as well. And if, by the representation of horrible scenes, you transform moral terror into physical fright, then you lose all the charm of imitation, you administer nothing but a nervous shock, and you may fail to make even this painful impression if you try to push it too far. For in the theatre, as in life, when there is overstatement we disregard even the reality.

In England the beauties of Shakespeare's work may triumph over his faults, but these faults greatly reduce his stature in other countries.

I shall not reproach Shakespeare with having cast aside

the rules of art; they are infinitely less important than those of taste, for the latter prescribe what must be done while the former limit themselves to forbidding what must be avoided. We cannot be mistaken about something that is bad, but it is impossible to set limits upon the ingenuity of a man of genius; he can follow entirely new paths without losing his way. The rules of art are a calculus of probability regarding the means to success; and if success is achieved it matters little whether one has followed the rules or not. But it is not the same with taste; for to put oneself above it is to stray from the beauty of nature itself—and there is nothing superior to that.

Chapter XIII. Shakespeare's Tragedies

A nation that has become free, whose passions have been powerfully stirred by the horrors of civil wars, is much more susceptible to the emotion aroused by Shakespeare than by Racine. When misfortune burdens nations for a long time, it gives them a character that even later prosperity cannot entirely efface. Shakespeare, though since equaled at times by English or German authors, was the first who portrayed human suffering in the highest degree; the bitterness of the pain he described might almost be taken to be pure invention, were it not that nature recognizes itself in it.

Another sentiment Shakespeare alone knew how to dramatize was pity unmixed with admiration for the sufferer, pity for an insignificant being and sometimes even for a contemptible one. It takes infinite talent to transfer this feeling from life to the stage while preserving all its power.

The national pride of the English, the feeling arising from a jealous love of liberty, lends itself less to fanatical devotion to a leader than did the spirit of chivalry in the French monarchy. In England they like to reward the services of a good citizen, but they have no inclination to that unlimited enthusiasm found in the institutions, customs, and character of the French. This proud aversion to eager obedience, which has in all times been characteristic of the English, must have inspired in their national poet the idea of achieving sympathy more through pity than through admiration. The tears we French offer to the exalted personalities of our tragedies the English author causes to flow for humble and forsaken suffering, for that succession of misfortunes one cannot understand in Shakespeare without also acquiring some knowledge of life itself.

The customs of the English regarding women were not yet formed in Shakespeare's time; political disorder had precluded social conventions. The position of women in tragedies was thus left entirely to the will of the author: so Shakespeare, in speaking of women, sometimes used the noblest language that love could inspire and at others words in the worst and most vulgar taste. This man of genius endowed by passion was inspired by it as priests are inspired by their god. He brought forth oracles when he was aroused but he was nothing more than a man when calm returned to his soul.

Chapter XIV. English Joking

We may distinguish various types of joking in the literature of every country; and nothing serves better to reveal the customs of a nation than the nature of the levity most widely adopted by its writers. Alone, we are serious; we are gay for others, above all in writing. We can make people laugh only by notions so familiar to those who hear them that they strike them instantly and do not require any mental effort.

The levity derived, so to speak, from the inspiration of taste and genius, the levity produced by the ingenuity of the mind, and the levity the English call *humor* are hardly related to one another. And in none of these types is natural cheerfulness of the disposition included because, as many examples prove, it is irrelevant to the talent for producing works of levity. Levity comes easily to anyone who is witty, but only the genius of one man and the good taste of many can inspire true comedy.

Let us now seek to discover why the customs of the English run against the true spirit of levity.

Most Englishmen, absorbed in business, seek pleasure only as a relaxation. Just as hunger caused by fatigue makes any dish acceptable, so continual, serious work disposes men to be satisfied with any kind of diversion. Family life, rather strict religious notions, serious pursuits, and an oppressive climate all make the English rather susceptible to the disease of boredom. For this very reason, refined amusements of the mind do not satisfy them. This kind of dejection requires strong shocks, and authors either share the taste of the audience in this regard or simply conform to it.

The type of levity that can be used in creating a good comedy presupposes a very subtle observation of character. For the comic genius to develop, people must live a great deal in society and attach great importance to social success. They must know one another and be brought together by the multitude of vain concerns that gives rise to every absurdity as well as to every scheme of vanity. The English are secluded in their families or gathered in public assemblies for national debates. The intermediary called *société* hardly exists among them; yet it is in this frivolous area of life that *finesse* and taste are formed.

The political relationship among men erases subtleties by

strongly accentuating individual personalities. The importance of the ends and the force of the means to attain them extinguish concern for everything that does not have a useful outcome. In monarchical states, where one is at the mercy of the personality and will of one man or of a small number of his deputies, every one takes pains to know the most hidden thoughts of others, the slightest gradations of individual feeling and weakness.* But when public opinion and popular reputation exert the principal influence, ambition abandons what it does not need: the mind does not bother to apprehend the ephemeral when there is no advantage in divining it.

The English do not have a comic author like Molière; and if they did they would not perceive all his subtleties.

There is now and then in Congreve some subtle wit as well as broad humor but no true affection is portrayed. By a curious contrast, the more simple and pure are the private manners of the English, the more they exaggerate the portrayal of every vice in their comedies.

It seems as if, wanting to be gay, they have deemed it necessary to deviate as much as possible from what they really are, or that, deeply respecting the sentiments that produce the happiness of their domestic life, they have not allowed them to be exhibited upon the stage.

One rarely finds true English characters in English comedies. Perhaps the dignity of a free people, among the English as among the Romans, does not permit them to represent their own manners upon the stage. The French readily make fun of themselves. Shakespeare and a few others have drawn in their plays some caricatures of common people but the exaggeration almost entirely excludes verisimilitude. The masses of every country are amused by coarse joking but it is only in

* England is governed by a king but all of its institutions are eminently guardians of civil liberty and security.

France that the raciest kind of joking may be at the same time the most refined.

Levity and eloquence are related only in that it is involuntary inspiration that can, in writing or in speech, lead to perfection in the one or the other. The spirit of those around us, of the nation in which we live, develops in us powers of persuasion or joking much more reliably than can deliberate thought and study. But the general disposition of most Englishmen does not stir their writers to levity.

There is nevertheless a kind of levity in some English writings that has all the characteristics of originality and fidelity to the national temper. The English language has created a word, humor, to express this sort of levity, which is almost as much a predisposition of the blood as of the mind; it derives from the nature of the climate and national customs and could not be imitated at all where the same causes did not develop it. Some writings of Fielding and Swift, *Peregrine Pickle, Roderick Random,* but above all the works of Sterne give a complete notion of this *genre* called humor.

There is a moroseness—I would say almost a sadness—in this levity; the one who makes us laugh does not experience the pleasure he brings to others. We can see that he writes in a gloomy frame of mind and that he would almost seem to be annoyed at us as he amuses us. But just as a brusque manner sometimes makes praise more enjoyable, so is a joke enhanced by the author's seriousness.* The English very seldom allow upon the stage the *genre* of wit they call humor; its effect would not be dramatic.

* In London I once visited an amusing gymnasium and I saw the most grotesque stunts of tilting, hurdling, and swinging executed by very old men of the grimmest demeanor and the most imperturbable gravity. They devoted themselves to these exercises for their health and did not seem to suspect that nothing in the world was funnier than the contrast between their stuffy appearance and their infantile games.

There is a certain misanthropy even in the joking of the English and a sociability in that of the French; the one ought to be read in solitude, while the other impresses all the more as the audience is larger. English levity leads almost always to a philosophical or moral outcome; the purpose of French levity is seldom anything but pleasure itself.

The English portray eccentric characters with great talent because there are many among them. Society obliterates distinctions but a squire's life preserves them.

Mimicry is especially unsuited to the English; their attempts at the kind of grace and levity that distinguish French literature for the most part lack subtlety and charm. They make all notions obvious and exaggerate all shades of difference; they do not think they are heard unless they shout, or understood unless they spell everything out. It is strange that idle people are much more particular than busy ones about the use of their leisure time. Men devoted to business are accustomed to long expositions, but men devoted to pleasure become weary much more quickly. A very refined taste is quickly sated.

There is rarely any subtlety in minds that always apply themselves to practical results. What is truly useful is very easy to understand and does not require a penetrating eye to be seen. A country that tends toward equality is also less sensitive to faulty etiquette. The nation being more uniform, the writer gets the habit of appealing in his works to the judgments and feelings of all classes. In short, free countries are and ought to be serious.

When government is based upon force, it can afford not to fear the nation's inclination toward joking; but when authority depends on general confidence, when public feeling is its mainspring, the talent and levity that reveal the absurd and delight in derision are extremely dangerous to liberty and political equality. We have spoken of the misfortunes that befell the Athenians because of their immoderate love of joking; and France would have provided us with another such example if the force of the revolutionary events had allowed people to develop naturally.

Chapter XV. English Imagination in Poetry and the Novel

The invention of incidents and the faculty of feeling and portraying nature are two absolutely distinct types of imagination. The first belongs more especially to the literature of the South, the second to that of the North. I have presented their various determinants. I must now examine the special character of the poetic imagination of the English.

They have not been inventors of new subjects of poetry, like Tasso and Ariosto. English fiction is not based upon improbable incidents or extraordinary events, like Arabian or Persian tales. They retain some images of Northern religion but not a brilliant and varied mythology like that of the Greeks. But their poets have an inexhaustible fund of those ideas and feelings that arise from the scenes of nature. The invention of supernatural incidents has its limit; they are very restricted conceptions and are not very capable of the kind of development that is characteristic of human truths of every kind. When poets take pains to invest their philosophical thoughts and ardent feelings with the colors of the imagination, they enter to some extent the path on which enlightened men advance continuously, unless ignorant and tyrannical power deprives them of all liberty.

The English, separated from the Continent, *Semotos orbe Britannos*,[8] did not share much at any time in the history and customs of the neighboring peoples. They have their own char-

[8] *Similar phrases to this, suggesting Britain's remoteness from the civilized world, occur in Horace and Virgil.*—Ed.

acter in every *genre;* their poetry is not like that of the French, nor even like that of the Germans, and they have not attained that inventive genius in story and poetic incident that is the greatest glory of Greek and Italian literature. The English observe nature and know how to portray it; but they are not creators. Their superiority consists in the talent for keenly expressing what they see and feel; they have the gift of intimately joining philosophical reflections with feelings produced by the beauties of the countryside. The sight of sky and earth, at any time of day or night, arouses changing thoughts in us. He who yields himself to whatever nature inspires in him feels a series of the purest and loftiest impressions most similar to the great moral and religious ideas that link man to the hereafter.

[A] gloomy imagination is the general color of English poetry. Their works in verse often contain more ideas than their works in prose. [But] they never weary us by surrendering themselves to their philosophical gloom, for it is in accord with the very nature of our being and its destiny.

We may ask why the English, who are contented with their government and customs, have an imagination so much more melancholy than was that of the French. The answer is that liberty and virtue, those two great results of human reason, require meditation, and meditation necessarily leads to serious pursuits.

In France persons distinguished for their mind or status had in general a great deal of levity, but levity in the highest classes of society is not a sign of happiness in a nation. For the political and philosophical condition of a country to meet the standard of nature's design, the fortune of the middle class must be the greatest of all; those who are superior in any way should be completely dedicated to and even sacrifice themselves for the general good of humanity.

Happy the country where the writers are gloomy, the merchants satisfied, the rich melancholy, and the masses content!

The English language, though not so harmonious to the ear as the language of the South, has, by virtue of the vigor of its pronunciation, very great advantages for poetry—every word that is strongly accentuated has an effect upon the soul because it seems to spring from a vivid feeling. The French language excludes from poetry a great many simple words that we must consider noble in English because of the way in which they are articulated. I offer one such example. When Macbeth, sitting down to the feast, sees in the place intended for him the shade of Banquo, whom he has just murdered, and cries out again and again in such terror, *The table is full,* the entire audience trembles.[9] If one were to say precisely the same words in French, *la table est remplie,* the greatest actor in the world could not in reciting them make us forget their ordinary meaning. French pronunciation would not permit that accent which ennobles words by enlivening them and makes sounds tragic because they imitate the soul's disturbance and make others share it.

The English can afford to be bold in every *genre* of their writings because they are ardent and because any true feeling, whatever it may be, has the power to transport the reader into the mental state of the writer. The impassive author, whatever spirit he may have, must adapt himself in many respects to the taste of his readers. They impose this obligation upon him as soon as they are aware that he can adapt himself in this way.

The English are pre-eminent in one *genre* of imaginative works: fiction without marvels, without allegory, without historical allusions, based solely upon the invention of characters and events of private life. Down to the present love has been

[9] *Macbeth says once (Act III, Scene 4): "The table's full."*—Ed.

the subject of this kind of novel. The life of women in England is the main reason for the inexhaustible productivity of English writers in this *genre*. The relations between men and women are infinitely multiplied by sensibility and refinement.

Tyrannical laws, coarse desires, or cynical ideas have settled the fate of women, whether in the ancient republics or in Asia or in France. Nowhere so much as in England have women enjoyed the happiness brought about by domestic affections. In poor countries, and above all in the middle classes of society, the most virtuous customs have often been found. But it is the duty of the upper classes to make their example more noteworthy. They alone can choose their mode of life; the others are forced to resign themselves to whatever destiny imposes upon them. When one is led to the practice of a virtue because of want of personal advantages or by the yoke of circumstance, one never has all the ideas and feelings that can give rise to this virtue out of free choice. In general, then, it is the customs of the upper classes of society that influence literature. When the customs of the upper classes are moral, they preserve love, and love inspires novels. Without philosophically examining here the destiny of women in the social order, it is in general certain that only their domestic virtues can draw from men all the love of which they are capable.

England is the country where women are most truly loved, though they are very far from enjoying the pleasures that society in France formerly afforded women. But an interesting novel cannot be made from the portrayal of the pleasures of vanity, though life often shows that people can be satisfied with such vain pleasures. English customs provide fictional talent with many fine distinctions and moving circumstances. We might at first believe that immorality, recognizing no limit, would broaden the scope for romantic ideas but we see that, on the contrary, this unfortunate talent can produce nothing but emptiness. Passions without conflict, sudden endings, sacrifices without sorrow, and relationships without modesty deprive novels of all their charm. The few examples of this *genre* in French have had scarcely any success even in the circles that were their model.

There are tedious passages in the novels of the English, as in all their writings, but these novels are created to be read by the people who have adopted the style of life portrayed in them—rural, domestic—in the time spared from regular pursuits and family affections. If the French tolerate the useless details piled up in these writings, it is only out of the curiosity that foreign customs excite. They tolerate nothing like it in their own works. These tediums indeed sometimes exhaust one's interest, yet English novels hold our attention by a steady succession of accurate and moral comments on life's tender emotions. Careful observation is useful to the English in everything, whether to portray what they see or to discover what they seek.

The old French tales describe the adventures of chivalry, which do not remind us at all of the events of real life. *The New Heloise*[10] is an eloquent and impassioned piece of writing which reveals the genius of a man and not the customs of the nation. All the other French novels we like are imitations of the English. The subjects are not the same, but the way they are treated and the general nature of this kind of invention belong exclusively to the English writers.

They were the first who ventured to believe that the representation of private feelings was enough to interest the mind and heart of man, that neither the luster of eminent people, nor magnitude of concerns, nor extraordinary events were necessary in order to captivate the imagination, and that the power of love was enough to provide an endless variety of

[10] *By Rousseau.*—Ed.

scenes and situations without ever exhausting one's interest. It is the English, in short, who have transformed novels into works of morality in which obscure virtues and destinies can find grounds for exaltation and create a kind of heroism for themselves.

Chapter XVI. The Philosophy and Eloquence of the English

There are three very distinct eras in the political situation of the English: the time prior to their Revolution, their Revolution itself, and their status since 1688. The character of their literature has necessarily changed in accordance with these changing circumstances. Before the revolution there was in [English] philosophy but one man, Chancellor Bacon.

Bacon's writings are more peculiar to his own character than to his age. He leaped alone into all the sciences; sometimes obscure, often Scholastic, he nevertheless had new ideas on all subjects, but could finish nothing. The man of genius takes a few steps along unknown paths, but it requires the combined power of the ages and nations to clear the highways.

English philosophy is scientific; that is to say, its writers apply to moral ideas the kind of abstraction, computation, and elucidation that scientists use to make discoveries and to explain them.

French philosophy depends more upon feeling and imagination, without being any the less profound for it. For these two human faculties, when they are directed by reason, light its way and help it to penetrate further into the understanding of the human heart.

The Christian religion as it is professed in England and the constitutional principles as they are set up allow a considerable latitude in intellectual inquiry, whether into human or political affairs. Yet the English philosophers, in general, do not venture to inquire into everything; utility, which is the mainspring of their efforts, at the same time restricts their independence to a certain extent.

The English have treated politics as a purely intellectual science. Hobbes, Ferguson, Locke, etc., inquire, in different ways, into the original state of society in order to understand the laws that must be established for mankind.

The English have advanced in the philosophical sciences in the same way they have in commercial activity: with the help of time and patience. Their philosophers' propensity to abstraction might have led them into doctrines contrary to reason. But the English philosophers have always been brought back to the practical by their pragmatic spirit, which tempers the application of abstractions; by morality, which is the most empirical of all human ideas; and by commercial interests and the love of liberty. What a large number of works designed to serve mankind!—for the education of children, relief of the unfortunate, economic welfare, criminal law, the sciences, morality, the essence of things. What philosophy in their conceptions! What respect for experience in the choice of methods!

It is to liberty that we must attribute this emulation and wisdom. In France one could so rarely hope to influence the country's institutions by one's writings that one aspired only to display cleverness even in the most serious discussions. A doctrine that was true in some respects would be pushed to the point of paradox. Reason being unable to have a useful effect, one hoped that at least the paradox was brilliant. Moreover, in an absolute monarchy one could, as Rousseau did in *The Social Contract,* sing the praises of pure democracy without risk, but one could not dare to approach more probable ideas.

The principle of utility, which has given, if I may put it that way, so much body to English literature, has nevertheless retarded among them the highest perfection of the art, which the French have achieved: brevity of style. Most English books, through sheer prolixity, are vague.

The French could make a book out of English ideas better than the English themselves; they would present them with greater order and precision. Because they omit many transitions, their works demand greater attention in order to be understood. But the ordering of ideas benefits from it, whether by greater speed or by the straightness of the path the mind is made to follow. In England fame almost always begins with the approbation of the multitude and then ascends to the higher classes. In France, it descended from the upper class to the populace. I do not consider here which is better for the national welfare. But the art of writing and the method of composition cannot be perfected in England to the point they reached in France when writers always had to look for approbation almost exclusively to the foremost people in their country.

In England people devote themselves to abstract systems or to researches whose goal is some real and practical utility. But the English have hardly any examples of that mediating style that unites thought and eloquence, instruction and interest, vivid expression and exact ideas, and their books have but one purpose at a time, utility or pleasure.

In their poems the English carry eloquence of spirit to the highest degree. They are great writers in verse but their prose works very rarely share the warmth and the vigor found in their poems. Since blank verse presents very few difficulties, the English have been able to reserve for their poetry everything that depends on the imagination. They consider prose the language of logic, in which the only goal of style is to make the line of reasoning understood and not to arouse interest through expressiveness. The English language has perhaps not yet achieved the degree of perfection of which it is capable. Having served commerce more often than literature, it still lacks a large number of *nuances*. A language needs much more *finesse* and polish for good prose than for good poetry.

Some English authors, however, like Bolingbroke, Shaftesbury, and Addison, have a reputation as good prose writers. Yet their style lacks originality and their images vigor; the character of the writer is not stamped upon his style, and his emotions are not felt by his readers. It seems that the English fear to abandon themselves, except to poetic inspiration: when they write in prose, a kind of modesty smothers their feelings; since they are at once timid and impassioned, they cannot surrender themselves by halves.

There are in England no *mémoires*, confessions, or autobiographies; the pride of the English character resists this *genre* of revelations and admissions. But eloquence in prose writers often suffers through a too severe self-abnegation of everything that seems to depend upon personal feelings.

In England the spirit of commerce is applied to the principles of literature. In these reasoned books every appeal to the emotions, everything that might in the least influence the disinterested exercise of judgment, is forbidden.

Parliamentary debates are more lively than the style of prose writers. The necessity to extemporize, the heat of the disputes, the conflict, and the repartee stimulate an interest and cause an excitement that can carry away the orators. Yet, argumentation is still the main characteristic of speech in parliament.

The English Revolution, which must have set in motion every popular passion, was caused by theological disputes. Eloquence, therefore, instead of receiving a great impetus in this period took the form of argumentation because of the very nature of the subjects it dealt with. Financial and commercial concerns have been the main subjects of every English Parliament, and whenever we are called upon to discuss their self-interests with men, only rationality can win their confidence. The diplomatic situation in Europe, another subject of parliamentary debates, has always required great circumspection because of the very importance of the stakes. The two parties that divided parliament did not combat each other, like the plebeians and patricians, with all the human passions. There were almost always some personal rivalries, but they were restrained by the very ambition that stimulated them. There were debates in which the opposition, wishing to provide the king a minister from its own party, always observed, even in its opposition, the amenity necessary to achieve this goal.

The English orators, like Cicero, often repeat ideas already understood; they sometimes revert to techniques of eloquence already used with success. In France, people are so chary in bestowing admiration that if an orator tried to succeed twice with the same sentiment, with the same happy expression, the audience would reproach him for his arrogant self-confidence and would not only deny him a second recognition of his talent but would virtually revoke the first one.

This mental disposition, among the French, must elevate true talent considerably, but it lures mediocrity into gigantic and ridiculous efforts. It as often encourages, banefully, the success of the most absurd assertions.

The language of prose being much more perfected among the French, such truly eloquent men as we had or have could stir human emotions more strongly; they could combine more varied gifts in the same speech. The English have considered the art of speech, as they do all talents, from the viewpoint of utility; and this happens with all nations after a certain period of peace based upon liberty.

Peace based upon despotism must produce the opposite result; it allows the potent needs of individual vanity to endure and makes us indifferent only to the national interest. The political importance of every citizen in a free country is such that he attaches greater value to his share in the public welfare than to any personal advantage that does not serve the common power.

*Chapter XVII. German Literature**

German literature goes back only to this century. Until then the Germans had been very successfully occupied with the sciences and metaphysics. But they had written more in Latin than in their native language, and as yet one could see no original character in the products of their mind. The forces that have retarded the progress of German literature still keep it from perfection in some respects. It is, moreover, a real disadvantage for a literature to take its shape later than that of several surrounding nations, for then the imitation of existing literatures often takes the place of national genius. Let us consider first the main influences affecting the spirit of literature

* I must recall here the purpose of this work. I have not pretended to analyze all the distinguished books that comprise a literature; rather, I have sought to characterize the general spirit of each literature in its relation to religion, customs, and government. Of course, I have not been able to treat such a subject without quoting many writers and books. But it is to support my arguments that I have presented these examples and not to assess and argue the merit of each author, as one might do in a literary survey. This observation applies to this chapter more than to all the others. There are many good books in German I have not mentioned because those that I have mentioned suffice to prove what I have said about the nature of German literature in general.

in Germany, the character of the truly beautiful works it has produced, and the dangers against which it must protect itself.

The division into several states excludes a single capital where all the resources of the nation are concentrated and all distinguished men gather; thus taste must take its shape with more difficulty in Germany than in France. Emulation multiplies its results in a large number of small spheres; but people do not judge or criticize severely when every city would like to have its own elite. The language must also have difficulty in assuming settled form when there are various universities and academies with equal authority over literary matters. Many writers thus consider themselves entitled to invent new words incessantly; but what looks like abundance leads to confusion.

It is recognized, I believe, that federation is a political system very favorable to happiness and liberty. But it almost always hinders the greatest possible development of the arts and of talents, for which the perfection of taste is necessary. Constant communication among all distinguished men and their meeting in a common center establishes a sort of literary legislation, which leads all minds into the best path.

The feudal regime to which Germany is subject does not permit it to enjoy fully the political advantages of federation. Nevertheless, German literature bears the stamp of the literature of a free people, and the reason for this is clear. The German men of letters maintain a republic among themselves; the more shocking abuses there are in the despotism of social status, the more do enlightened men avoid society and public affairs.

[The Germans] excel in the portrayal of sorrowful emotions and melancholy images. In this respect they resemble all other literatures of the North, Ossianic literatures. But their meditative life inspires in them a kind of enthusiasm for what is fine and an indignation toward social evils that protects them against the boredom to which the English are susceptible in the ups and downs of their existence. In Germany enlightened men live only for study and their spirit sustains itself internally by a kind of inner energy, steadier and more lively than that of the English.

The works of the Germans are less practical than those of the English. They devote themselves more to systematic thinking because, having no influence through their writings upon their country's institutions, they surrender themselves without any tangible goal to the vagaries of their thoughts. They adopt every mystical religious sect in succession; in a thousand different ways they while away their time and their lives, which they are able to use only for meditation. But there is no country where writers have probed more deeply the feelings of men of passion and the sufferings of the soul, or the philosophical resources that can help people to withstand them.

After having surveyed the principal merits of German literature, I must examine the faults of its writers and the probable consequences of these faults if not corrected.

The impassioned style is the one in which it is easiest to go wrong. It requires great talent not to depart from the truth in portraying a nature that is above the ordinary feelings, and in the portrayal of enthusiasm inferiority is intolerable. The Germans are much more indulgent than we are. They put up with and often even approve a certain number of trivial ideas in philosophy, on wealth, charity, birth, merit, etc.—commonplaces that in France would dampen every sort of interest. The Germans even listen with pleasure to the most familiar ideas, though their intelligence discovers new ones every day.

The German language is not fixed; every writer has his own style, and thousands of people consider themselves writers. How can literature take shape in a country where nearly three thousand books are published annually? It is much too easy to write German well enough to be published. Too many obscurities are permitted, too many abuses of freedom tolerated, too many ordinary ideas welcomed, too many words joined together or newly created. The achievement of good style ought to be so difficult as to discourage at least the complete mediocrities. True talent can hardly get its bearings in the midst of this ocean of books. It ultimately succeeds in standing out, but the general taste deteriorates increasingly from so much insipid reading, and the literary profession itself must end by losing esteem.

[The Germans have] a certain weakness for metaphysical analysis of feelings, which often chills the most touching situations. As they are by nature thoughtful and meditative, they put their abstract ideas and the elaborations and definitions with which their heads are filled into the emotional scenes. So the heroes, the women, the ancients and the moderns, all sometimes hold forth in the language of a German philosopher.

Sometimes the Germans make the mistake of trying to mingle philosophical works with a kind of lightness that is in no way appropriate to serious writings.* They believe that in this way they come down to the level of their readers. But we ought never to attribute to our readers faculties inferior to our own. It is better to express our ideas just as we have conceived them. We should not put ourselves at the level of the majority but should reach for the furthest possible limit of perfection: the public's judgment is always, ultimately, that of the most distinguished people in the nation.

Sometimes it is also from a mistaken desire to please women

* A German lithologist, discussing in one of his writings a stone that he has not yet been able to track down, expresses himself in this way in speaking of it: *This fugitive nymph escapes our quest;* and then enthusing over the properties of another stone, he exclaims in mentioning it: *Ah, siren!*

that the Germans try to combine the serious with the frivolous. The English do not write for women, while the French have, by the rank which they have accorded them in society, made them excellent judges of intelligence and taste.

Soberness in thought and eloquence in feeling must be the special province of German literature. Its attempts in other styles have always been less successful.

There is no nation more especially suited to philosophical studies. Their historians, of whom Schiller and Müller[11] must be considered the best, are as eminent as it is possible to be in the writing of modern history.

What a large number of works in the sciences and metaphysics do honor to the German nation! What researches! What perseverance! The Germans do not have one political fatherland, but they have created for themselves a literary and philosophical fatherland, for the glory of which they are filled with the most noble enthusiasm.

A voluntary yoke, however, prevents the Germans in some respects from achieving the degree of enlightenment they could. This is the spirit of sectarianism. In an uneventful existence it takes the place of a spirit of partisanship, and it has some of its disadvantages. A sect, however philosophical its purpose, cannot be so in its methods. A sort of blind trust must always be inspired to obliterate individual dissent. For the many, so long as their reason is free, never give full consent to all the opinions of one.

To conquer empires, disciplined forces must recognize a leader. But to make progress in the arena of truth, each man must travel by himself, guided by the knowledge of his time, not by the teachings of a given party.

O enlightened people, inhabitants of Germany, who perhaps

[11] *Johannes von Müller (1752–1809), a Swiss historian who lived many years in Germany.*—Ed.

will one day be, like us, enthusiasts of all republican ideas, remain always faithful to a single principle, which by itself is enough to keep you from committing irreparable errors. Never allow yourselves to do something morality might reprove, never listen to what some contemptible casuists will tell you about the difference between the morality of private individuals and that of public men. This distinction comes from an unsound mind and a narrow heart. If we perished, it would be because we had adopted it.

Chapter XVIII. Why Did the French Have More Charm, Taste, and Levity than Any Other People in Europe?

French levity and good taste have become proverbial throughout Europe and are generally attributed to the national character. But what is a national character if it is not the result of the institutions and events that affect the happiness, concerns, and customs of a nation?

Religions and laws determine national similarities or differences almost entirely. Climate can also cause changes in national character, but the general education of the highest classes in society is always the result of the dominant political institutions. The government being the focus of most of the people's concerns, their habits and thoughts conform to these concerns. Let us study what advantages may be found in France for distinction through the charm of elegance and levity, and we shall know why this country presented such perfect models of both.

Giving pleasure or displeasure was the real source of those rewards and punishments not decreed by law. Other countries had monarchical governments, absolute monarchs, and sumptuous courts; but none combined the same circumstances that influenced the spirit and customs of the French.

In limited monarchies like England and Sweden, the love of liberty, the exercise of political rights, and the almost continual civil disturbances taught the kings that they needed favorites with a certain willingness to stand up to them, and taught the courtiers that to be preferred by their kings they must be able to support their authority by independent and personal means.

In Germany, long wars and federations of petty states prolonged feudalism and offered no center where enlightenment and all interests could meet.

The Oriental and Northern despots needed so much to inspire fear that they could not stimulate the minds of their subjects in any way; and the desire to please is a kind of familiarity with masters that only stirs their tyranny.

In republics, however constituted, men needed to defend themselves or to help one another so much that they could not establish relations among themselves merely for pleasure and amusement.

Moorish gallantry and the life it afforded women might have allowed the Spanish to approach the French spirit in some respects; but the superstitions they indulged in halted all progress in pleasurable or serious realms. The indolent spirit of the South left everything to the diligence of the priesthood.

It was thus only in France that, the royal authority being consolidated by the tacit consent of the nobility, the king had power unlimited in fact and yet uncertain in law. This situation obliged him to be solicitous toward his courtiers as part of that body of conquerors who at the same time both yielded to him and safeguarded for him their conquest, France.

Sensitivity to points of honor, one of the obsessions of the privileged order, obliged the nobles to embellish the most loyal submission with the guise of liberty. In their situation charm was, so to speak, a political necessity, for it alone could lend an aspect of choice to obedience.

The king, on his part, considering himself in some respects the dispenser of glory and the representative of public opinion, could reward only by flattering and could punish only by censuring. He had to rest his power upon a kind of public consent of which his will was no doubt the prime mover but which often showed itself to be independent of his will. Delicate bonds and skillfully handled prejudices formed the understanding between the leading subjects and their master. This relationship required a great shrewdness. The monarch had to have charm or at least his agents did. Taste and subtlety were required in the selection of favors and favorites so that neither the beginning nor the end of the royal power could be made out. Some of his rights had to be exercised without being acknowledged and others acknowledged without being exercised. And public opinion was so finely attuned to social position that even the slightest want of tact was felt by everyone and could ruin a minister no matter how much the government might try to support him.

Charm and elegance of manner passed from the customs of the court into the writings of men of letters. The highest realm, the source of all favors, is the object of everyone's attention. Just as in free countries the government provides the impetus to public virtues, so in monarchies the court influences the intellectual style of the nation. People usually seek to imitate the highest class.

Spirited levity, much more than even polite elegance, smoothed social differences without destroying them. It made nobles dream of equality with kings, and poets with nobles.

Elegance and taste not only advanced the highest interests in France but protected the individual against the most dreaded misfortune, ridicule. Ridicule is in many respects an aristocratic force. The more social ranks there are in society, the more conventional relations there are between the ranks and the more they must be understood and respected.

The class in France that dominated the nation was skilled in discerning the finest shades of difference. Since the ridiculous shocked them above all, the ridiculous had to be avoided above all. This fear often impeded originality and perhaps could even be an obstacle to political influence. But it developed a truly remarkable kind of perspicacity in the mind of the French. Their writers understood and portrayed moods and dispositions better than did those of any other nation. Obligated continually to study what could injure or please in society, they were made very observant.

Levity brings us back to simple truths. Though good form in French society was based entirely on artificial relations, we must attribute all that remains of truthfulness in ideas and in their manner of expression to the levity of society.

There was no doubt not much philosophy in the behavior of most enlightened men. They often had the very weaknesses they condemned in their books. But their writings and conversations were seasoned by a kind of homage to philosophy that was meant to show that they were as acquainted with reason as the mind could be and that they could, when called for, laugh at their own ambition, their pride, and even their social position, though they were determined not to give them up.

The court wanted to please the nation, and the nation the court. The court had pretensions to philosophy, the town to good form. In associating with the inhabitants of the capital, the courtiers wanted to display personal merit and a character and spirit peculiar to themselves, while the inhabitants of the capital were always irresistibly attracted by the brilliant manners of the courtiers. This mutual stimulation did not accelerate the progress of strict and deep truths, but there was not a single subtlety or *nuance* that self-interest did not reveal to the mind.

The influence of women is necessarily very great when the *salon* is the scene of all important events and when all personalities prove themselves in speech. In such a state of affairs, women are a power, and one cultivates what pleases them. It was neither through labor nor study that one attained power in France; a *bon mot,* a certain elegance, was often the reason for the most rapid advancement. When amusement is not only tolerated but is often useful, a nation must attain perfection in this *genre.*

Nothing like this will ever be seen again in France under a different kind of government, no matter what its nature. I shall demonstrate fully that what was called French wit and French elegance was only the direct and inevitable effect of the monarchical institutions and customs such as had prevailed in France for several centuries.

Chapter XIX. Literature in the Age of Louis XIV

The age of Louis XIV, the most noteworthy of all in literature, was much inferior in philosophy to the following era. The monarchy (and above all a monarch who counted admiration among the acts of obedience), religious intolerance, and still dominant superstitions limited the horizon of thought. One could not conceive a comprehensive view or venture an analysis in a certain realm of beliefs; one could not follow an idea wherever it led. Literature, in the age of Louis XIV, was the greatest work of the imagination but it was not yet a philosophical force, for it was encouraged by an absolute monarch and did not offend his despotism.

Chapter XX. The Eighteenth Century, to 1789

This is the era in which literature stimulated philosophy. After the death of Louis XIV, abuses being no longer protected by the same power, reflection turned toward questions concerning religion and politics. And the intellectual revolution began. The English philosophers known in France have been one of the main causes of the analytical spirit that has taken French writers so far. But independent of this particular cause, in every country, as I have tried to prove, the age of thought succeeds the age of literature.

The courtiers, unaware of the close connection that must obtain among all prejudices, hoped at once to continue in a status based upon error and to sport a philosophical spirit. They wanted to disdain some of their advantages but to preserve them nevertheless. They thought that it was only the perpetrators of abuses who could be made to realize that they were abuses. They thought that the populace would continue to be trusting while a small number of men, continuing to enjoy the superiority of their status, would add to this superiority that of enlightenment. They deluded themselves that they could, for a long time, consider their inferiors as dupes without these inferiors ever wearying of such a condition. No man was better able than Voltaire to thrive on this disposition of the French nobility, because it is quite possible that he himself shared it.

He loved the nobility and royalty. He sought to enlighten society more than to change it. The stimulating elegance and exquisite taste that prevailed in his works almost made it necessary that he be judged by the aristocratic spirit. He wanted learning to be considered good form and philosophy to be fashionable, but he did not arouse the powerful feelings of nature. He did not, as Rousseau did, summon from the depth of the forests the tempest of primitive passions to shake the government upon its obsolete foundations. The value and interest of most of his jests depend upon the existence of the prejudices he derides.

In the age of Louis XIV the principal object of writers was the perfection of the art of writing itself. But in the eighteenth century literature already assumes a different character. It is no longer only an art, it is a means. It becomes a weapon for the human mind, which until then it was content merely to inform and amuse.

From the moment literature began to involve itself with serious matters, from the moment writers glimpsed a sign of hope that they might influence the condition of their countrymen by the development of certain principles and by the interest they could lend to some truths, prose style improved.

In countries where ability can change the fate of empires, it grows with the goal it sets itself. A lofty goal inspires eloquent writings by the same impulse that makes courageous acts possible. All the rewards of a monarchy, all the distinctions it can offer, will never provide a stimulus equal to that which comes from the hope of being useful.

Here end my reflections upon the past. I shall now examine the contemporary mind and offer some conjectures as to the future. More active interests and emotions, still living, shall be applied in this new kind of investigation. But I feel, nevertheless, that I can analyze the present with as much impartiality as if time had long ago devoured the years we are living through.

Part Two. The Present State of Enlightenment in France and Its Future Progress

Chapter I. General View of Part Two

I have followed the history of the human mind from Homer to 1789. In my national pride, I considered the period of the French Revolution as a new era for the intellectual world. Perhaps it is only a dreadful event! Perhaps the influence of old customs will not allow this event to bring forth either a productive institution or a philosophical result for a long time. In any case, since this second part contains some general ideas on the progress of the human mind, it may be useful to develop these notions even if they should be applicable only to another country or another age.

I believe it always worth while to consider what must be the character of the literature of a great nation, an enlightened nation, where liberty and political equality are established, and where customs are consistent with its institutions. There is only one nation in the world to which some of these reflections are already appropriate: the Americans. They do not yet have a well-developed literature, but when their civil officials are called upon to appeal to public opinion in any way, they are eminently talented in stirring all the emotions by the expression of simple truths and honest sentiments—which is already to understand the most useful secrets of style.

These observations, applied to France, cannot be divorced from the results already produced by the Revolution; and these results, it must be admitted, are detrimental to manners, letters, and philosophy. In the course of this work I have shown how the mingling of Northern and Southern peoples led to barbarism for a time, though it eventually resulted in very great progress for learning and civilization. The introduction of a new class into the government of France had to produce a similar effect. This Revolution may in the long run enlighten a greater mass of men but for several years the vulgarity of language, manners, and opinion must cause taste and reason to retrogress in many respects. It is in the very nature of revolution to arrest the progress of enlightenment for some years and then to give it a new impetus. We must first examine the two principal obstacles to the development of the mind: the loss of refinement of manners and of that emulation that the rewards of public opinion can stimulate. When I have presented the various ideas pertinent to this matter, I shall consider to what extent literature and philosophy are perfectible if we overcome the mistakes of revolution without renouncing with them the truths that give thinking Europe an interest in the foundation of a free and just republic.

Chapter II. Taste, Refinement of Manners, and Their Literary and Political Influence

For some time, people in France believed that it was necessary to make a revolution in literature too, and to grant the widest latitude to the rules of taste in every *genre.* Nothing would be more contrary to the progress of literature, to that advancement that so effectively promotes the spread of philosophic learning, and consequently to the maintenance of liberty. Nothing could be more fatal to the improvement of morals, one of the chief goals at which republican institutions ought to aim. The exaggerated refinements of some communities in the Old Regime no doubt have no relation to the true principles of taste, which always conform to reason. But we can banish some conventional rules without upsetting the boundaries that mark the path of genius and preserve decency and dignity in both speech and writing.

The French nation was too civilized in some respects; its institutions and social customs took the place of natural feelings.

Vanity alone absorbed almost every class. Men lived only to produce an effect around them, to obtain a conventional superiority over their immediate rivals in order to stir up the envy that they themselves would experience in their turn. From individual to individual and class to class, long-suffering vanity was never at rest except upon the throne. In every other status, from the highest to the lowest, men spent their lives comparing themselves with their equals or superiors.

By being extended too far, this despotism of public opinion could ultimately injure true talent. The rules of good manners and taste became daily more refined and further removed from the mark of nature. There was freedom of manners without abandonment of awareness of difference. Good manners graded people instead of uniting them.

Yet people wanted to establish a sort of equality, the sort that on the surface placed all minds and personalities on the same level, an equality that burdened distinguished men and relieved jealous mediocrity. The art of avoiding the dangers of the mind was the sole use of the mind.

After having refined taste, the tyranny of ridicule, which was especially characteristic of the last years of the Old Regime, ended by using force; and literature could have been affected. To lend greater nobility to writings and greater vigor to persons, taste should not be surrendered to the elegant and mannered customs of aristocratic communities, however noteworthy they may be for their perfection of charm. Their despotism would bring about serious disadvantages for liberty, political equality, and even higher literature. Yet, on the other hand, how much would not bad taste, pushed to the point of vulgarity, hinder literary glory, morality, liberty, and everything good and lofty in the relations among men?

Since the Revolution, a revolting vulgarity of manners has often been attached to the exercise of the least authority. The defects of power are contagious. In France especially it seems that power influences not only deeds and speech but almost the inner thoughts of the sycophants who surround powerful men.

Bad taste, such as has prevailed for several years of the Revolutionary period, is not only detrimental to the relations between society and literature but also strikes at morality. People make so bold as to joke about their own baseness and vices, to acknowledge them shamelessly, and to flout those timid souls who still shrink from this degrading levity.

People are rather generally convinced that the republican spirit calls for a change in the character of literature. I consider this notion correct but in a different sense from that given it. The republican spirit calls for more rigor in good taste, which is inseparable from good manners. It also undoubtedly permits literature to convey a more forceful kind of beauty, a more philosophical and more moving portrait of the great events of life. Montesquieu, Rousseau, and Condillac belonged in advance to this republican spirit. They began the desirable revolution in the character of French works: this revolution must be completed. Since a republic necessarily brings forth stronger emotions, the art of portrayal must grow as its subjects grow. But by an odd contrast, it is largely the licentious and the shallow *genre* that has sought to take advantage of the liberty that literature was believed to have acquired.

The precepts of taste as they apply to republican literature are more simple but no less rigorous than those adopted by the writers of the age of Louis XIV. Under the monarchy, convention was sometimes substituted for reason and propriety for true feelings. But since in a republic taste should consist only in perfect understanding of all true and enduring relations, to lack the elements of taste is to be unaware of the real nature of things.

Under the monarchy, it was often necessary to disguise bold condemnation, to veil a new opinion under the form of received prejudices. The taste that had to be brought to these various appearances required an unusually delicate *finesse.* But the guise of truth, in a free country, is in harmony with truth itself. Expression and feeling ought to spring from the same source.

Formerly, people combined nobility of manners with an almost habitual practice of jesting. This combination presupposes a perfection of taste and refinement, a sense of one's superiority, power, and status which education for equality does not develop. This elegance, grand and trivial at the same time, probably does not suit republican manners; it is too distinctively characteristic of the practices of great wealth and high status. Intellect is more democratic; it waxes at random among all men independent enough to have some leisure. It is intellect, therefore, that we must encourage above all in literature, by devoting ourselves less to subjects that depend exclusively upon formal elegance.

Politeness is the tie society has established between strangers. Certain qualities attach us to family, friends, and the unfortunate. But in all those relations that have not yet assumed the character of a duty, civility of manners anticipates sympathy, moderates firm beliefs, and maintains for every one the place in the world that his merit ought to bring him. It marks the degree of respect to which each person has raised himself; in this sense, it distributes the rewards that are the goal of life's labors.

Women and great men, love and glory, are the only ideas and feelings that can find a strong echo in the mind. But how shall a pure and proud model of woman be found in a country where social relations are not guarded by the most rigorous propriety? Where shall we find standards of virtue when women themselves—those independent judges of life's struggles—have permitted their noble instinct for lofty sentiments to wither? A woman loses her charm not merely by the indelicate speech she may indulge in but also by what she hears, by what others may dare to say in her presence. In the bosom of her family, modesty and simplicity suffice to maintain the respect a woman ought to demand. But in the social world, more is necessary: the elegance of her speech and the loftiness of her manners form part of her dignity and can alone command respect.

Under the monarchy, the spirit of chivalry, the ceremony of rank, the magnificence of wealth—everything that strikes the imagination—compensated in some respects for the lack of true merit. But in a republic women no longer count for anything if they do not inspire respect everywhere by their natural nobility. As soon as an illusion is banished, a reality must be substituted. As soon as an ancient prejudice is destroyed, a new virtue is needed. So a republic, far from having to afford greater liberty in customary social relations, must protect itself much more scrupulously against all kinds of lapses from propriety; for all distinctions in it are based only on personal qualities. If a reputation is in the slightest injured it is no longer possible, as in a monarchy, for a man to improve his position by his rank, birth, or any privilege extraneous to his own merit.

It is essential in France to establish ties that can reconcile opposing groups, and civility is an effective means to achieve this goal. It would unite all enlightened men, who would constitute a court of opinion which would dispense blame or praise with some justice.

This court would also exert an influence upon literature. Writers would know where to rediscover national taste and intellect, and would labor to portray and enlarge it.

Civility alone can soften the asperities of the partisan spirit. It permits mutual toleration long before affection, and intercourse long before agreement. And so our profound aversion for those we did not know is gradually weakened by conversation, consideration, and solicitude, which kindles sympathy and leads us ultimately to find fellow men among those we formerly regarded as enemies.

Chapter III. Emulation

I certainly cannot deny that for several years the condition of France has been much more adverse to the development of talent and the mind than most periods of history.

It would appear, on first glance, that civil disturbances, by overturning the old social ranks, must afford natural ability the exercise and development of all its powers. That was undoubtedly the case in the beginning. But at the end of a short time the rebels conceived a hatred for enlightenment at least equal to what the old defenders of prejudices felt.

If revolutionary movements extend beyond the goal they sought to achieve, power falls into the hands of increasingly ignorant classes of society.

To encourage men of letters is to place them under whatever power rewards them. To do so is to consider literary genius apart from the world of society and political interests, to treat it like the talent for music or painting or any art outside of intellect itself, that is to say, the whole of man.

It is only in free states that the genius for action and the genius for reflection can be united. In the Old Regime it was desirable that literary talent should almost always imply the absence of political talent.

In absolute monarchies people want a kind of mystery to suffuse the qualities suited to government so that an influential and barren mediocrity may push aside a superior intellect.

Great talent is no doubt necessary in order to govern well. But it was only in order to brush aside talent that people tried to argue that the reflection that creates the profound philosopher, the great writer, and the eloquent orator has no connection with the rules that should guide the leaders of nations. Chancellor Bacon, Temple the *chevalier*, L'Hôpital,[12] etc., were philosophers, literary men, yet proved themselves to be leading statesmen.

For the happiness of mankind, the great men charged with its destiny must have a certain number of very different qualities in almost equal degrees. A single type of superiority is not enough to win over the various forms of opinion and worth, nor does it, if I may put it so, adequately personify the conception we like to develop of a man of renown.

But, it may be said, what ought to be feared above all in a republic is enthusiasm for one man.

Nothing is less philosophical—that is to say, nothing would lead less to happiness—than the jealous narrow-mindedness that would deprive nations of their place in history by equalizing the reputations of men. Every effort should be made to spread general education. But along with this great concern for the promotion of knowledge we must allow the goal of individual glory. A republic must give much more scope to this motive of emulation than any other form of government,

[12] *Sir William Temple (1628–99), and Michel de L'Hôpital (1505–73).*—Ed.

for it grows richer with the manifold labors emulation inspires. Only a small number of men succeed, but all may aspire. And if fame crowns only success, the effort itself often has some hidden use.

The guiding principle of a republic in which political equality is sacred ought to be the establishment of the most pronounced distinctions among men in accordance with their talents and qualities.

Conquerors fear the soldiers who have helped them conquer their empire, priests fear the very fanaticism on which all their power depends, and the ambitious mistrust their own devices —but enlightened men who reach the highest rank in the state do not cease to love and to disseminate knowledge. Reason has nothing to fear from reason, and philosophic minds base their strength upon their peers.

Chapter IV. Women Who Cultivate Literature

The place of women in society is still uncertain in many respects. The desire to please stirs them to action but reason counsels them to remain obscure, and everything in their success as well as their failure is arbitrary. In the present state of things, they are for the most part in neither the world of nature nor of society. What succeeds for some ruins others. Their virtues sometimes injure them and their defects aid them. They are now everything, now nothing.

It would certainly be much better, in general, if women devoted themselves solely to the domestic virtues. But men's judgment of them is strange: they more readily forgive women failure in their obligations than when they attract attention by their distinguished talents. They tolerate degradation of feeling in women if it is accompanied by mediocrity of intellect, while they cannot forgive genuine superiority in a woman of the most perfect integrity.

I shall develop the various causes of this oddity. I shall begin by examining the fate of women who cultivate literature in monarchies and in republics. I shall try to describe the principal differences these two political conditions must create in the destiny of women who aspire to literary fame, and I shall then consider in a general way the degree of happiness renown can promise them.

In monarchies they have to fear ridicule, in republics hate.

It is in the nature of things that in a monarchy, where sensitivity to the proprieties is so refined, every unusual action, every motion to depart from one's proper place, must at first appear ridiculous.

Men can always conceal their vanity and their desire for approval under the guise or the reality of greater and nobler emotions. But when women write, the public, generally assuming that the primary motive is the desire to show their cleverness, only reluctantly bestows its approval. It senses that they cannot do without approval, and this gives rise to the temptation to withhold it.

Some of these disadvantages cannot be found in republics, especially in one whose goal is the promotion of knowledge. It would perhaps be natural that, in such a state, literature properly so called would become the assignment of women and that men would devote themselves solely to higher philosophy.

The education of women has in all free countries been in accordance with the nature of the country's constitution. In Sparta they were conditioned to the practices of war. In Rome austere and patriotic qualities were required of them. If the principal drive in the French Republic is to be emulation in knowledge and philosophy, it would be reasonable to encourage women to cultivate their minds so that men could converse with them upon ideas that would hold their interest.

Yet since the Revolution men have thought it politically and morally useful to reduce women to the most absurd mediocrity. They have addressed women only in wretched language as devoid of refinement as of wit. Women have had no incentive to develop their minds: manners have thus not improved.

As soon as a woman is marked as a distinguished person, the public in general is prejudiced against her. The common people never judge except according to certain universal rules to which they can cling without risk. Men of intellect, astonished to meet rivals among women, can judge them with neither the generosity of an adversary nor the indulgence of a protector. In this new conflict they follow neither the rules of honor nor of kindness.

If, as a crowning misfortune, a woman acquired a noteworthy fame in the midst of political discord, her influence would be considered unlimited even if she exercised none at all. She would be blamed for all the acts of her friends, and would be detested for everything she loved. People would first attack this defenseless object before taking on those whom they might still fear.

In this description I have spoken only of the injustice of men toward distinguished women. But is not that of women themselves also to be feared? Do they not secretly stir up the malevolence of men? Do they ever join a famous woman in order to help her, to defend her, to support her unsteady footsteps?

That is still not all. Opinion seems to release man from all obligations toward a woman whose superior intellect is acknowledged. Toward her, he may be ungrateful, false, and wicked—opinion will not avenge her. *Is she not an unusual woman?* Say no more.

Chapter V. Works of the Imagination

It is easy to indicate the defects that good taste always prohibits in literature, but it is not so easy to point the road the imagination should follow in the future in order to produce new impressions. The Revolution has necessarily destroyed the basis of certain literary techniques. Let us begin by examining these methods, and we shall be led naturally to some notions about the new resources that can still be discovered.

Imaginative works act upon us in two ways, by presenting us clever pictures that give rise to levity, or by stirring our emotions. These emotions spring from relations inherent in human nature. Levity is often only the result of the various and sometimes arbitrary relations created by men in society. Though levity depends in several respects upon circumstances of the moment, the soul's emotions have an enduring foundation that scarcely changes with political events.

The more we simplify institutions, the more we obliterate the distinctions from which the philosophic mind can draw striking contrasts. Voltaire's works serve best to show how a rational political order deprives levity of its material. Voltaire ceaselessly contrasted what ought to have been with what was, pedantry in form with frivolity in essence, the austerity of religious doctrines with the loose habits of those who taught them, the ignorance of great men with their power.

The Americans would hardly sense the merit of a comic situation that alluded to institutions entirely foreign to their form of government. They might listen to such things because of their connections with Europe, but their writers would never think of exerting themselves upon such a subject. Every jest that strikes at civil and political institutions contrary to natural reason loses its effect when it attains its goal, the reform of the social order.

When society advances along the path of reason, discouragement especially must be avoided. But jests, after having been useful in destroying the power of prejudices, can then work only upon the power of true feelings, attacking the basis of moral life that must support individuals and mankind.

Clever works undoubtedly have a different kind of levity than the one that depends almost entirely upon jests concerning the social order or human destiny. This is the precise and subtle observation of passions and dispositions. The genius of Molière is the most sublime example of this superior talent. Voltaire was not able to produce any dramatic effect in this *genre,* however sharp his habitual turn of mind. So it remains for us to discover what subjects of comedy can best succeed in a free state.

There are two very distinct kinds of ridicule among men, that which depends upon nature itself, and that which changes as society changes. Absurdities of the latter type must be far less numerous in countries where political equality prevails, for there social relations come closer to natural relations and the proprieties are in greater accord with reason. One could have been a man of great merit under the Old Regime and yet be made to look ridiculous by an absolute ignorance of the ways of society. The true decencies, in a free state, can be offended only by real defects of mind or character.

Under the monarchy, it was often necessary to know how to reconcile dignity with material interest, the appearance of courage with the private plan of flattery, the air of indifference with the persistence of concern for personal interest, the reality of bondage with the affectation of independence. The necessity to overcome so many difficulties could easily make anyone who did not know the art of evading them look ridiculous. In a republic, more simplicity in manners and attitudes provide authors with many fewer comic scenes.

Among Molière's plays there are some based solely upon established prejudices, such as *Le Bourgeois Gentilhomme*, *George Dandin*, etc., but there are also some, such as *L'Avare*, *Le Tartuffe*, etc., which portray men of all countries and all times; and these would suit a free government, if not in every detail then at least as a whole.

The comedy that attacks human failings is more striking but also more bitter than the one that recalls ordinary absurdities or odd practices. We experience a feeling mixed with pathos in the most comic scenes of *Le Tartuffe* because they recall the malice that is natural to mankind. But when the jests attack the failings that derive from certain prejudices—or the prejudices themselves—the hope we retain of correcting them suffuses a milder levity over the impression caused by the ridicule. In a government based upon reason there can be neither talent nor cause for this kind of mild levity, so creative minds must turn rather toward higher comedy, the most philosophical of all works of the imagination, which presupposes the most profound study of the human heart. A republic can stimulate a new emulation in this domain.

In a monarchy, people like to hold up to ridicule those manners that do not conform to received practices. In a republic, the subject of the shafts of ridicule ought to be the human failings that harm the general welfare. I shall mention one noteworthy example of the new subjects comedy can deal with and the new goal it ought to set for itself.

In *Le Misanthrope*, it is Philinte who is rational and Alceste at whom we laugh. A modern author,[13] developing these two personalities in a continuation of their lives, has shown Alceste

[13] *Fabre d'Eglantine, in* Le Philinte de Molière (*1790*), *cited by Paul van Tieghem, ed. of* De la Littérature, *Vol. II, p. 348, n. 1.*—Ed.

to be generous and loyal in friendship, and Philinte privately greedy and tyrannically self-centered. I believe that in his play the author has taken the point of view that comedy must offer from now on. The negative failings, so to speak, those arising from the want of certain qualities, ought now to be attacked in the drama. It is necessary to draw attention to certain forms behind which so many men withdraw in order to be themselves at peace or to be false with decency. The republican spirit requires positive virtues, public virtues.

One may well ask: what will provide contrast and variety, and how will vivid impressions originate? Some rather unexpected ones must emerge from this new *genre*. The immoral behavior of men toward women, for example, has been continually presented on the stage deliberately to ridicule the deceived women. The trust women may have in the feelings they inspire can be, with reason, the subject of ridicule. But the author's talent would be greater, and the subject treated more noble, if ridicule were directed rather toward the deceiver, if the oppressor were attacked and not the victim. It is easy to attack what is wrong in itself, but it would be more to the point to coat immorality with a veneer of folly—and it can be done.

Men who would impose their vices and depravities as so many more charms, whose pretension to ingenuity is such that they would practically boast even to you of having cleverly betrayed you if they did not anticipate that you might one day realize it, these men who would conceal their incapacity by their wickedness, flattering themselves no one will ever discover that an intellect so forcefully opposed to universal morality may be so weak in its political notions, these personalities so indifferent to the opinion of decent men but so afraid before powerful men, these false purveyors of vice, these scoffers at noble principles, these mockers of sensitive souls—it is they who must be subjected to the ridicule they devise for others, who must be exposed as wretched beings, and abandoned to children's jeers.

Tragedy concerns unchanging feelings; and since it portrays grief, the source of its effects is inexhaustible. It is nevertheless altered, as are all products of the human mind, by social institutions and the customs that rest upon them.

The themes of the ancients and their imitators produce fewer effects in a republic than in a monarchy. Distinctions of rank make the pains of reverses of fate more poignant, and place a huge gap between misfortune and the throne, which the mind cannot bridge without a shudder.

The ancients often exiled and destroyed royalty, but in our day it is merely analyzed, and nothing could be more damaging to dramatic effect. The splendor of power, the respect it inspires, the pity felt for those who lose it when they are believed to be entitled to it—all these feelings act upon the mind independent of the author's ability, and their vigor would be greatly reduced in the political order I am assuming. Man merely as man has suffered too much to be capable of a special emotional response to the misfortune of those in high places or to conditions peculiar to only a few people.

We must, however, avoid transforming tragedy into tragi-comedy,[14] and to do so we must understand the difference between these two *genres.* This difference does not lie entirely in the social position of the characters but in the nobility and depth of the emotions the author portrays.

The events of private life are adequate for a tragi-comedy, whereas for an event to become a theme for tragedy it must

[14] *The French word* drame *referred to a mixture of tragedy and comedy in which there were characters of high and low station and the ending was happy though the action was fundamentally serious or tragic.* —Ed.

generally involve the concerns of whole nations. Nevertheless, tragic nobility must be sought in the loftiness of ideas and in the depth of feelings rather than in recollections of historical allusions.

The philosophical bent that provides generalizations, and the system of political equality, must give our tragedies a new character. This is no reason to reject historical themes, but great men must be portrayed as having feelings that arouse the sympathy of all people, and humble deeds must be exalted through nobility of character. We must elevate character instead of perfecting notions of conventionality.

Conventionality on the stage is inseparable from aristocracy of social rank in government; the one cannot be sustained without the other. The dramatic art, deprived of all of these artificial resources, can grow only through philosophy and sensibility. And in this sense it has no limits, for grief is one of the most powerful means of development for the human mind.

Life slips by, so to speak, unnoticed by contented people. But when the soul is in travail, reflection is exerted to seek some hope or to find some cause of regret, to probe the past or divine the future. In tranquillity and happiness, this faculty of observation is directed almost entirely toward external objects, but in misfortune we exercise it only upon our own impressions.

Philosophy covers all the arts of the imagination as well as works of reason. In this age, men are interested only in human emotions. Externals are clear and decided; only moral existence, in its hidden workings, is still an object of surprise and can alone produce a strong impression.

Poetry of the imagination will no longer make progress in France. Philosophical ideas and strong emotions will be put into verse, but in our age the human mind has reached a point that no longer allows either illusions or the enthusiasm that creates scenes and fables calculated to stun the mind.

A weariness of life, when it does not lead to despair but allows complete detachment, together with the love of renown, can inspire great beauty of feeling. Everything is contemplated from a certain height, everything appears in strong colors. Among the ancients, the more readily was one's imagination delighted, the better poet one was. In our day, the imagination must be as disenchanted with hope as with reason. It is only thus that the philosophical imagination can produce great results.

In order to succeed in works of the imagination, we must perhaps offer a lenient moral code where there are strict morals, but where morals are corrupt an austere moral code must be steadfastly presented. This general maxim is especially applicable to our age.

Chapter VI. Philosophy

We must not tire of saying that philosophy should be regarded only as the search for truth through reason. Religious ideas are not contrary to philosophy, since they are in agreement with reason. The maintenance of the rules that constitute the basis of the social order cannot be contrary to philosophy, since these rules are in agreement with reason. Providence has not given us any human faculty of which we are forbidden to make use. And the more knowledge we have, the more we penetrate to the essence of things, at least if we have subjected this knowledge to the method that can unify and guide it. The method itself is nothing but the result of all knowledge and human thought. It is to the physical sciences that we owe the soundness of argument and analysis that affords the certainty of reaching the truth when one sincerely wants it. So by applying, to the extent that it is possible, the philosophy of the exact sciences to the philosophy of intellectual ideas, we can make effective progress in the human and political domain, where the emotions never cease to block our path.

In some respects, the mathematical method has already been successfully applied to the essence of human understanding. It has been employed to explain the theory of the intellectual faculties; this is a triumph for the philosophical spirit. If the same path were followed in the human sciences, the triumph would have even more useful results. How much might human happiness and peace increase if political issues could ever reach a degree of certainty to which the great majority of men would give their assent as they do to mathematical truths?

It would undoubtedly be difficult to subject human affairs to measurement, even to the calculus of probability. In the exact sciences all the foundations are unchanging, but in human matters everything depends upon circumstances. Things can be settled only by a multitude of considerations, some of which are so ephemeral that they often elude even expression—and measurement all the more. Condorcet, nevertheless, in his work on probability,[15] has shown clearly how we might know in advance, almost with certainty, the opinion of a group on any subject. Applied to a large number of cases, the calculus of probability yields a virtually infallible result.

15 *Among Condorcet's several essays on probability, Madame de Staël, most likely, was referring to* Essai sur l'application de l'analyse à la probabilité des décisions rendues à la pluralité des voix *(1785), or to* Tableau général de la science qui a pour objet l'application du calcul aux sciences politiques et morales *(1795). The latter appears in* Oeuvres de Condorcet, *ed. by O'Connor and Arago (12 vols., Paris, 1847–49), Vol. I, pp. 539–73.*—Ed.

Gamblers use it as a guide, however much their goal may seem to be subject to the whims of chance. It may likewise be applicable to the multitude of events making up the political sciences.

Mortality and birth tables present results that are certain and invariable, as long as the regular order of events continues. The number of divorces that will take place annually, the number of thefts and murders that will be committed in a country of a given population and religious and political condition—such numbers can be calculated precisely. So the events that depend upon the daily concurrence of all the human emotions occur as regularly and punctually as those subject only to the physical laws of nature.

By taking the mean proportional of a decade, we can know that each year there are so many divorces in Berne and so many murders in Rome; and this calculation will be correct. If this is so, is it not then possible to show that the affairs of the human order are as regular as those of the physical order, and to base exact predictions upon these known events?

These predictions must be based upon the unchanging uniformity of a mass and not upon the diversity of individual units. Individually, all units of the human order are different. But if you take a hundred thousand persons at random you can make a fair approximation of the proportion who are enlightened, weak, wicked, and intellectually superior. You can determine this even more precisely if you introduce into the calculation the influence of the interests of class, that is, as in physics, the momentum that a certain slope or inclination gives to movement. By adding to this calculation the tested knowledge of the effects of this or that institution, one could base governmental functions upon almost certain foundations, measure the resistance one could expect to meet, and balance these functions among themselves in accordance with their real operation and the force of the obstacles to this operation.

Why should we not one day succeed in drawing up tables that would contain the solution of every political issue in accordance with statistical information and precise data collected on every country? One might then say the following: If we want to govern a particular people, we must require such and such a sacrifice of individual liberty—consequently, certain laws and a certain regime are appropriate to that realm. Or: For a country of a particular wealth and size, such and such a degree of force is necessary in the executive power—consequently, a certain degree of authority would be proper in one region though regarded as tyrannical in another. Such and such an equilibrium is necessary in order to establish a proper balance among governmental powers—consequently, one constitution might be inapplicable and another might be necessarily despotic. We could give more examples but it is enough to point out the idea, because the real problem is not to conceive of it in the abstract but to apply it with precision.

Politics is a science yet to be created. One can as yet make out only vaguely the combination of experiment and principles that will lead to such precise results that all the problems of the human sciences may be successfully subjected, so to speak, to mathematical sequence, inference, and proof. The elements of the science are not fixed. What we call general ideas are only particular facts.

In America many political problems seem to be solved, for the citizens there are happy and free. But this good fortune depends upon special circumstances and so offers no guide to anything, neither the invariable rules themselves nor their applicability in another country.

Even less may we offer as a proof of the progress of the human mind in politics the long duration and almost indestructible stability of some governments in Europe, which, maintaining themselves by their power and keeping domestic peace and tranquillity, secure to mankind some benefits of association. Despotism dispenses with political science, just as force dispenses with knowledge and authority makes persuasion unnecessary. But these methods cannot be admitted to the discussion of mankind's interests. Force is an affair of chance, destructive of everything pertaining to thought and reasoning, the exercise of which always presupposes freedom.

In politics, then, the philosophers should set themselves the task of arranging the facts known to them in precise combinations, in order to draw sure results in accordance with the number and nature of the probabilities.

It is true that no calculation requires a larger number of different combinations. If a physical experiment can fail because a slight difference in the processes or a slight degree more or less of heat or cold has not been taken into account, what study of the human heart is not required in order to determine the degree of respect that ought to be given to government so that it may be obeyed, but without its power becoming unjust, and to determine the power legislators need to unite the nation in a single spirit, but without shackling individual genius! What a practiced glance is required to indicate the precise point where executive authority ceases to be a benefit and its absence an evil! There is no problem composed of a greater number of terms, and none in which error would have more dangerous consequences.

Philosophy today must rest upon two bases, morality and calculation. But there is one rule from which we must never depart: whenever the calculation does not agree with morality, the calculation is false, however incontestable its exactitude may appear at first glance.

It has been said that in the French Revolution barbarous theorists took mathematical calculations as the basis of their bloody laws and coldly sacrificed the lives of several thousand individuals to what they regarded as the happiness of the greater number.

These atrocious men thought they could simplify their calculations by omitting suffering, feeling, and imagination; they had no conception of the nature of general truths. These truths are made up of every fact and every individual being. Calculation is neither good nor useful unless it recognizes all exceptions and regularizes all differences. If a single case is allowed to escape, the result will be false, just as the slightest numerical error makes the solution of a problem impossible.

Politics is subject to calculation because, applying always to men united in a mass, it is based upon a scheme that is general, and therefore abstract. But morality, whose purpose is the preservation of the rights and happiness of each person, is necessary to force politics to respect, in its combinations, the happiness of individuals. Morality must guide our calculations, and our calculations must guide politics.

The person who loses his way in the physical sciences is led back to the truth by the necessity of applying his abstractions to material facts. But what of the person who devotes himself to the abstract ideas that make up the human sciences? How can he be sure that his conceptions will be correct and good in practice? How can he reduce the cost of experimentation and yet predict the future with some certainty? Only by subordinating reason to virtue. Without virtue nothing can endure, and against virtue nothing can succeed. The comforting idea of an eternal Providence can take the place of every other thought. But when men refuse to recognize God as its creator, they deify morality itself.

Chapter VII. The Style of Writers and of Governors

Style must change through the revolution that has been wrought in our minds and institutions. For style does not consist only of grammatical constructions, is not a mere external form; it depends upon the foundation of ideas, the nature of the mind. Style in literature is like character in a person; and character cannot be divorced from one's opinions or feelings but influences one's entire being.

Let us inquire then which style ought to suit philosophical writers in a free nation.

Images, feelings, and ideas represent the same truths to man in three different forms. The same logic of sequence and inference prevails in these three realms of understanding. When a new idea is discovered, there is an image in nature that will help to represent it, and a sentiment in the heart that corresponds to it through connections that reflection discovers. Writers cannot raise conviction and enthusiasm to the highest degree unless they know how to touch at once these three notes, whose chord is the very harmony of creation.

We can determine the merit of various authors according to how completely they united these means of affecting sentiment, imagination, and judgment. No style is worthy of praise if it does not contain at least two of these three qualities that, when united, constitute perfection in the art of writing.

A book on the principles of taste, on painting, on music, can become a philosophical book if it addresses the whole man and arouses in him feelings and thoughts that enhance the significance of all matters. And a discussion of the most important concerns of human society can weary the mind if it contains only ephemeral ideas, or presents only the narrowest aspects of the most important subjects, or does not lead the mind to the broad considerations of concern to it.

Since the Revolution, people have fallen into an error that is especially destructive of all the beauties of style; they have sought to make all terms abstract and to shorten all sentences by some new verbs which strip style of all its charm without giving it greater precision. Nothing is more opposed to the real talent of a great writer. Conciseness does not consist in the ability to reduce the number of words; even less does it consist in the lack of images. The conciseness we must envy is that of Tacitus, which is at once eloquent and forceful; and metaphorical expressions, far from impairing that conciseness that is justly admired, summon up the most ideas with the fewest words.

It is especially in style that one may notice the nobility of mind and heart that proclaims the character of the human being in the writer. In all countries—but especially in a state where political equality is established—propriety, nobility, and purity of language add much to the respect for those who govern. True nobility of language is the best way to demonstrate moral superiority, to inspire a respect that improves those who feel it. The talent for writing can become one of the influences in a free state.

When the leaders of a country have this sort of influence, it constitutes a voluntary tie between governors and governed. Deeds are undoubtedly the best warrant of a man's morality, yet I should think there is a tone in language, and therefore a character in the forms of style, that attests the qualities of the soul with greater certainty even than deeds. This kind of style is not an art that can be acquired through the intellect; it is the impress of the self.

What noble ideas and emotions were summoned up when an American said, in announcing the death of Washington:

It has pleased Divine Providence to remove from our midst this man, first in war, first in peace, first in the hearts of his countrymen.[16] Does not this turning toward Providence show us that in this enlightened country no ridicule is hurled upon religious ideas or upon regrets expressed with heartfelt tenderness?

In our own revolutionary crises no man ever spoke this language, some of the remarkable words of which I have just quoted. In everything that reaches us concerning the relations that have prevailed, through writing, among the governors and citizens of America, we find this true, noble, and pure style inspired by the conscience of honest men.

Undoubtedly, the greatest men have not all been distinguished writers, but few among them did not wield the power of the word.

Chapter VIII. Eloquence

In free countries, since the peoples' will determines their political destiny, men seek and acquire to the highest degree the means of influencing that will; and the greatest of these is eloquence. Efforts always increase in proportion to rewards. When the character of government is such that it promises

[16] *Madame de Staël ran together two distinct quotations. The first part, "It has pleased . . . this man," comes from President John Adams's letter to Congress transmitting the news of Washington's death. (See Charles Francis Adams,* The Works of John Adams, *Boston, 1854, Vol. IX, p. 163.) The second part, "first in war, etc." is from a Congressional resolution on Washington's death. (See* Journal of the House of Representatives of the United States, *6th Congress, 1st Session, Philadelphia, 1799, p. 45.) Madame de Staël was an admirer of John Adams, as she told his son John Quincy when they met in Russia in 1812. (See Richmond L. Hawkins,* Madame de Staël and the United States, *Cambridge, Massachusetts, 1930, pp. 48–49.)*—Ed.

power and glory to men of genius, contestants fit to carry off such a prize are not long in appearing. Emulation develops talents that would remain unknown in states unable to offer a first-class mind any suitable goal.

Let us, then, examine why, since the first years of the Revolution, eloquence in France has been declining and deteriorating instead of continuing its natural progress in the deliberative assemblies. Let us inquire how it may revive and improve, and then conclude with a general view of its value for the progress of the human mind and the maintenance of liberty.

Effectiveness in speech cannot be separated from restraint. If everything is permitted, nothing can produce a great effect. To observe human decencies is to respect men's talents, services, and virtues, to respect the right to that public esteem each person has earned. If the marks of natural inequality are confounded by a crude and envious sense of equality, social life will resemble the confusion of combat in which only the cries of war or fury are heard. What means, then, are left to eloquence to impress people with happy ideas or expressions, by the contrast of vice and virtue, by praise or blame distributed with justice?

In a country where every influence of moral ideas is reduced to nothing, only the fear of death can move people. Speech still maintains the power of a deadly weapon, but it no longer has intellectual influence. Contempt for the decencies deprives eloquence of every effect that depends upon men's discretion and knowledge, nor can reason exercise any influence in a country where even a semblance of respect for truth is scorned.

Several times during our Revolution only the most revolting sophisms filled certain speeches. Partisan language, which orators vied with each other in repeating, wearied the ear and withered the heart.

No one will deny that for several years eloquence in France has been completely debased, but many assert that it cannot revive and improve. Others maintain that the talent for oratory disturbs the tranquillity and even the liberty of a country. I think it useful to refute these two errors.

I may be asked: In the hope of what do you desire eloquent men to make themselves heard? After ten years of revolution, who stirs himself for virtue, refinement, or even goodness?

These objections can discourage me for a time, yet it seems to me impossible that all that is intrinsically good should not in the end acquire a great influence. I still believe that if speech uttered before a large number of people and books judged by the entire public have no effect whatever, then it is the orators and the writers who are to blame.

Undoubtedly, if you address a few individuals united by the tie of a common self-interest or fear, you can exert no influence over them no matter what your talent; that natural source that could flow even from a stone at the command of a divine prophet has long ago dried up in their hearts. But if you are surrounded by a multitude containing all kinds of people—fair-minded and sensitive people, and weak people whose fears are overcome beside the strong—if you appeal to human nature, it will respond to you. If you can ignite the spark in every human being, you need not fear the imperturbability of the indifferent, or the mockery of the perfidious, or the calculations of the egotist, or the vanity of the envious—this whole multitude is yours. Do the beauties of tragedy, or the divine sounds of heavenly music, or the enthusiasm of songs of war escape them?—then why should they resist eloquence? The soul has need of exaltation—kindle this desire, and you will carry off opinion as well.

How can we perfect eloquence, assuming it can indeed still exert influence? Since eloquence belongs to the realm of sentiments more than of ideas, it appears less capable of infinite progress than philosophy is, yet, since new ideas develop new sentiments, the progress of philosophy will probably provide eloquence with new resources.

For some time there has been an absurd stereotype concerning eloquence. Stunned by the abuse of speech since the Revolution, people have inveighed against eloquence and sought to guard against that danger, which is, to be sure, not yet imminent. It is no longer felt that even decent people should summon sentiment to the aid of sound ideas, as if the French people were condemned to wander unceasingly through a circle of false ideas merely because unjust causes have been upheld by force and often even by vulgarity.

I believe, on the contrary, that it can be maintained that everything eloquent is true. That is, in a plea for an evil cause it is the reasoning that is false. Eloquence, properly so called, is always based upon a truth, though it is easy then to go astray in the application or in the consequences of this truth—but the error lies in the reasoning. Since eloquence always requires a stirring of the mind, it addresses itself only to the feelings of man, who in large numbers is always in favor of virtue. An individual person, appealed to in isolation, is often led astray by dishonest motives; but man in the presence of other men yields only to what he can endorse without shame.

Finally, if one persists in believing that eloquence is dangerous, reflect a moment upon all that it would take to smother it, and you will realize that it is the same as with learning, liberty, and all the great developments of the human mind. Some dangers may well be connected with these benefits, but to be secure against these dangers all that is useful, noble and generous in the exercise of the human faculties would have to be reduced to nothing. It is this last idea that I propose to develop in concluding this work.

Chapter IX. Conclusion

It is said that enlightenment and everything that arises from it—eloquence, political liberty, and independence in religious ideas—disturb the peace and happiness of mankind. But think of the means that must be used to check mankind's inclination toward enlightenment! Ask yourself how to prevent this evil—if it be one—short of resorting to means horrible in themselves and in the end fruitless!

I have tried to show the strength with which philosophical reason, despite all obstacles and misfortunes, has always cleared a path for itself and has expanded to every country as soon as any degree of toleration, however limited, has allowed men to think. How, then, can the human mind be forced to retrogress? And even if such an unhappy result were somehow attained, how could one ward off all the circumstances that might give human faculties a new impulse? If the Spanish Inquisition or Russian despotism were to be imitated, one would still have to be assured that other institutions would not be established in any other European countries. For commercial relations alone, even if others were prohibited, would communicate to one country the enlightenment of its neighbors.

Since the goal of the physical sciences is an immediate utility, no government would or even could prohibit them. And how could the study of nature not banish the belief in certain dogmas? How could independence of religious controls not lead to the free examination of all earthly authorities as well? It might be said that excess could be curbed without blocking the reason for it. But who would curb the excess—the government? Can the government ever be regarded as an impartial power? Would not the boundaries it would place upon intellectual inquiry be precisely those that eager minds would want to cross?

If you deliver a nation to amusement and sensuality, if all of its power and courage is drained in order to deter thought, who will defend it against warlike neighbors?

I have tried in this work to bring together all the grounds that can inspire a love for the progress of learning, to show the necessary effects of such progress, and accordingly to enlist keen minds to guide this irresistible force whose basis is in human nature, just as the laws of motion are contained within physical nature. Yet, I confess that on every page of this book where the love of philosophy and liberty that their enemies—or friends—have not yet stifled in me recurs, I fear that an unjust and false interpretation may represent me as being indifferent to crimes I detest and to the misfortunes I have tried to relieve with all the power of a mind without cunning and a soul without disguise.

Some may defy malevolence, others may resist calumnies with indifference or scorn. For myself, I cannot boast such courage, I cannot say to those who accuse me unjustly that they do not disturb my life. No, I cannot say it. Whether, by acknowledging this power over my happiness, I invite injustice or disarm it, I shall not pretend to a strength of mind that every day of my life would belie.

I am aware how easy it is to reproach me with thus confounding my soul's passions with the general ideas this book ought to have. But I cannot separate my ideas from my feelings. How can we impose silence upon the feelings that live within us and yet not lose any of the ideas that these feelings enable us to discover? And what sort of writing could result from such unceasing efforts? Would it not be better to surrender to all the faults entailed by the unconventionality of a natural lack of restraint?

Section VI

Essay on Fiction

This Section retains Madame de Staël's original title of this work, first published in 1795.—Ed.

The pleasure it affords is not the sole benefit of fiction. When it reaches only the reader's eyes, it can do nothing but amuse, but when it moves the heart, it can have a great influence upon all human conceptions. So this ability is perhaps the most powerful means of guidance or enlightenment. Man has only two distinct faculties, reason and imagination; all the others, even sentiment, are dependent upon or made up of them. The domain of fiction, like that of the imagination, is thus widespread. Far from being hindered by the passions, it makes use of them. Philosophy ought to be an invisible power that guides fiction's effects, but if it becomes obvious it destroys its magic.

In speaking of fiction, then, I shall consider it at once in respect to its purpose and its fascination because this *genre* can afford pleasure without utility but never utility without pleasure. Fiction is designed to captivate. The more we should like its effect to be moral and philosophical, the more necessary it is to adorn it with all that can stir people and to lead to the goal without revealing it in advance.

Fiction may be divided into three groups: (1) supernatural or allegorical inventions, (2) inventions based upon historical events, (3) events at once entirely invented and imitated, in which nothing is true but everything is believable.

This subject might require a rather extended treatise, for it could embrace most works of literature. But I have sought only to demonstrate that novels that show life as it is—with insight, eloquence, depth, and morality—must be the most useful of all forms of fiction, and I have excluded from this essay everything unrelated to this purpose.

III

The third and final part of this essay will consider the usefulness of what I have called pure fiction, in which everything is invented and imitated, and nothing is true but everything is believable. Tragedies whose theme is entirely a product of the imagination are excluded from this class because they portray an exalted character, an extraordinary social rank and condition. The verisimilitude of these plays rests upon rather rare occurrences whose moral is applicable to only a small number of people. Dramas, comedies, have in the theatre a place corresponding to that of the novel in other works of fiction, for they, too, take their themes from private life and real events. But the conventions of the theatre deprive us of the author's elaboration of the moral to be drawn from specific events. It seems to me that only the modern novel can achieve the effect of exactness of circumstantial detail that can be derived from the portrayal of our ordinary feelings. A special class has been created called the philosophical novel. All novels ought to be philosophical, since they all should have a moral goal. But when they relate the entire story to a leading idea, they lose verisimilitude in the train of events and thus perhaps lead less certainly to the moral goal. Each chapter becomes a kind of allegory in which the events are nothing but an illustration of the maxim that follows. *Candide, Zadig,* and *Memnon,*[1] fascinating as they are in other ways, would have a more widespread effect if, first, they were not supernatural, if they presented realities instead of symbols, and if, as I have already said, the entire story did not inevitably lead to the same moral.

Novels like those of Richardson and Fielding stay close to human life by following its slow movement toward climax, its gradual unfoldment, and its lack of logical sequence, and yet they also regularly alternate between pointing out the moral lessons of experience and the benefits of virtue. These events are invented, but the sentiments are so natural that the reader often thinks that it is he himself he is reading about under another name.

The art of writing novels does not have the reputation it merits because a host of poor authors have worn us down with their insipid works in this *genre,* in which perfection requires the most elevated genius but mediocrity is within everyone's reach. The countless number of insipid novels have almost exhausted the very emotion they portray; one fears to rediscover in his own past even the slightest connection with the circumstances they describe. It has taken nothing less than the authority of the great masters to restore the reputation of this *genre* against the writers who degraded it. Other authors have debased it even further by injecting disgusting scenes of vice.

There is, however, a justifiable reason for the fact that the general public holds the talent for writing novels in less es-

[1] *By Voltaire.*—Ed.

teem than it merits. It is that novels are regarded as dedicated to portraying only love—the most violent, universal, and genuine of all the emotions but one that, exercising its power only upon the young, does not arouse our interest in other stages of life. Undoubtedly we may regard every profound and tender feeling to be in the nature of love. The destiny of women and the happiness of men not summoned to govern empires often depends, in their later life, upon the place they allowed the power of love in their youth. Yet at a certain age they completely forget the impression it left upon them. They assume another disposition, totally absorbed by other purposes and other emotions. And the themes of novels should be extended to these new concerns. It seems to me that a new realm thus opens itself to authors who have the talent to portray it and can intimately understand all the emotions of the human heart. Ambition, pride, avarice, vanity, might be the main subjects of novels whose incidents would be fresher and whose situations would be as varied as those arising from love. It may be said that such a portrayal of the emotions can be found in works of history, and that it would be better to seek it there. But history does not reach down into the life of ordinary people and to feelings and personalities that have no effect upon public affairs. History does not have a sustained moral influence upon us. Truth is often hidden. Moreover, the gradual unfolding of events, which alone can make a deep impression upon us, would slow down the quick pace necessary to historical narration and give dramatic form to a work that ought to have an entirely different kind of value. History, in a word, cannot make its lesson perfectly clear, whether because we cannot always prove that their inner feelings punished the wicked in the midst of their prosperity and rewarded the virtuous in their misfortune, or because the fate of man is not confined to this life. Lessons for moral development, based upon the rewards of virtue, do not always emerge from a reading of history.

The great historians, and especially Tacitus, certainly try to attach a moral significance to the events they relate—for example, to make us envy Germanicus as he is dying and to detest Tiberius at the pinnacle of success. But they can portray only those feelings warranted by the facts. And what emerges from the reading of history is more the exalting influence of talent, the brilliance of fame, and the privileges of power than that quiet morality, refined and gentle, on which individual happiness and human relationships depend. It would be absurd of me to depreciate the value of history and to prefer fiction to it, for inventions themselves derive from experience, and all the subtle *nuances* that novels bring out derive from philosophy and the fruitful conceptions that the great drama of public affairs presents. But there is only morality in history taken *en masse,* for its uniformities stem from the recurrence of probabilities. The lessons of history regularly apply, therefore, to multitudes and not to individuals. These lessons are appropriate to nations because in their broad aspects they are unchanging.

Novels, on the contrary, can portray personalities and feelings with such intensity and detail that no other kind of literature can produce so profound an aversion to vice and love of virtue. The morality of novels depends more upon the unfolding of the inner emotions of the heart than upon the events they relate. A practical lesson may be drawn not from the arbitrary event the author invents to avenge crime; rather, indelible impressions remain of the truth of the pictures drawn, the gradual unfolding of a chain of errors, the willingness to sacrifice, and the sympathy for misfortune. Everything is so believable in these novels that one is easily convinced it could very well have happened just that way. A novel is not a story of the past but often seems to be one of the future.

It has been maintained that novels give a false conception of mankind. That is true of the poor ones, as it is of paintings that copy nature poorly. But when a novel is good, nothing gives such an intimate understanding of the human heart as these representations of all the events of private life and of the feelings they generate; and nothing so stimulates thought, which finds much more to learn in specific examples than in general ideas. *Mémoires* might achieve the same goal, were it not for the fact that, like history, they deal only with famous men and public affairs. Novels would be useless if most men had enough wit and sincerity to give a faithful and colorful account of what they had experienced in life; yet, even such sincere accounts would not combine all the advantages of novels. It would be necessary to add to the truth a kind of dramatic effect, which does not dilute it but makes it stand out the more by compressing it. This is the technique of the painter who, far from falsifying his subjects, represents them more vividly. Nature may often reveal their elements on the same level, hiding their contrasts. By copying nature too slavishly, therefore, one would not succeed in portraying it. The most exact account is always an imitative truth; like a painting, it demands its own harmony. A true story, though noteworthy for its *nuances*, emotions, and characters, could not arouse interest without the help of the talent necessary to create fiction.

But while admiring the talent that probes the recesses of the human heart, it is nevertheless impossible to endure the minute details with which even the most famous novels are burdened. The author thinks they add to the credibility of the picture, but he does not realize that everything that reduces interest destroys the single truth of fiction: the impression it produces. If one were to represent on the stage everything that happens in private life, the dramatic illusion would be absolutely destroyed. The novel, too, has its dramatic rules. Fiction ought not to be filled with useless detail. If a glance, a motion, or an unnoticed event is useful in portraying a personality or in revealing a sentiment, the simpler the technique the better. But the precise details of an ordinary event diminish its credibility rather than adding to it. Reduced by details to a narrow conception of truth, we escape the illusion and soon weary of ever finding in such fiction either the facts of history or the fascination of the novel.

The capacity to affect us emotionally is the great power of fiction. Virtually all moral truths can be made perceptible by putting them into action. Virtue has so great an influence upon our happiness and unhappiness that most classes of people can be said to depend upon it. There are stern philosophers who condemn all the emotions and would like morality to prevail through the mere statement of the obligations it calls for; but nothing is less suited to the nature of mankind than such an opinion. Virtue must be animated to struggle effectively against the passions, to create an exalted feeling so that we may be attracted to sacrifice—in brief, to beautify misfortune so that it will be preferred to sinful pleasures. Fiction that really moves us to noble emotions makes them habitual with us. It leads us unwittingly to make a pledge to ourselves that we would be ashamed to go back on. But the more genuine is this capacity to move us, the more important it is to extend its influence to the emotions of people of all ages and to the obligations of all classes. Love is the main theme of novels, and other dispositions are treated as secondary. By following another pattern, one might discover a multitude of new themes. *Tom Jones* has a broader morality than any similar kind of work. In this novel love is presented only as one of the means to emphasize the philosophical effect. The real purpose of *Tom Jones,* one of the most useful and justly famous novels, is to show the doubtfulness of judgments based upon appearances and the superiority of natural—and, so to speak, instinctive—qualities over those based only upon superficial conventionality.

There is always a great objection to novels about love. It is that they portray this emotion in such a way as to stimulate it; and, it is said, there are times when this danger outweighs every sort of benefit. But this drawback does not pertain to novels that deal with the other emotions. By describing even the most obscure signs of a dangerous inclination from their very outset, one can deter oneself and others from it. Ambition, pride, and avarice often exist unknown even to those who yield to them. Love is stimulated by its portrayal. But the best way to combat the other passions is to reveal them.

Even if purely philosophical works could, like novels, allow for all the *nuances* of actions, there would still be a great advantage in the *genre* in which morality is dramatized: the power to inspire feelings of indignation, exaltation, sweet melancholy—that is, the results of various romantic situations and a kind of supplement to one's own experience. This impression resembles that produced by real events witnessed by the readers. Always directed toward the same end, however, the impression produced by fiction does not confuse us so much as the disconnected picture of events around us does. There are, in short, men upon whom the sense of duty has no influence who might nevertheless be saved from evil by developing in them the capacity to be moved by emotion.

There are some writings, such as the letters of Abélard, works by Pope, *Werther,* the *Portuguese Letters,* etc., and a unique work, *The New Héloise*,[2] whose chief merit is eloquence of emotion. Though their theme may often be moral, what stands out above everything else in them is the all-powerfulness of the feelings. Such works of fiction are in a class by themselves. In a hundred years we find only one mind, one genius, that can create them. So they cannot become a type, or a goal. Yet should one prohibit these miracles of language, these deep impressions that gratify all the emotions of people with strong feelings? There are only a few enthusiastic readers of such works, which always benefit those who admire them. Let these passionate and sensitive souls enjoy such works—they cannot make themselves heard. The feelings that move them are hardly understood. Ceaselessly condemned, they might believe themselves alone in the world and might soon come to abhor their own character that isolates them from others, did not some impassioned and melancholy works enable them to hear a voice in the desert of life and to find in solitude some rays of happiness that elude them in society. This pleasure in withdrawal gives them peace from the vain efforts of disappointed hope. As the whole world seethes far from such an unfortunate individual, an eloquent and tender piece of writing remains close to him, like the most faithful friend who best understands him.

[2] *These references are to Abélard's letters to Héloise; Alexander Pope; Goethe's* Sorrows of Werther; Letters of a Portuguese Nun, *published in French in 1669 and purporting to be letters from Marianna Alcaforado to her French lover; and Rousseau's* The New Héloise.—Ed.

Three

NATIONAL CHARACTER AND INSTITUTIONS

Section VII

On Germany

This Section retains the title Madame de Staël gave to the book, De l'Allemagne *(1813) from which it comes. I have retained the original division into Parts and Chapters as well as their titles.*—Ed.

Chapter XXVIII. Novels
Chapter XXXI. The Literary Riches of Germany and Its Most Renowned Critics, A. W. and F. Schlegel
Chapter XXXII. The Fine Arts in Germany

from Part Three. Philosophy and Ethics

Chapter IV. The Frivolity Deriving from a Certain Kind of Philosophy
Chapter V. General Observations on German Philosophy
Chapter VI. Kant
Chapter IX. Influence of the New German Philosophy upon Literature and the Arts
Chapter X. Influence of the New Philosophy upon the Sciences
Chapter XI. The Influence of the New Philosophy upon the Character of the Germans
Chapter XV. Scientific Ethics

from Part Four. Religion and Enthusiasm

Chapter I. General Considerations on Religion in Germany
Chapter II. Protestantism
Chapter IV. Catholicism
Chapter VIII. The Spirit of Sect in Germany
Chapter X. Enthusiasm
Chapter XI. The Influence of Enthusiasm upon Learning
Chapter XII. The Influence of Enthusiasm upon Happiness

Preface

London, October 1, 1813

In 1810 I gave the manuscript of this work on Germany to the publisher who had published *Corinne.* Since I revealed in it the same opinions and maintained in it the same silence regarding the present government of the French as in my previous writings, I imagined that I would be allowed to publish it too. A few days after the dispatch of my manuscript, however, there appeared a decree of a very remarkable nature on the freedom of the press. It said that no work could be printed without having been examined by the censors. So be it. Under the Old Regime in France people were accustomed to submitting to censorship. Public feeling was then moving in the direction of liberty and made such a restriction hardly to be feared. But a brief article at the end of the new regulation said that when the censors had examined a work and permitted its publication, publishers would in fact be authorized to print it, but the chief of police would then have the right to suppress it entirely if he judged it appropriate to do so—which means that such and such procedures would be adopted until it was deemed advisable to follow them no longer. A law was not necessary to decree the absence of laws; it would have been better to rely on plain absolute power.

My publisher, nevertheless, took upon himself the responsibility of the publication of my book by submitting it to the censor, and thus our agreement was made. I came to a place forty leagues from Paris to follow the printing of the work, and it was there that I breathed the air of France for the last time.[1] Yet I had denied myself, as will be seen, any observa-

[1] *In October 1803, Napoleon ordered Madame de Staël to come no closer to Paris than forty leagues (around a hundred miles). She returned to France, to Paris in fact, in May 1814, after Napoleon's defeat.*—Ed.

tion on the political state of Germany; I imagined myself to be fifty years from the present time, but the present does not allow itself to be forgotten. Several censors examined my manuscript and suppressed the various sentences I have restored and indicated by footnotes. Except for these sentences, they permitted the book to be printed just as I now publish it, for I did not think I ought to change anything in it. It seems to me to be interesting to show what kind of work it is that can, in France today, bring down the most cruel punishment upon the head of its author.

At the moment when this work was to appear, and when the first edition of ten thousand copies had already been printed, the chief of police, known under the name of General Savary, sent his *gendarmes* to the publisher with an order to destroy the whole edition and to post sentries at the various exits of the warehouse lest a single copy of this dangerous piece of writing escape.

While my book was being destroyed in Paris, I received in the country the order to give up the copy from which it had been printed and to leave France within twenty-four hours. I do not know anyone but a recruit for whom twenty-four hours is enough to start on a journey. I therefore wrote to the chief of police that I needed eight days to obtain money and my carriage. Here is the letter he sent in reply.

General Police
Office of the Minister

Paris, October 3, 1810

I have received, Madame, the letter which you have done me the honor to write to me. Your son must have informed you that I saw no objections to your postponing your departure by seven or eight days. I trust they will be enough for the arrangements you still have to make, because I cannot grant you any more.

You must not seek the cause of the order which I have sent you in the silence you have maintained in your latest book with respect to the Emperor. That would be a mistake. No place could be found in it that would be worthy of him. Your exile is a natural consequence of the course you have constantly followed for several years. It has seemed to me that the air of this country did not agree with you, and we are not yet reduced to seeking models among the nations you admire.

Your latest work is not French. It is I who stopped the printing of it. I regret the loss to the publisher, but I cannot allow it to appear.

You understand, Madame, you were allowed to leave Coppet only because you had expressed the desire to go to America. If my predecessor allowed you to reside in the *département* of Loir-et-Cher, you are not to regard that tolerance as a revocation of the rules established in your case. You now oblige me to have them strictly executed, and you have only yourself to blame for it.

I am instructing M. Corbigny to see to the execution of the order I have given him upon the expiration of the delay I have granted you.

I am very sorry, Madame, that you have forced me to resume my correspondence with you by a harsh measure. It would have been more pleasant to be able to offer you only the evidence of the high esteem with which I have the honor to be,

Madame,

Your most humble and obedient servant,
[Signed] The Duke of Rovigo.

Madame de Staël.

P.S. I have reasons, Madame, for indicating to you the

ports of Lorient, La Rochelle, Bordeaux, and Rochefort as the only ones from which you may embark. I request you to let me know which one you choose.*

I think it important to make this slandered book known to the public—this book that has caused so much trouble. General Savary asserted to me in his letter that my work *was not French,* but since I shall certainly not recognize in him the representative of France it is to the French people I have known that I trustingly address a piece of writing in which I have tried with all my might to enhance the glory of the works of the human mind.

Germany, because of its geographical position, can be considered the heart of Europe, and the great Continental coalition cannot regain its independence except through the independence of that country.

General Remarks

The origin of the principal nations of Europe may be traced to three large distinct strains: the Latin, Germanic, and Slavic.

The Germanic nations steadily resisted the Roman yoke; they were civilized later and solely by Christianity. They passed directly from a sort of barbarism to Christian society. The era of chivalry and the spirit of the Middle Ages are their strongest memories. Though their learned men have studied the Greek and Latin authors even more than have the Latin nations themselves, the genius natural to German writers belongs to an earlier era but not to antiquity.

The resemblance among the Teutonic nations is unmistakable. Independence and loyalty always distinguished these

* The purpose of this postscript was to bar the Channel ports to me.

nations; they have always been good and faithful, and it is perhaps for that very reason that their writings bear the mark of melancholy. For it often happens that nations, as individuals, suffer for their virtues.

It might be said with reason that the French and the Germans are at the two extremes of the human chain, since the former regard external things as the source of all ideas, and the latter regard ideas as the source of all impressions. These two nations get on well in their social relations but there are none more opposed in their literary and philosophical doctrine. Intellectual Germany is almost unknown to France; very few men of letters among us concern themselves with it. It is true that a much larger number have an opinion on the matter. This blithe frivolity, which makes people judge things they know nothing about, may seem smart in conversation but not in writing. The Germans make the mistake of often putting into conversation things appropriate only to books, while the French sometimes put into their books things appropriate only to conversation.

I have therefore believed that there might be some advantage in making known that country of Europe where study and meditation have been carried so far that it may be regarded as the fatherland of thought. The reflections that the country and its books have suggested to me will be divided into four sections. The first will deal with Germany and the customs of the Germans, the second with literature and the arts, the third with philosophy and ethics, the fourth with religion and enthusiasm. These various subjects necessarily overlap. National character influences literature, literature and philosophy influence religion, and the whole can make fully known each part.

I am aware that I am about to present, in literature as well as in philosophy, views strange to those prevailing in France.

But whether they appear just or not, whether they are adopted or combated, they nevertheless make us think. "We have not yet, I imagine, come to wish to raise around literary France the Great Wall of China in order to prevent the entrance of all ideas from the outside."*

It is impossible that the German writers, the best-informed and most thoughtful men in Europe, should not deserve a moment's attention to their literature and their philosophy. The former is criticized as lacking good taste, the latter as full of nonsense. It is quite possible for a literature not to conform to our rules of good taste and yet to contain new ideas from which we could benefit by adapting them to our own style. It is in this way that we are indebted to the Greeks for Racine and to Shakespeare for some of Voltaire's tragedies. The sterility with which our literature is threatened might convince us that the French spirit itself needs to be renewed by a stronger sap.

After having rejected German literature in the name of good taste, people think they can also get rid of German philosophy in the name of reason. Good taste and reason are words it is always pleasant to utter, even at random. But can people honestly bring themselves to believe that writers of vast erudition, who know all the French books as well as we ourselves know them, have for twenty years busied themselves with pure absurdities?

Superstitious eras easily accuse new ideas of impiety and

* These quotation marks indicate the passages whose suppression the censors of Paris required. In the second volume they found nothing reprehensible, but the chapters of the third [*Part Four*—Ed.] on enthusiasm and especially the last passage of the book did not win their approval. I was prepared to yield to their criticism negatively, that is, by omitting without ever adding anything; but the *gendarmes* sent by the Chief of the Police exercised the function of censors in a most brutal way, by tearing the whole book into pieces.

skeptical eras accuse them no less easily of absurdity. In the sixteenth century Galileo was handed over to the Inquisition for having said that the world turned around, and in the eighteenth some people wished to make J.-J. Rousseau seem a religious fanatic. Views that differ from the prevailing spirit, whatever it may be, always offend the vulgar mind. Study and inquiry alone can provide that liberality of judgment without which it is impossible to acquire new knowledge or even to preserve what we have. For we submit to certain received ideas not because they are true but because they are powerful. And it is thus that human reason becomes accustomed to servitude even in the field of literature and of philosophy.

Part One. Germany and the Customs of the Germans Chapter II. The Customs and the Character of the Germans

Only a few basic characteristics are held in common by the entire German nation, for the diversities of this country are such that one is at a loss to combine from one viewpoint religions, governments, climates, and even peoples so different. The Germany of the South is, in many respects, entirely distinct from the North; the commercial cities are unlike the cities famous for their universities; the small states differ considerably from the two great monarchies of Prussia and Austria. Germany was an aristocratic federation. This domain had no common center of enlightenment and public spirit; it was not a solid nation, for the separate elements were not tied together. This division of Germany, fatal to her political influence, was nevertheless very favorable to all efforts of talent and the imagination. In respect to literary and metaphysical ideas, there was a sort of mild and peaceful anarchy that permitted each person to develop fully his own way of looking at things.

Since there is no capital where the elite of Germany gathers, the spirit of society exercises little power there: the sway of taste and the weapon of ridicule have no influence. Most writers and thinkers work in solitude or surrounded only by a little circle that they dominate.

In literature, as in politics, the Germans have too much consideration for foreigners and not enough national predilections. This self-abnegation and esteem of others is a virtue in individuals, but the patriotism of nations ought to be self-centered.

I shall examine separately the Germany of the South and of the North but I shall confine myself now to some reflections applicable to the whole nation. The Germans are in general sincere and faithful; they rarely break their word, and deceit is foreign to them.

The power of work and reflection is another distinctive trait of the German nation. They are naturally literary and philosophical; but the separation of the classes, which is more pronounced in Germany than anywhere else because society does not subdue its distinctions, is in some respects harmful to the understanding properly so called. The nobility have too few ideas and the men of letters too little practical experience. It is imagination, rather than understanding, that characterizes the Germans.

In leaving France, it is very difficult to get used to the slowness and dullness of the German people. They never hurry, and they find obstacles to everything. You hear "it is impossible" a hundred times in Germany for one time in France. When it comes to action, the Germans do not know how to wrestle with difficulties. Their respect for power arises more from its resemblance to destiny than from self-interest. The lower classes have rather coarse manners, especially when they are rubbed the wrong way. They naturally feel, more than the nobility, that holy antipathy for foreign manners, customs, and languages that strengthens the national bond in every country. The offer of money does not disturb their usual ways, nor does fear; in short, they are very capable of that steadiness in all things that is an excellent basis for morality; for the man who is always moved by fear, and even more by hope, passes easily from one opinion to another whenever his interest requires it.

Once we rise a little above the lowest class of people in Germany, we can easily observe the inner life, the poetry of the soul, that characterizes the Germans. Almost all the inhabitants of town and country, the soldiers and the peasants, know music. I had the experience of entering poor homes blackened by tobacco-smoke and of suddenly hearing not only the mistress but also the master of the house improvising on the harpsichord, as the Italians improvise in verse.

We must also be grateful to the Germans for the good will they display in the respectful bows and in politeness filled with formalities that foreigners have so often held up to ridicule. They might easily have substituted cold and indifferent manners for the grace and elegance they are accused of being unable to reach. Indifference always silences mockery, for mockery applies itself especially to useless efforts. But benevolent people would rather expose themselves to mockery than preserve themselves from it by the haughty and reserved air so easy for anyone to assume.

One is constantly struck, in Germany, by the contrast between sentiments and habits, between talents and tastes: civilization and nature do not yet seem to be well blended. Sometimes the most truthful men are affected in their expressions and appearance, as if they had something to hide. Sometimes, on the other hand, gentleness of soul does not prevent rudeness in manners: often this contradiction goes still further, and weakness of character reveals itself through the rough language and conduct. Enthusiasm for the arts and poetry is joined to rather common behavior in social life. There is no country where the men of letters or the young people studying in the universities are better acquainted with ancient languages and antiquity, but also there is none where superannuated practices more generally still persist. The memories of Greece and the taste for the fine arts seem to have reached them indirectly, but feudal institutions and the old customs of the Germans are still held in honor there, although, unhappily for the military power of the country, they no longer have the same strength.

There is no more bizarre combination than the military appearance of all Germany—the soldiers one meets at every step, and the kind of domesticated life people lead there. They are afraid of hardship and bad weather, as though the nation were entirely made up of merchants and men of letters; yet all their institutions tend—and necessarily so—to give the nation military habits.

Stoves, beer, and tobacco-smoke surround the lower classes of Germany with a heavy and hot atmosphere from which they do not like to emerge. This atmosphere is harmful to alertness, which is no less important than courage in war. Determination is sluggish and discouragement is easy because such a generally melancholy life does not afford much confidence in fortune.

The demarcation of classes, much more positive in Germany than it was in France, necessarily destroyed the military spirit in the middle class. This demarcation is not offensive, for, I repeat, amiability suffuses everything in Germany, even aristocratic pride. Differences in rank are reduced to a few court privileges, to a few gatherings that do not afford enough pleasure to warrant much regret. Nothing is bitter, no matter how regarded, when society—and through it, ridicule—has little influence. Men can wound their own souls only by duplicity or mockery; in a serious and truthful country there is always justice and happiness. But the barrier in Germany that separated the nobles from the citizens necessarily made the entire nation less warlike.

Imagination, which is the dominant feature of artistic and literary Germany, inspires the fear of danger if this natural emotion is not combated by the influence of judgment and the exaltation of honor. It is important to know whether domestic affections, the habit of reflection, and the very gentleness of soul do not lead to the fear of death; and if all the power of a state consists in its military spirit, it is essential to examine the causes that have weakened this spirit in the German nation.

Three chief motives usually lead men to battle: love of country and of freedom, love of glory, and religious fanaticism.

There cannot be much love of country in a realm divided for several centuries, where Germans fought Germans almost always through foreign instigation. Love of glory has little vitality where there is no center, no capital, no society. The type of impartiality, a luxury of justice, that characterizes the Germans makes them susceptible to being more inflamed by abstract ideas than by the concerns of life. The general who loses a battle is more certain of indulgence than the general who wins one is of applause. In such a nation there is not enough difference between success and failure to excite much ambition.

Religion in Germany is deep-seated, but it has a character

of meditation and self-containment that does not inspire the vigor necessary to exclusive feelings. That same separateness in opinion, individuals, and states, so harmful to the power of the German Empire, is found in religion too: a large number of different sects divide Germany. Even Catholicism, which by its nature exerts a uniform and strict discipline, is interpreted by each one in his own way. A political and social bond among peoples, one government, one religion, one law, common interests, a classical literature, a prevailing point of view—none of these things is found among the Germans.

The love of liberty is not developed among the Germans; they have not learned its value through possession or deprivation of it. There are several examples of federated governments that lend as much vigor to public spirit as does unity in government, but they are associations of equal states and of free citizens. The German federation was composed of strong and weak states, citizens and serfs, rivals and even enemies—these were old elements joined by circumstances and respected by men.

The very independence enjoyed in Germany, in almost all respects, made the Germans indifferent to liberty. Independence is a possession, and liberty is a right. And precisely because no one in Germany was injured in respect to his rights or possessions, no need was felt for any means to preserve this happy condition.

The Germans, with a few exceptions, are hardly able to succeed in anything that calls for tact and facility. Everything makes them anxious, everything hinders them, and they feel the need of a method in doing things just as much as they feel the need of independence in ideas. The French, on the contrary, approach action with the freedom of art, and ideas with the bondage of custom. The Germans, who cannot endure the yoke of rules in literature, prefer everything to be laid out for them in advance when it comes to behavior. They do not know how to deal with people; and the less occasion they have in this respect to decide for themselves, the more satisfied they are.

Only political institutions can shape the character of a nation. The nature of the government of Germany was antithetical to the philosophical enlightenment of the Germans. That is why they combine boldness of thought with the most obedient character. The pre-eminence of the military regime and the distinctions of rank have accustomed them to the strictest submission in the relations of social life. Among them obedience is a matter of regularity, not servility; they are scrupulous in the execution of the orders they receive, as though every order were a duty.

The enlightened men of Germany heatedly argue among themselves in the domain of theory, where they will brook no interference. But they rather willingly abandon to the powerful of this earth all the realities of life. "These realities, which they so despise, nonetheless find purchasers, who then disturb and repress the realm of the imagination."* The mind and character of the Germans appear not to be in touch with each other: the one cannot bear any restriction, the other submits to every yoke. The one is very venturesome, the other very timid. In short, the enlightenment of the one rarely lends strength to the other, and that is easily explained. The spread of knowledge in modern times only weakens character when the latter is not fortified by the practice of business and the exercise of the will. To see and understand everything is a great cause of uncertainty; and vigor of action develops only in those free and powerful countries where patriotic senti-

* A sentence suppressed by the censors.

ments are to the soul like blood to the veins and grow cold only as life ends.*

Chapter III. The Women

Nature and society have given women a great capacity for endurance, and it seems to me that it cannot be denied that in our day they are in general more meritorious than men.

German women have a charm all their own—a touching voice, fair hair, a dazzling complexion. They are modest, but less timid than English women; it seems that they less often meet men who are superior to them and that, moreover, they have less to fear from harsh judgments of the public. They seek to please by their sensibility and to interest by their imagination. They are familiar with the language of poetry and the fine arts. They flirt wholeheartedly, whereas French women do so wittily and jokingly. The perfect loyalty that is peculiar to the character of the Germans makes love less dangerous for the happiness of women, and they possibly approach this sentiment with more confidence because it is clothed in more romantic colors, and disdain and infidelity are less to be feared there than elsewhere.

Love is a religion in Germany, but a poetic religion that too readily tolerates whatever sensibility excuses. It cannot be denied that the ease of divorce in Protestant areas strikes at the sacredness of marriage. Husbands and wives are changed

* I do not have to say that it was England that I meant to indicate by these words. When proper names are not stated, most censors, who are enlightened men, are pleased not to understand. It is not the same with the police. They have a truly remarkable kind of instinct against liberal ideas no matter what form they take, and in this way the police track down, like a clever hunting dog, everything that might awaken in the mind of Frenchmen their old love of learning and liberty.

there as calmly as if it were a matter of arranging the incidents of a play. Owing to the good nature of men and women, no bitterness enters into these easy separations; and since the Germans have more imagination than genuine passion, the most bizarre events occur with extraordinary tranquillity. But it is in this way that manners and character lose all solidity. The spirit of paradox shakes the most sacred institutions, and there are no fixed rules on any subject.

One may justifiably laugh at the absurdities of some German women who become enthusiastic to the point of affectation, and whose saccharine expressions obliterate everything pointed and striking in mind and character. They are not frank, yet neither are they false. It is merely that they see and judge nothing accurately, and real events pass before their eyes like a phantasmagoria. Even when it occurs to them to be gay, they still maintain a tinge of that sentimentality that is so honored in their country.

Despite these absurdities, there are many German women with genuine feelings and simple manners. Their careful upbringing and natural purity of soul make them a gentle and steady influence. But we seldom find among them the quick wit that animates conversation and stimulates ideas; this kind of delight is hardly to be found except in the smartest and wittiest Paris society.

Chapter V. Southern Germany

It has been rather generally acknowledged that only Northern Germany has had a literature and that the inhabitants of the South devoted themselves to the physical pleasures of life while the Northern regions relished more exclusively those of the soul. Many men of genius have been born in the South, but they have developed in the North. The finest academies and the most distinguished scholars and men of letters are to be found near the Baltic. And from Weimar to Koenigsberg, from Koenigsberg to Copenhagen, the mists and frosts seem to be the natural element of men of strong and profound imagination.

When the climate is neither harsh nor mild, when people live without fear or hope from the heavens, they are preoccupied with hardly anything but the practical concerns of life. It is the delights of the South and the rigors of the North that vigorously stir the imagination. Whether one has to struggle against nature or becomes intoxicated with its bounty, the power of creation is no less strong and awakens in us a feeling for the fine arts or an aptitude for the mysteries of the soul.

Southern Germany, moderate in every respect, maintains itself in a monotonous state of well-being singularly harmful to vitality both in business and in thought. The strongest desire of the inhabitants of this calm and fertile region is to continue to live as they do. And what can one achieve with such a desire? It is not even enough to maintain what they are content with.

Chapter X. Arrogant Stupidity and Benevolent Mediocrity

Superiority of mind and soul is very rare in any country. Thus, in order to assess the character of a nation, we must study the ordinary mass of the people.

A Frenchman can speak even when he has no ideas but a German always has in his head a little more than he can express. A German, if he does not think, can say nothing.

Stupidity in France is lively but arrogant. Since the country's opinion is that success determines everything, even fools, in their capacity as spectators, think they can influence the intrinsic value of things by not approving them, and thus enhance their own importance. On the other hand, ordinary people in Germany are full of good will. They would blush at their inability to rise to the height of a famous writer's ideas. And far from setting themselves up as judges, they aspire to become disciples.

In France there are so many commonplaces on every subject that a fool can with their help speak well enough and even seem momentarily to be a man of intelligence. In Germany, an ignorant man would not dare to state his opinion confidently on anything. For, since no opinion is accepted as incontestable, one cannot advance any without being ready to defend it. So ordinary people are for the most part silent and contribute no amenity to society except a friendly benevolence.

Chapter XI. The Spirit of Conversation

The kind of pleasure that a lively conversation affords does not precisely consist in its subject; neither the ideas nor the knowledge it unfolds are its main interest. Rather, it is a certain way of interacting, of giving mutual and immediate pleasure, of speaking at the moment you think, of enjoying oneself instantly, of gaining approval effortlessly, of revealing your understanding in all its *nuances* by accent, gesture, look—in short, of stimulating spontaneity like a kind of electricity that makes sparks fly, relieving some people of their excess of vitality and wakening others from oppressive apathy.

Nothing is more foreign to this capacity than the character and mentality of the Germans; they seek a serious result in everything. But we must admit that the taste for and intoxication with the life of society makes people singularly incapable of diligence and study, and the virtues of the Germans perhaps depend in some aspects upon the very absence of this spirit.

The older forms of politeness, which are still in effect in almost all of Germany, are contrary to the ease and familiarity of conversation. The longest but most inconsequential title is bestowed and repeated twenty times during a meal. Every dish, every wine, must be offered with a solicitude and earnestness that is mortally tiresome to foreigners. There is good nature at the bottom of all these practices, but they would not last a moment in a country where one might risk a joke without offending sensitive natures. And how can society have grace and charm if one does not allow that gentle banter that relaxes the mind and lends even to benevolence a pointed way of expressing itself?

The desire to please is a very agreeable quality, but it differs considerably from the need to be loved. The desire to please makes us dependent upon general opinion, the need to be loved frees us from it. One might want to please even those one would harm, and this is precisely what is called coquetry. Coquetry is not found among women only but in all conduct that displays more affection than one really feels. Their honesty does not permit Germans anything like this. They take grace literally and regard charm of expression as a promise of conduct, and their sensitivity stems from this. For they never hear a word without drawing a consequence from it and do not conceive that speech may be treated as a liberal art that has no purpose or result but the pleasure one finds in it.

In Germany everyone stays in his social position like a sentry at his post, and there is no need for clever appearances, explanations, and hints to show the advantages of birth or title one thinks he enjoys over his neighbor.

The talent for telling a story, one of the great charms of conversation, is very rare in Germany. The audience is too tolerant and not quickly enough bored; so the *raconteurs,* confident of their listeners' patience, are too relaxed in telling their stories. In France every speaker is a usurper conscious of being surrounded by jealous rivals and trying to keep his ground through success; in Germany he is a legitimate proprietor who can peacefully exercise his acknowledged rights.

The Germans do better in poetic than in epigrammatic tales. When one appeals to the imagination, details can please and make a scene more real, but when a *bon mot* is involved, the preliminaries cannot be too brief.

The Germans would do well to take advantage, in some vital respects, of the benefits of the spirit of society in France. They ought to learn from the French to show themselves less irritable in small matters in order to reserve all their strength for the important ones. They ought to learn from the French not to confuse obstinacy with vigor, rudeness with firmness.

Chapter XII. The German Language in Its Relation to the Spirit of Conversation

By studying the spirit and character of a language, one comes to know the historical causes of national opinions, customs, and usages; the changes a language undergoes ought to throw much light upon the process of thought. But such an analysis would necessarily be highly theoretical and would require a great deal of knowledge that we almost always lack concerning foreign languages and often even concerning our own. So we must be content with the general impression that a nation's language makes today. French, having been spoken more than any other European dialect, is at once polished through use and sharpened for its target. No language is clearer and swifter, or suggests more readily and explains more clearly just what one wants to say. German is much less adapted to the precision and speed of conversation. By the very nature of its grammatical construction, the meaning is not generally understood until the end of the sentence. Thus the pleasure of interrupting, which makes argument so lively in France and forces one to make one's points quickly, is impossible in Germany. Since the beginning of a sentence means nothing without the end, everyone must be allowed all the time he wants. This is better for getting to the bottom of things and is more civil but less stimulating.

German politeness is warmer but less subtle than French; it shows more consideration for rank and more caution in everything. The German language is very brilliant in poetry, very rich in metaphysics but very matter-of-fact in conversation.

German is better adapted to poetry than to prose, and to written prose than to spoken prose. It is a very useful instrument for describing or explaining everything but one cannot in German, as one can in French, touch lightly on a variety of subjects. The Germans fill time profitably, the French make us forget it.

Chapter XV. Weimar

Of all the principalities of Germany, none demonstrates better than Weimar the benefits of a small state when its leader[2] is a man of great understanding and can seek to please his subjects without ceasing to be obeyed. Such a state is a private association in which everyone is closely related to

[2] *Charles Augustus, grand duke of Saxe-Weimar (1757–1828).* —Ed.

everyone else. The Duchess Louise of Saxe-Weimar is the true model of a woman destined by nature for the most illustrious position. Without pretension, as without weakness, she inspires trust and respect in the same degree, and the heroism of the time of chivalry has entered her soul without depriving her at all of the gentleness of her sex. The military talents of the duke are universally esteemed, and his stimulating and thoughtful conversation continually reminds us that he was formed by Frederick the Great. It is his influence and his mother's that have attracted the most distinguished men of letters to Weimar. Germany has thus had a literary capital for the first time. But since this capital has been at the same time a very small town, it has had no influence except through its enlightenment; fashion, which leads to uniformity in everything, could not arise from such a narrow circle.

Herder had just died when I arrived at Weimar, but Wieland, Goethe, and Schiller were still there. I shall describe each of these men separately in the following section. I shall describe them mainly through their works, for their books perfectly reflect their characters and conversation. This rare agreement is a proof of sincerity. When a writer's main purpose is to produce an effect upon others, he never reveals his real self, but when he writes to satisfy an internal urge with which his soul is possessed, he involuntarily reveals through his writings even the slightest *nuances* of his way of living and thinking.

Living in small towns had always seemed to me very boring. The mind of man contracts there and the heart of woman freezes. People there live so much in each other's presence that one is oppressed by one's fellow men. Distant ideas no longer animate people and reverberate from afar like the clamor of fame. There is rather a minute inspection of all one's actions, an observation of each detail, which makes it impossible to understand the totality of one's character. The more independent and elevated one is, the less one can breathe through all these petty barriers. This painful restraint did not exist at Weimar; it was not a small town but a large country palace. A select circle discussed with interest each new product of the arts.

In the same principality, near the leading literary center of Germany, was Jena, one of the most noteworthy centers of science. A rather confined area thus assembled brilliant luminaries in every field.

Chapter XVI. Prussia

To know Prussia one must study the character of Frederick II. It was a man who created this empire, which nature had not favored and which became a power only because a warrior was its master. There are two very distinct men in Frederick II: a German by nature and a Frenchman by upbringing. Everything the German did in a German realm has left enduring impressions; everything the Frenchman attempted has not been fruitful.

Frederick II was formed by French philosophy of the eighteenth century. This philosophy is harmful to nations when it dries up the source of enthusiasm; but when there is an absolute monarch, it is desirable that liberal principles should temper his despotic action.[3] Frederick brought freedom of speech and writing to a position of honor; for he never pun-

[3] *Madame de Staël clearly intended this chapter as a commentary on Napoleon as well as Frederick. The censors understood this too and suppressed the two passages she put within quotation marks. When she praised Frederick, it was also to contrast him to Napoleon; when she criticized Frederick, it was also to draw attention to her criticism of Napoleon and all despotism.*—Ed.

ished those who criticized him orally or in print, but displayed in nearly all his actions the philosophy whose principles he professed.

Frederick's great misfortune was that he did not have enough respect for either religion or morality. His tastes were shameless. Though love of glory had raised the level of his thoughts, his licentious way of expressing himself on the most sacred subjects insured that even his virtues did not inspire trust: they were appreciated and approved but were believed to be calculated. In Frederick, everything appeared to be political. So the good that he did improved the condition of the country but did not improve the morality of the nation. He flaunted unbelief and scoffed at female virtue: nothing less suited German character than this way of thinking. In freeing his subjects from what he called prejudices, Frederick extinguished patriotism in them; for people to become attached to countries that are naturally gloomy and unproductive, very strict opinions and principles must govern there.

Frederick's rule was based on military force and civil justice: he reconciled them by his wisdom, but it was difficult to combine two essences whose nature is so opposite. Frederick wanted his soldiers to be military machines, blindly obedient, and his subjects to be enlightened citizens capable of patriotism. He did not establish subordinate authorities in the cities of Prussia—municipalities like those in the rest of Germany—out of fear that they might delay the urgent actions of his military forces. Yet he wanted enough of a spirit of liberty in his rule to make obedience appear voluntary. He wanted the military profession to be the leading one of all, since it was the one most indispensable to him, but he would have liked the civil order to continue independently by the side of force.

The wonderful mixture of all classes of society is scarcely

attainable except through the rule of law, the same for all. A man may reconcile opposing elements but "at his death they separate."* Frederick's influence, continued by the wisdom of his successors, manifested itself for some time. But one always sensed in Prussia the two nations that poorly composed one: the army, and the civil estate. The prejudices of nobility continued alongside the most decided liberal principles. In short, the image of Prussia presented a double aspect, like that of Janus: one military, the other philosophical.

One of Frederick's greatest errors was to become a party to the partition of Poland. Silesia had been acquired by sheer force, but Poland was a Machiavellian conquest, "and it could never be expected that subjects snatched in this way would be loyal to the sleight-of-hand artist who claimed to be their sovereign."*

Frederick II would have liked French literature to be the only literature in his realm. He placed no value upon German literature. Doubtless it was not in his time nearly so noteworthy as it is today, yet a German ruler ought to encourage everything German.

Klopstock nobly reproached Frederick with neglecting the German muses which, unbeknown to him, tried to proclaim his glory. Frederick had no idea of what the Germans were achieving in literature and philosophy; he did not think they were innovators.

Chapter XVII. Berlin

Berlin is a big city, with very broad streets that are perfectly straight, beautiful houses, and a general appearance of orderliness. But since it has only recently been rebuilt, it has

* Suppressed by the censor.

no traces of earlier times. Not a single Gothic monument remains amid the modern dwellings; this newly created locality is in no way impeded by the old. What could be better, it may be said, whether for the buildings or the institutions, than to be unhampered by ruins? I feel that in America I should like new cities and new laws: there, nature and liberty speak to the soul in such a way that people do not need mementos. But in our old land we need a sense of the past. Berlin, this entirely modern city, however beautiful it may be, does not make a serious enough impression. It shows no imprint of the country's history or the character of its inhabitants, and these magnificent newly built dwellings seem intended only as comfortable centers of pleasure and industry. The most beautiful palaces in Berlin are built of brick; a stone is hardly to be found even in the triumphal arches. The capital of Prussia resembles Prussia itself; the buildings and institutions are no older than the age of manhood because one man alone is their creator.

No spectacle in Germany equals that of Berlin. This city, being in the center of Northern Germany, may be considered its seat of learning. The sciences and letters are cultivated there. At dinner parties, at the homes of ministers and others, the separation by social rank so harmful to Germany is less rigid, and talented men of all classes gather. This happy mingling does not yet extend to the society of women. There are some women whose talents and charms attract to them all who are distinguished; but in general, in Berlin as in the rest of Germany, the society of women is not well mixed with that of men.

When there are, as in England, important political concerns to discuss, gatherings of men are always animated by an elevated common interest, but in countries without representative government the presence of women is necessary to preserve the feelings of refinement and purity, without which love of the beautiful must vanish. The influence of women is more wholesome to soldiers than to civilians. The rule of law can better dispense with women than can the rule of honor, for it is only they who preserve the spirit of chivalry in a purely military monarchy. Ancient France owed all its brilliance to that power of public opinion brought about by the influence of women.

Military practices have harmed rather than promoted the martial spirit of the Prussians. These practices were based upon old ways that separated the army from the nation, whereas in our own day there is no real strength except in the national character. Prussian character is nobler and more exalted than recent events would lead us to believe—"and the passionate heroism of the unfortunate Prince Louis ought still to cast some glory upon his companions in arms."* [4]

Chapter XVIII. The German Universities

All of Northern Germany is filled with the most learned universities of Europe. In no country, not even in England, are there so many means of education and of improving one's faculties. Why is it, then, that the people lack energy and seem in general to be dull and narrow, though they have a small number of the most intellectual men in Europe? This

* Suppressed by the censor. I fought for several days to obtain the liberty to render this homage to Prince Louis, and I pointed out that the glory of France was enhanced by praise of the bravery of those whom they conquered, but it seemed easier to the censors to allow nothing of the kind.

[4] *Prince Louis Ferdinand of Prussia, nephew of Frederick the Great and a bitter enemy of Napoleon, died in the war against France in 1806. The "recent events" were Napoleon's defeat of Prussia and his triumphal entrance into Berlin in 1806.*—Ed.

extraordinary contrast must be attributed to the nature of the government, not of education. Intellectual education is perfect in Germany, but everything is theoretical. Practical education depends entirely upon doing things; it is only by action that the character acquires the firmness necessary for guidance in the management of life. Character is an instinct; it pertains to nature more than does the understanding, and yet only events give men the opportunity to develop it. Governments are the true instructors of nations; yet public education, however good, can create men of letters but not citizens, soldiers, or statesmen.

In Germany philosophy has progressed farther than anywhere else; nothing stops it. The very absence of political life, so fatal to the mass of the people, gives more freedom to thinkers. But a great distance separates minds of the first and second ranks because there is no incentive for men who cannot rise to the level of the most comprehensive ideas. In Germany a man who does not concern himself with the universe might as well do nothing.

The German universities have a long reputation going back several centuries before the Reformation. Since that period, the Protestant universities have been unquestionably superior to the Catholic universities, and all of Germany's literary renown rests upon these institutions. The English universities have contributed greatly to the spread among the English people of that knowledge of languages and of ancient literature that gives to orators and statesmen in England so liberal and brilliant an education. It is in good taste to know something besides business—when one knows *that* well; moreover, the eloquence of free nations is linked not merely to their own history but also to that of the Greeks and Romans. But the German universities, though founded on principles analogous to those of England, differ from them in many respects. The multitude of students gathered at Göttingen, Halle, Jena, etc., constituted almost an independent body within the state; the rich and poor students distinguished among themselves only by their personal merit, and the foreigners who came from all corners of the world submitted with pleasure to this equality that only natural superiority could upset.

The students had independence and even a military spirit. If, therefore, upon leaving the university they had been able to devote themselves to the public interest, their education would have promoted vigor of mind and character. But they returned to the monotonous and domesticated life that prevails in Germany and gradually lost the spark and determination that university life had inspired in them. Nothing of it remained with them but a very broad education.

In every German university several professors competed in each branch of learning. Thus the teachers themselves had a spirit of emulation, for they were anxious to surpass each other in the number of students they attracted. Those who planned to take up a certain profession, such as medicine, law, etc., were naturally impelled to learn other subjects, from which arose that universality of knowledge one notices among almost all educated Germans. The universities had their own property, like the clergy. They had their own jurisdiction. It was a good idea of our ancestors to make the institutions of education entirely independent. Middle age may yield to circumstances, but at least upon entering life young men should draw their ideas from an uncorrupted source.

The study of languages, which is the basis of education in Germany, is much more favorable to the development of the faculties in childhood than is the study of mathematics or physical science. Children occupied so early with calculation lose all vigor of imagination, so beautiful and fruitful at that age, and do not acquire in its place a surpassing accuracy of understanding. For arithmetic and algebra are restricted to teaching us the same propositions in a thousand ways. The problems of life are more complicated; none is precise or fixed. We must predict and choose with the help of estimates and assumptions that have no connection with the infallible process of the calculus.

Proved truths do not lead us to conditional truths, the only ones that can guide us in business, as in the arts and human relations. There is undoubtedly a point at which mathematics itself demands that brilliant power of invention without which the secrets of nature cannot be penetrated. At the summit of thought, the imagination of Homer and Newton seem to meet —but how many children without talent in mathematics devote all their time to it! They are drilled in only a single faculty, whereas it is necessary to develop the entire moral being at a time when the mind as well as the body may be so easily disturbed by strengthening only a part.

Nothing is less applicable to life than a mathematical argument. A proposition expressed in numbers is definitely false or true. In all other relations the truth is so mingled with the false that often only instinct can help us to decide among various influences, sometimes equally as strong in one direction as in the other. The study of mathematics, habituating us to certainty, makes us annoyed with all opinions different from our own, whereas the most important thing for the direction of this world is that we understand others—that is to say, that we understand everything that leads them to think and feel differently from us.

So it seems to me that, for the benefit of morality as well as the understanding, the study of mathematics should come in due course and as part of a whole education, rather than be made the basis of education and therefore the determining principle of character and mind.

There are some systems of education that recommend beginning instruction with the natural sciences. In childhood these are only a pure entertainment, an erudite toy that accustoms us to systematic amusement and superficial study. People have supposed that, to the extent that it is possible, we ought to spare children effort, turn all their studies into diversions, and give them at an early age collections of natural history for playthings and experiments in physics for a show. It seems to me that this is likewise an erroneous method. Even if it were possible for a child to learn anything well while amusing itself, I should still regret the failure to develop one faculty, the attention, which is much more essential than simply another bit of information.

Education through amusement dissipates thought. In every domain labor is one of the great secrets of nature. The mind of the child ought to become accustomed to the effort of study, as our soul to suffering. Improvement in infancy depends upon work, in later life upon suffering. But it is doubtless to be hoped that neither parents nor fate will abuse this double secret too much. You may show your child a lot of things with pictures and cards, but you will not teach him to learn; and the propensity for amusement, which you direct toward the sciences, will soon follow another course when the child is no longer under your control.

Thus it is not without reason that the study of ancient and modern languages has been the basis of all the educational institutions that have molded the most able men in Europe. The meaning of a sentence in a foreign language is at once a grammatical and an intellectual problem, which can correspond perfectly to the child's intelligence. At first he understands only the words, then he advances to the apprehension of the sentence, and soon afterward to the charm of the expression, its power, its harmony—the child who translates gradually perceives everything in the language of man. The number of faculties such study stimulates at once makes it more advantageous than all other kinds. And we should be very happy to use the child's flexible memory in retaining a kind of knowledge without which he would be confined all his life to the circle of his own nation—a circle that is narrow, like everything exclusive.

The study of grammar requires the same coherence and power of attention as mathematics, but it depends much more upon thought. Grammar connects ideas as calculation links numbers. The logic of grammar is just as exact as that of algebra, and yet it applies to everything that is alive in the mind. The theory of grammar thus combines precision of reason with independence of thought.

Chapter XIX. Private Institutions of Education and Charity

It will seem at first glance inconsistent to praise the old system which made the study of languages the basis of education and to consider Pestalozzi's[5] school one of the best institutions of our time, but I think these two views can be reconciled.

By leading him conscientiously through each level of reasoning, Pestalozzi puts the child in a position to discover himself what he wishes to teach him.

It is noteworthy that neither punishments nor rewards are necessary to make [children] study. This is perhaps the first

[5] *Johann Heinrich Pestalozzi (1746–1827), Swiss educator who advanced a theory of education based upon the development of the individual.*—Ed.

time that a school of a hundred and fifty children has succeeded without the stimulus of competition and fear.

It is rather generally feared that Pestalozzi's method may stifle the imagination and discourage originality of mind. Education for genius would be difficult to devise, and only nature and government can prompt it. But a perfectly clear and certain basic knowledge cannot be an obstacle to genius; it gives the mind a kind of firmness that later makes the highest studies easier. We must judge Pestalozzi's school as limited, until now, to childhood. The education he gives is terminal only for the lower classes, but for that very reason it may exert a very salutary influence upon the national mind. Education for the rich should be divided into two periods: in the first, the children are guided by their masters; in the second, they teach themselves voluntarily, and this superior form of education ought to be adopted in great universities. The education acquired at Pestalozzi's gives every man, of whatever class he may be, a foundation upon which he may build, as he pleases, a poor man's cottage or the palaces of kings.

The example of England and America shows us that free institutions suffice to develop the people's understanding and wisdom; but it is a step further to give them something beyond the merely necessary in education. There is something revolting about the necessary in every domain when it is meted out by those who enjoy the superfluous. It is not enough to be concerned about the lower classes only in regard to their useful employment; they must also share in the pleasures of the imagination and the heart.

There is much charity in the world, and he who cannot serve his fellow men by the sacrifice of his time and tastes may readily help them with his money: this is still something, and no virtue is to be scorned. But the great mass of private alms in most countries is not wisely directed.

Part Two. Literature and the Arts
Chapter III. Principal Periods of German Literature

German literature has never had what is usually called a golden age, that is to say, a period in which the progress of letters was encouraged through the patronage of sovereigns. Perhaps this literature has owed its greater originality and vigor to this abandonment and independence.

For a thousand years the German language has been cultivated, first by monks, then by knights, then by artisans like Hans Sachs, Sebastian Brand,[6] and others at the approach of the Reformation, and recently by scholars who have made it a language suitable to all the subtleties of thought.

In examining the works that make up German literature, we find, in accordance with the author's genius, the traces of these different forms of cultivation, just as we see in mountains the strata of various minerals caused by the earth's changes. Style changes its nature almost entirely with each writer, and foreigners must make a fresh study to understand each new book.

The Germans, like most European nations in the time of chivalry, had troubadours and warriors who sang of love and battle. An epic poem has just been discovered, entitled the *Nibelungenlied* and composed in the thirteenth century.[7] We see in it the heroism and fidelity that characterized men in those days, when everything was true, strong, and pro-

[6] *Sachs (1494–1576) was a leading Meistersinger and poet. Brand (1458–1521), a moralist and poet, was the author of the allegory,* Ship of Fools.—Ed.

[7] *In an earlier manuscript of* De l'Allemagne, *Madame de Staël says it was composed in the twelfth century, which is now regarded as correct. See Comtesse Jean de Pange,* De l'Allemagne, *Vol. II, p. 35, nn. L. 15 and 1.*—Ed.

nounced, like the primary colors of nature. The German in this poem is simpler than today's; general ideas had not yet been introduced and only traits of character were related.

Luther conspicuously improved his language by making it serve theological discussion; his translation of the Psalms and the Bible is still a fine model. The poetic truth and brevity he gives to his style are in perfect harmony with the nature of the German language, and even the sound of the words has an indefinable kind of vigorous simplicity that we can confidently trust. The political and religious wars, in which the Germans had the misfortune of fighting among themselves, diverted people from literature. When they resumed their concern with it, it was under the guidance of the Age of Louis XIV, a period when the desire to imitate the French possessed most of the courts and the writers of Europe.

The works of Hagedorn, Gellert, Weiss,[8] etc., were only labored French, with nothing original and nothing in harmony with the natural character of the nation. Another school soon succeeded the French school, arising in German Switzerland; this school was at first based upon imitation of English writers. Bodmer, supported by the example of the great Haller, tried to prove that English literature agreed with the nature of the Germans better than French literature. Gottsched,[9] a scholar without taste and talent, contested this view. A great illumination flashed from the dispute between these two schools. Some men then began to blaze a new trail by themselves.

Since there are in all the Teutonic nations some sparks of

[8] *Friedrich von Hagedorn (1708–54), Christian Fürchtegott Gellert (1715–69), and probably Christian Felix Weisse (1726–1804), according to Comtesse Jean de Pange in* De l'Allemagne, *Vol. II, p. 37, nn. 1–3.*—Ed.

[9] *Johann Jakob Bodmer (1698–1783), Albrecht von Haller (1708–77), and Johann Christoph Gottsched (1700–66).*—Ed.

the sacred fire that time has covered with ashes, Klopstock, at first imitating the English, succeeded in awakening the imagination and character peculiar to the Germans, and almost at the same moment Winckelmann in the arts, Lessing in criticism, and Goethe in poetry founded a truly German school, if this name may be applied to something that admits as many differences as there are individuals or varying talents. I shall examine separately poetry, dramatic art, novels, and history; but since every man of genius forms, so to speak, a separate school in Germany, it seems to me necessary to begin by revealing the principal traits that distinguish each writer as an individual and by personally describing the most renowned men of letters, before analyzing their works.

Chapter VII. Goethe

Goethe might well represent all of German literature, not that there are no writers superior to him in some respects; but only he combines all that distinguishes the German spirit.

Goethe is a man of great genius in conversation; and, say what you will, genius should be able to talk. Some examples of silent men of genius may be offered; timidity, misfortune, contempt, or boredom are often the cause of it. But in general breadth of ideas and warmth of soul must inspire the need to communicate with others. Men who do not wish to be judged by what they say may well not merit any more interest in what they think. When one knows how to induce Goethe to talk, he is admirable. His eloquence is rich in ideas. His humor is at once full of grace and philosophy. His imagination is impressed by external things, as was that of the ancient artists; nevertheless, his reason has only too much of the maturity of our time. Nothing impedes the force of his mind, and the very limitations of his character—bad temper, irritability, constraint—pass like clouds at the foot of the mountain upon whose summit his genius was placed.

Goethe no longer has that lively eagerness that inspired *Werther*, but the warmth of his thought is still enough to animate everything. It would seem that he is not affected by life and that he describes it only as a painter: he now attaches more value to the pictures he offers us than to the emotions he feels. Time has made him a spectator. When he still had an active part in scenes involving the emotions, when he himself experienced things with his heart, his writings gave a more vivid impression.

Since a poet draws his poetics from his own character, Goethe now maintains that an author must be calm even when he is creating an impassioned work, and that an artist should retain his composure in order to affect his readers' imagination the more vigorously. Perhaps he would not have believed this in his youth, when he may have been possessed by his genius instead of mastering it. He may then have felt that since the sublime and the divine enter the heart of man for but a fleeting moment, the poet is inferior to the inspiration that moves him and cannot judge it without losing it.

In his writings as well as in his conversation, Goethe likes to break the thread he himself has woven, to dispel the emotions he stirs up, to overturn the idols he has made us admire. When, in his fiction, he inspires sympathy for a character, he soon reveals deviations that dissipate it. He commands the poetic world as a conqueror does the real world. He thinks himself strong enough to introduce, as nature does, the spirit of destruction into his own works. If he were not a worthy man, we should fear this kind of superiority that rises above everything, degrades and then exalts, moves and then mocks, affirms and doubts in turn—and always with the same success.

I have said that Goethe combines in himself the principal traits of the German spirit to a high degree: a great depth of ideas, the grace that springs from the imagination—a grace more fresh than that formed by the spirit of society; in short, a sometimes incredible sensibility, but for that very reason one more likely to interest readers who seek in books something to give variety to their monotonous lives and who want poetry to take the place of real events for them.

The admiration for Goethe is a kind of fraternity in which the rallying cries reveal the adepts to one another. When foreigners also want to admire him, they are rejected with scorn, if it may be supposed from their reservations that they have dared to analyze those works which are indeed worth analysis. Only power, in whatever domain, can be feared so much as to be loved in this way; a man cannot stir such fanaticism without having a great capacity for both good and evil.

Chapter VIII. Schiller

Schiller was a man of rare talent and absolute sincerity; these two qualities should be inseparable, at least in a man of letters.

There is no more noble career than literature when followed in Schiller's manner. He loved poetry, dramatic art, history, and literature for their own sake. Even if he had decided not to publish his works, he would have given them the same care. No consideration—of success, fashion, prejudice or in short of anything that comes from others—could have made him alter his writings. For his writings were himself, they expressed his soul, and he could not conceive the possibility of changing an expression if the inner feeling that inspired it had not changed.

I saw Schiller for the first time in the *salon* of the Duke and

Duchess of Weimar, in company as enlightened as it was imposing. He read French very well but had never spoken it. I avidly maintained the superiority of our dramatic method above all others. He did not decline to fight me. Without worrying about the impediments and delays he met in expressing himself in French, and without fearing, either, the opinion of his audience, which was contrary to his own, his profound conviction impelled him to speak. To refute him, I used French weapons at first—spirit and wit. But I soon made out through the barrier of words so many ideas in what Schiller said; I was so impressed by the simplicity of character that led a man of genius to engage thus in a struggle where words were unequal to his thoughts; I found him so modest and so indifferent to what related merely to his own success, so proud and so lively in defense of what he believed to be the truth, that I pledged to him from that moment a friendship full of admiration.

Chapter IX. Style and Versification in the German Language

In learning the accent of a language we enter more intimately into the spirit of the nation that speaks it than by any other kind of study. That makes it amusing to pronounce foreign words: we listen as if it were someone else speaking. There is nothing so subtle and so difficult to apprehend as an accent; it is a thousand times easier to learn the most complicated musical airs than the pronunciation of a single syllable. Only many years, or the first impressions of childhood, can enable us to imitate pronunciation, which pertains to what is most subtle and indefinable in the imagination and in national character.

The air we breathe has a great deal of influence upon the sounds we utter: variation in soil and climate causes very different ways of pronouncing the same language. As we approach the sea, words become softer; the climate there is moderate and perhaps, too, the habitual sight of this image of infinity inclines people to revery and gives pronunciation more gentleness and indolence. But when we climb toward the mountains, accent becomes stronger, and it might be said that the inhabitants of these high places wish to make themselves heard by the rest of the world from the height of their natural platforms.

German is perhaps the only language in which verse is easier to understand than prose; for the poetic sentence, being necessarily broken by the very meter of verse, cannot be prolonged.

Undoubtedly there are more fine distinctions and more connections between ideas in those sentences that comprise a whole and that bring together under the same viewpoint various aspects of the same subject. But if we carried to its logical conclusion the connection of all ideas among themselves, we should end up by wanting to put everything into the same sentence. The human mind must break up unities in order to understand them.[10]

German is the only modern language that has long and short syllables like Greek and Latin; all the other European dialects are more or less accented. But verse cannot be scanned, as the ancients did, according to the length of the syllables. Accent gives unity to sentences as well as to words.

10 *In these two paragraphs Madame de Staël seems to argue that poetry, by its very meter, shortens German sentences and thus makes them easier to understand. Prose in German does not force such a breaking up of sentences and thoughts, and is therefore more difficult to understand.*—Ed.

It is connected with the meaning of what is said—we stress what is to determine the meaning; and pronunciation, by making this or that word stand out, arranges everything in relation to the main idea. This is not the case with the musical duration of sounds in language; this is much more favorable to poetry than accent is, because it has no precise function and merely affords a lofty and indefinable pleasure, as do all enjoyments without purpose. Among the ancients, syllables were scanned according to the nature of the vowels and interrelations of the sounds—harmony alone determined everything. In German, all the subordinate words are short, so it is the grammatical significance—that is, the importance—of the root syllable that determines its value. There is less charm in this kind of prosody than in that of the ancients because it depends more upon abstract combinations than upon natural feelings. It is nevertheless always a great advantage for a language to have in its prosody something that can substitute for rhyme.

One of the great advantages of the German dialects in poetry is the variety and beauty of their epithets. In this respect, too, German may be compared to Greek. One senses several images in a single word, just as in the basic note of a chord we hear the other sounds of which it is composed, or just as certain colors stir in us the feeling of those colors subordinate to them. In French we can say only what we want to, and we do not see hovering around words those clouds of a thousand shapes that surround poetry in the Northern languages and stir a host of memories. To the liberty of forming a single epithet of two or three is added that of enlivening the language by making nouns out of verbs: *living, willing, feeling* are less abstract terms than life, will, sentiment.[11] Anything

[11] *In English the same word, feeling, is the verbal noun and the abstract noun.*—Ed.

that changes thought into action always lends more liveliness to style. The ease of reversing the construction of a sentence at will is likewise very favorable to poetry and enables one, by the various means of versification, to stimulate impressions like those of painting and music. In short, the general spirit of Teutonic dialects is independence. Writers seek above all to transmit what they feel.

Chapter XI. Classic Poetry and Romantic Poetry

The name *romantic* has been recently introduced in Germany to designate the poetry whose source is the songs of the troubadours and which arose from chivalry and Christianity. If we do not acknowledge that paganism and Christianity, the North and the South, antiquity and the Middle Ages, chivalry and Greek and Roman institutions, have divided the realm of literature, then we shall never succeed in judging ancient and modern taste philosophically.

The word *classic* is sometimes taken as a synonym for perfection. I use it here in another sense, regarding classic poetry as that of the ancients, and romantic poetry as related in some way to the traditions of chivalry. This division is equally appropriate to the two historical eras of the world: that which preceded the establishment of Christianity and that which followed it.

In various German works ancient poetry has been likened to sculpture and romantic poetry to painting. In short, the progress of the human mind has been described in every way in its passage from materialist to spiritual religions, from nature to divinity.

The French nation, the most cultivated of the Latin nations, inclines toward classic poetry modeled upon the Greeks and Romans. The English nation, the most renowned of the Germanic nations, prefers romantic and chivalrous poetry and is proud of its masterpieces in this *genre.* I shall not examine here which of these two kinds of poetry merits preference; it is enough to show that diversity of taste in this connection arises not merely from accidental causes but also from primitive sources of the imagination and thought.

There is a kind of simplicity in the epic poems and tragedies of the ancients that arises from man's identification with nature in that era and his belief that he was controlled by fate just as nature was controlled by necessity. Not very reflective, man still manifested externally all the workings of his mind. Even conscience was represented by external things, and the torches of the Furies shook remorse over the heads of the guilty. The event was everything in antiquity, but character has more importance in modern times.

The ancients had, so to speak, a corporeal soul all of whose emotions were strong, direct, and pronounced. It is not the same with the human heart unfolded by Christianity; modern men have derived from Christian repentance the habit of constantly turning inward upon themselves.

But to reveal this inward existence, a great variety of external events must display the infinite subtleties of the soul in all their forms. If in our day the fine arts were confined to the simplicity of the ancients, we would not attain their characteristic pristine power, but we would lose the intimate and manifold feelings of which we are capable. Simplicity in art, among the moderns, could easily turn into coldness and abstraction, whereas among the ancients it was full of life. Honor and love, valor and pity are the sentiments that marked Christianity in the age of chivalry; and these tendencies of the soul could manifest themselves only through perils, exploits, loves, misfortunes—in short, romantic concerns that ceaselessly vary the scene of action. Thus the sources of the effects of art differ, in many respects, in classic poetry and romantic poetry. In the one it is fate that rules, in the other it is Providence. Fate ignores the feelings of men, while Providence judges deeds only in accordance with these feelings. Poetry must indeed create a world of an entirely different nature when it seeks to describe the workings of a destiny that is blind and deaf, always in a struggle with mortals, or that intelligent order guided by a Supreme Being to whom our heart may address itself and be answered.

Pagan poetry is necessarily as simple and pronounced as external objects, but Christian poetry needs the myriad colors of the rainbow to prevent it from being lost in the clouds. The poetry of the ancients is purer as art, whereas that of the moderns makes us shed more tears. But the issue for us is not between classic poetry and romantic poetry but between imitation in the former and inspiration in the latter. To the modern era the literature of the ancients is a transplanted literature; romantic literature is indigenous to us, and it is our religion and customs that have made it blossom. Writers who imitate the ancients have submitted to the strictest rules of taste; not being able to consult their own nature or their own recollections, they must conform to those formulas by which the masterpieces of the ancients may be adapted to our taste, even though all the political and religious conditions that gave birth to those masterpieces are changed. But poems modeled on the ancient, however perfect they may be, are seldom popular, for they do not relate in our own time to anything native to us.

French being the most classic of all modern poetry, it is the only one not familiar to the populace. The stanzas of Tasso are sung by the gondoliers of Venice, Spaniards and Portuguese of all social classes know by heart the verses of Calderón and Camões. Shakespeare is as much admired by the populace in England as by the upper classes. The poems of Goethe and Bürger are set to music and you can hear them repeated from the banks of the Rhine to the Baltic. Our French poets are admired by all cultivated minds among ourselves and in the rest of Europe, but they are completely unknown to the common people and even to the middle class in the cities, because the arts in France are not, as elsewhere, native to the country where their beauty is revealed.

Some French critics maintain that the literature of the German people is still in its infancy as art. This view is entirely wrong. The most learned men in languages and the works of the ancients are certainly not ignorant of the disadvantages and advantages of the *genre* they adopt or reject, but their character, habits, and reflections have led them to prefer the literature based upon memories of chivalry, on the wonders of the Middle Ages, to that based upon Greek mythology. Romantic literature alone is still capable of improvement because, having its roots in our own soil, it alone can grow and revitalize itself. It expresses our religion and recalls our history. Its source is old but not antique.

Classic poetry must pass through the recollections of paganism in order to reach us, but the poetry of the Germans belongs to the Christian era of the fine arts: it uses our personal impressions to move us. The spirit that inspires it appeals directly to our heart and seems to recall our very existence like the most powerful and awful of phantoms.

Chapter XXVIII. Novels

Since the novel is the easiest of all the forms of fiction, there is no field in which writers of the modern nations have more often tried their hand. The novel is, so to speak, a transition from real to imaginary existence. Every one's history is, with only a few changes, a novel rather like those that are being published,[12] and personal recollections, in this respect, often take the place of invention.

I shall not ignore the fact that novels, even the purest ones, do harm; they have told us too much about the most hidden of our feelings. We can experience nothing any more without almost remembering that we have already read about it; all the veils of the heart have been torn away. The ancients would never thus have made their soul a theme of fiction. A sanctuary remained for them that even their own glance would fear to penetrate.

The Germans, like the English, are very fertile in novels that portray domestic life. The portrayal of customs is more elegant in English novels but more varied in the German. There is in England, despite people's individuality, a general style of life that is set by polite society; in Germany nothing is a matter of convention in this respect. Several of these novels based upon feelings and customs, which have in literature the place of tragi-comedies in the theatre, deserve to be mentioned. But *Werther* is the one without equal; we can see in it everything that Goethe's genius could produce when he was impassioned. It is said that he now attaches little value to this work of his youth. The effervescence of the imagination, which almost inspired him with enthusiasm for suicide, now probably seems to him to be blameworthy.

[12] *Comtesse Jean de Pange, who has prepared the definitive edition of* De l'Allemagne, *states (Vol. III, p. 243, n. 1): "Mme. de Staël, who is often wrongly judged to be a novelist, had little imagination. She wrote only two novels,* Delphine *and* Corinne, *which are in effect only a transposition of her personal impressions and recollections; and contrary to the advice she gives here, she strove to combine with fiction a great deal of history, philosophy and even archeology!"*—Ed.

Novels in the form of letters always deal more with feelings than with action. The ancients would never have thought of giving this form to their fiction, and it is only in the last two centuries that philosophy has been sufficiently developed in us to permit so great a place in literature to the analysis of our feelings. This manner of conceiving novels is certainly not so poetic as that of pure narration. But the human mind is now much less interested in even the best plot than in comments on what goes on in our hearts. This disposition results from the great intellectual changes that have taken place in man; he tends more and more, in general, to fall back upon himself, seeking religion, love, and thought in the deepest recess of his being.

Several German writers have composed stories of ghosts and witches and think there is more talent in these inventions than in a novel based upon an event of ordinary life. It is all very well if a writer is inclined to it by a natural aptitude, but in general poetry is required for the realm of the extraordinary—prose is inadequate.

Chapter XXXI. The Literary Riches of Germany and Its Most Renowned Critics, A. W. and F. Schlegel

Though they are not a direct part of literature, treatises on the fine arts and works of erudition and philosophy must nevertheless be included among its riches. Germany has treasures of ideas and knowledge which the rest of the nations of Europe will not be able to exhaust for a long time.

Poetic genius, if Heaven restores it to us, may also receive a happy impetus from the love of nature, the arts, and philosophy that seethes in the Germanic lands. But at the least I venture to assert that any man today who wants to devote himself to some serious work of any kind, on history or philosophy or archeology, cannot avoid acquainting himself with the German writers who have concerned themselves with these matters.

Before going on to philosophy, which always constitutes a part of letters wherever literature is free and powerful, I shall say a few words on what may be regarded as the rules of that domain, criticism. There is no branch of German literature that has been carried further; just as in certain cities there are more doctors than sick people, so there are sometimes in Germany more critics than authors. But the analyses of Lessing, the creator of style in German prose, are composed in such a way that they may themselves be regarded as artistic works.

Among the younger writers Schiller and the two Schlegels have shown themselves far superior to all the other critics. Schiller is the first disciple of Kant who has applied his philosophy to literature.

The writings of A. W. Schlegel are less abstract than Schiller's. Since he has a knowledge of literature that is rare even in his own country, he is constantly stimulated by the pleasure he finds in comparing various languages and kinds of poetry with one another. So universal a point of view ought almost to be regarded as infallible, if bias did not sometimes mar it; but this bias is not arbitrary, and I shall point out its direction and purpose.

W. Schlegel has given a course on dramatic literature at Vienna, embracing the most noteworthy compositions for the theatre from the Greeks down to our own day. It is not a sterile catalogue of the works of various authors; rather, it captures the essence of every literature with the imagination of a poet.

I was in Vienna when W. Schlegel gave his public lectures

there. I expected merely understanding and instruction from these lessons whose purpose was educational, but I was amazed to hear a critic as eloquent as an orator, and one who, far from merely hunting down defects—the eternal forage of jealous mediocrity—sought only to bring creative genius to life again.

This is the only honest way to be a critic. Any craftsman can point out the faults and laxities to be avoided, but the ability to recognize and admire genius is the nearest thing to genius itself.

After having done justice to the rare talents of the two Schlegels [A.W. and F.] we must now inquire into the nature of the bias of which they are accused and from which, it is true, some of their writings are not free. They have a decided preference for the Middle Ages and its outlook.

Opinions whose tendency is so pronounced must necessarily mar impartiality of judgment of works of art. Undoubtedly, as I have constantly reiterated in the course of this work, it is desirable that modern literature be based upon our history and our creed. But the point is not that we should be forcing art backward in time but that we should combine, as much as possible, the various fine qualities displayed by the human mind in all eras.

Chapter XXXII. The Fine Arts in Germany

The Germans in general can conceive art better than they can practice it; no sooner do they have an impression of something than they extract a host of ideas from it. They make much of mystery, but only in order to reveal it, and no kind of originality can be shown in Germany without everyone explaining how it comes about. This is a great drawback, above all for the arts, where everything is feeling. The arts are analyzed even before they are felt, and it is useless to say afterward that analysis should be abandoned: one has already tasted the fruit of the tree of science and the innocence of genius is lost.

I certainly do not recommend for the arts the ignorance that I have always condemned in literature. But we must distinguish those studies relating to the practice of art from those whose only goal is to explain genius. The latter, pushed too far, stifle invention. The artist is impeded by the memory of everything that has been said of every masterpiece; he senses between himself and the object he wants to portray a swarm of treatises on painting and sculpture, the ideal and the real, and he is no longer alone with nature.

Before the age of the Reformation the Germans had a school of painting that the Italian school would not have scorned. Albert Dürer, Lucas Cranach, and Holbein are related, in their manner of painting, to the predecessors of Raphael, Perugino, Andrea Mantegna, etc. Holbein more closely resembles Leonardo da Vinci. There is in general, however, more hardness in the German school than in the Italian but no less expression and contemplation in the faces. These painters of the fifteenth century had little acquaintance with artistic techniques, but a touching sincerity and modesty are conspicuous in their works.

In these portraits of the fourteenth and fifteenth centuries, the folds of clothing are entirely straight, the hair-styles a bit stiff, the postures very ordinary, but there is something in the expression of the faces that we never tire of contemplating. These portraits inspired by the Christian religion produce an impression like that of the Psalms, which combine poetry and piety with so much charm.

The second and the finest era of painting was that in which

the painters retained the truth of the Middle Ages, adding to it all the splendor of art. But nothing among the Germans matched the age of Leo X.[13] Toward the end of the seventeenth century down to the middle of the eighteenth, the fine arts almost everywhere fell into an extraordinary decline, and taste degenerated into affectation.[14]

Almost all German artists had adopted the views of Winckelmann until the new literary school[15] extended its influence to the fine arts. Goethe, whose universal genius we meet everywhere, has shown in his works that he understands the real spirit of painting much better than Winckelmann. Yet, convinced like him that Christian subjects are not favorable to art, Goethe seeks to revive enthusiasm for mythology—but this is an effort that cannot succeed. Perhaps, in the fine arts, we are not able to be either Christian or pagan. But whenever the creative imagination of mankind is reborn, it will certainly not be through imitation of the ancients that it will be influential.

I have already said, in speaking of Germany, that there are few noteworthy modern buildings. In the North, one sees in general nothing but Gothic, and both nature and poetry also foster the predispositions that such buildings arouse.

There are in Germany a large number of picture galleries and collections of drawings, which implies a love of the arts in all social classes. In the homes of noblemen and leading men of letters there are very fine reproductions of the masterpieces

[13] *Leo X, Pope from 1513 to 1521, was greatly interested in literature and the arts. He was Raphael's patron.*—Ed.

[14] *This denigration of the baroque was common in the nineteenth century.*—Ed.

[15] *Comtesse Jean de Pange, in the definitive edition of* De l'Allemagne *(Vol. III, p. 362, n. 1), notes that Madame de Staël refers here not to the Sturm und Drang school but to the later Romantic movement whose organ was* Das Athenäum.—Ed.

of the ancient world. Goethe's house is very remarkable in this respect; he seeks not only the pleasure afforded by the sight of these pictures and statues of the great masters, but he believes that they deeply affect our spirit and mind. "I should improve," he would say, "if I had before my eyes the head of the Olympian Jupiter which the ancients so admired."[16]

Sculpture has not been cultivated with much success among the Germans, mainly because they lack the marble that makes these masterpieces immortal, and also because they scarcely have the delicacy and grace of posture and gesture that only gymnastics and the dance can facilitate.

The Germans excel in instrumental music, for the knowledge it requires and the patience necessary to perform it well are entirely natural to them. They also have composers whose imagination is versatile and productive. I shall offer only one objection to their talent as musicians: they put too much intellect into their works, they reflect too much upon what they are doing. The fine arts need more instinct than thought. German composers follow the meaning of the lyrics too exactly. This is a great merit, it is true, for those who like lyrics better than music; moreover, no one can deny that a clash between the meaning of the former and the expression of the latter would be unpleasant. Yet the Italians, who are truly musicians by nature, suit the melodies to the lyrics only in a general way. In ballads and musical plays, since there is not much music, what little there is may be subordinated to the lyrics, but when it comes to the melody's profound impression, one must go straight to the heart by a direct sensation.

At Vienna I heard the *Requiem* Mozart composed a few days before he died, and which was sung in church the day of his

[16] *In* De l'Allemagne, *Comtesse Jean de Pange states (Vol. III, p. 367, n. 1) that Goethe made this remark to Madame de Staël at Weimar in 1803.*—Ed.

funeral. It is not solemn enough for the occasion, though we still find ingenuity in it, as in all that Mozart created. Yet, what is more touching than a man of superior genius thus commemorating his own funeral, inspired at once by the premonition of his death and of his immortality! The memories of life ought to adorn a tomb; a soldier's weapons are hung upon it. And the masterpieces of art create a solemn impression in the temple where the remains of the artist repose.

Part Three. Philosophy and Ethics
Chapter IV. The Frivolity Deriving from a Certain Kind of Philosophy

The philosophical system adopted in a country exerts a great influence upon the inclination of the mind. It is the universal mold in which all thoughts are cast; even those who have not studied it unconsciously conform to the general predisposition it inspires. For nearly a hundred years we have seen in Europe the birth and growth of a kind of scoffing skepticism whose foundation is the metaphysics that attributes all ideas to sensations. The leading principle of this philosophy is to believe only what can be proved like a fact or a calculation. To this principle are added a scorn for noble sentiments and a fondness for material pleasures. These three elements of the doctrine embody all the forms of irony to which religion, sensibility, and morality can be subjected.

It is therefore essential to inquire whether the nation that constantly protected itself against the metaphysics from which such inferences have been drawn was not right in principle and even more so in the application of this principle to the development of the faculties and the moral conduct of mankind.

Chapter V. General Observations on German Philosophy

Speculative philosophy has always found many advocates among the Teutonic nations, and experimental philosophy among the Latin nations. And among the nations of the North the Germans have always shown themselves more inclined to contemplative philosophy than any other nation. Leibniz is their Bacon and their Descartes. We find in this noble genius all the qualities the German philosophers boast: vast erudition, complete honesty, enthusiasm concealed by restrained forms.

Leibniz was an idealist who based his system exclusively upon rationality; the result is that he pushed abstractions too far and did not rest his theory sufficiently upon inner conviction, the only true foundation of everything higher than the understanding. In short: reason upon the liberty of mankind, and you will not believe in it; rely upon your conscience, and you will not be able to doubt it.

It seems to me, then, that while admiring the intellect and profound genius of Leibniz, one might wish, in his writings on metaphysical theology, more imagination and sensibility, so that the feelings might provide a respite from thought. Leibniz hesitated to resort to them, fearing he might thereby seem to be beguiling people in favor of the truth. He was wrong, for sentiment is truth itself in such matters.

The objections I have ventured to the works of Leibniz relate to questions that cannot be solved by reasoning; they do not apply to his writings on the formation of ideas in the human mind. The opinions of Leibniz in this respect tend above all to moral improvement if it is true, as the German philosophers have tried to prove, that free will rests upon the doctrine that frees the mind from external objects and that virtue could not exist without the complete independence of the will.

With admirable logical power Leibniz opposed Locke's system, which attributes all our ideas to our sensations. People acted upon the well-known axiom that there is nothing in our intellect that has not first been experienced in our sensations. Leibniz added this sublime limitation: *except the intellect itself*. From this principle comes the entire new philosophy that exerts so much influence upon people in Germany. This philosophy is also experimental, for it seeks to understand what happens within ourselves. It merely substitutes observation of our inner feelings for that of our external sensations.

Chapter VI. Kant

Kant lived to a very advanced age but never left Koenigsberg. There, in the midst of the Northern ice, he spent his whole life meditating upon the laws of human understanding.

At the time *The Critique of Pure Reason* appeared, there were among thinkers only two doctrines concerning human understanding. Locke attributed all our ideas to our sensations. Descartes and Leibniz sought to establish the spirituality and action of the mind, the free will—in short, the whole doctrine of idealism; but these two philosophers rested their doctrine upon purely speculative proofs.[17] I have shown, in the preceding chapter, the disadvantages of such abstraction, which, so to speak, stops the blood in our veins so that our intellectual faculties may reign alone within us.

Kant sought to find out whether the human mind could attain absolute certainty, and he found it only in necessary ideas, that is to say, in all the laws of our understanding.

[17] *That is, intellectual, logical proofs that ignore sentiment.*—Ed.

The nature of these laws is such that we cannot conceive of anything except as these laws represent it.

The leading imperative forms[18] of our understanding are space and time. Kant demonstrated that everything we perceive is subject to these two forms. He concludes that they are in ourselves and not in external objects, and that in this sense it is our understanding that imposes laws upon external nature rather than receiving them from it.

Far from rejecting experience, Kant considered life to be only the action of our innate faculties upon the knowledge that comes to us from outside. He believed that experience without the laws of understanding would be nothing but chaos, but that these laws of understanding have nothing upon which to work except the elements provided by experience. It follows that metaphysics itself can teach us nothing beyond its own limits and that it is to sentiment that we must attribute prescience and certainty concerning everything that transcends the visible world.

Mankind's finest eras have been those in which truths of a certain kind were never contested in writing or speech. The passions might lead men to sinful acts, but no one doubted the religion he disobeyed. Sophisms of every kind and abuses of a certain philosophy have destroyed, in various countries and eras, that noble firmness of belief, the source of heroic devotion. Is it not then a fine idea for a philosopher to prohibit the very science he professes from entering the sanctuary and to use all the power of logic to prove that there are some regions from which it must be excluded?

[18] *Madame de Staël adds the following note two paragraphs later (Vol. IV, p. 123 of the edition prepared by Comtesse Jean de Pange), indicating that these terms, "necessary ideas" and "imperative forms," refer to Kant's "categories":* Kant gives the name *categories* to the various necessary ideas of the understanding, which he presents in a table.—Ed.

Despots and fanatics have tried to prevent human reason from inquiring into certain subjects, but reason has always shaken off these unjust shackles. But the limits reason imposes upon itself, far from enslaving it, give it new strength—the kind that always results from the authority of laws freely consented to by those who submit to them.

Chapter IX. Influence of the New German Philosophy upon Literature and the Arts

In countries where it is believed that all ideas come to us through external things it is natural to place a higher value upon the rules of propriety, whose authority lies outside ourselves. But where, on the contrary, people are convinced of the immutable laws of moral existence, society has less power over each man.

In style, some qualities depend upon the truth of sentiment and others upon grammatical correctness. It would be difficult to make the Germans understand that the main thing to look for in a work is the way it is written and that the execution should be more important than the conception. Experimental philosophy assesses a work primarily in accordance with the ingenious and lucid method in which it is presented. Idealist philosophy, on the contrary, always attracted to the center of the soul, admires only those writers who approach it.

It must also be acknowledged that the practice of burrowing into the most hidden mysteries of our being results in an inclination for what is most profound and sometimes most obscure in thought: so the Germans too often mix metaphysics with poetry.

The new philosophy inspires the need to rise to boundless thoughts and sentiments. This impulse may be favorable to genius but only to it, and it often produces rather ridiculous pretensions in those who lack genius.

The taste the Germans show for the simple, of which I have already had occasion to speak, seems to be in contradiction to their inclination for metaphysics, an inclination that arises from the need for self-knowledge and self-analysis. But this taste for the simple must also be related to the influence of a systematic doctrine, for there is philosophy in everything in Germany, even in the imagination. One of the main characteristics of the simple style is to express what is felt or thought without considering any effect or leading toward any goal; and it is in this respect that it is in harmony with the theory of the Germans regarding literature. Unlike most people, the Germans do not consider the imitation of nature to be the principal aim of art; it is ideal beauty that seems to them the main element of all masterpieces, and in this respect their poetics are in perfect accord with their philosophy.

The literary theory of the Germans differs from all others in that it does not subject writers to certain practices or tyrannical restrictions. It is a completely creative theory, a philosophy of the fine arts which, far from restraining them, seeks, like Prometheus, to steal fire from the heavens to bestow it upon poets.

It must be acknowledged, however, that there are often intrinsic disadvantages to these systems of philosophy applied to literature. German readers, accustomed to reading Kant, Fichte, etc., regard a lesser degree of obscurity as clarity itself, and the writers do not always give works of art that striking lucidity so necessary to them.

Ingenious ideas derived from theories deceive us as to the true nature of talent. One cleverly demonstrates that such and such a play should not have pleased; but it does please, so people start to condemn those who like it. One demonstrates that another play, composed in accordance with certain rules, ought to interest us; but when one wants to see it acted out, when one says, *arise and walk,* the work does not move, and so people must then condemn those who do not enjoy a play composed according to the laws of the ideal and the real. People are almost always wrong when they criticize the public's judgment in the arts, for the popular impression is more philosophical than even philosophy itself. When the learned man's ideas do not agree with this impression, it is not because these ideas are too profound but rather because they are not profound enough.

Yet it seems to me infinitely better for a country's literature that its poetics be based upon philosophical ideas, even if a bit abstract, than upon simple, superficial rules, for these rules are merely rails to prevent children from falling.

Chapter X. Influence of the New Philosophy upon the Sciences

Unquestionably the idealist philosophy leads to contemplation and, by disposing the mind to turn in upon itself, increases its ability to penetrate and persevere in intellectual labors. But is this philosophy equally favorable to the sciences, which consist of the observation of nature? The following reflections are directed to the examination of this question.

The progress of the sciences during the last century has been widely attributed to experimental philosophy, and since observation is indeed important in this domain it is believed that the more importance we attach to external things the more certain we are to attain scientific truths. But the country of Kepler and Leibniz is not to be scorned with respect to science. The principal modern discoveries, gunpowder and printing, were discovered by the Germans, yet the tendency of the mind in Germany has always been toward idealism.

The new philosophy has already exerted its influence upon the physical sciences in Germany in many respects; in the first place, the same spirit of universality that I noted among the literary men and philosophers is found among the scientists as well.

Literature spreads light upon the sciences, just as the sciences do upon literature.

Universality of knowledge necessarily leads to the desire to find the general laws of the physical order. The Germans descend from theory to experience while the French ascend from experience to theory.

Yet the Germans scholars, who are at the same time philosophers, show an extraordinary interest in the contemplation of the phenomena of this world. They do not inquire into nature haphazardly, according to the accidental course of experience; rather, they predict by thought what observation must then confirm.

The scientists of Germany may be divided into two groups: those who devote themselves entirely to observation, and those who claim the honor of anticipating the secrets of nature. The most distinguished minds of these two groups approach and understand each other, for the philosophical physicists could not scorn experience nor the profound observers deny the possible results of lofty thinking.

Experience daily leads scholars to acknowledge phenomena that were no longer believed because they were mixed with superstitions and had formerly been regarded as portents.

What we call errors and superstitions perhaps depended upon laws of the universe still unknown to us. And who knows whether there is not a germ of truth concealed in all the fables and beliefs branded with the name of madness? Certainly it does not follow that the experimental method, so necessary in the sciences, ought to be renounced. But why not provide as supreme guide for this method a wider philosophy that would embrace the universe in its entirety?

The universe resembles a poem more than a machine. If to conceive it we had to choose between the imagination and the mathematical mind, the imagination would come closer to the truth. But again, it is not necessary to choose, because all of our capacities must be applied in so important an endeavor.

Chapter XI. The Influence of the New Philosophy upon the Character of the Germans

It would appear that a system of philosophy that attributes an all-powerful influence to something that depends upon ourselves, that is, to our will, must strengthen the character and make it independent of external circumstances. But there is ground for believing that only political and religious institutions can create a public spirit and that no abstract theory is effective enough to give vigor to a nation; for, it must be confessed, the Germans of our day do not have what can be called character. They are virtuous and honest as private individuals, as fathers, as administrators. But their obliging and ingratiating eagerness before the powerful distresses those who are fond of them and who consider them the most enlightened theoretical advocates of human dignity.

The wisdom deriving from the philosophical spirit has taught them only the cause and effects of everything that happens, and it seems to them that once they have found a theory for a fact it is justified. Military spirit and patriotism have carried various nations to the highest possible degree of vigor;

but these two sources of self-sacrifice hardly exist among the Germans taken as a whole. They know scarcely anything of the military spirit except a pedantic kind of tactics that authorizes them to be beaten according to the rule-book; and of liberty they know only the subdivision into small states that, accustoming the citizens to feel weak as a nation, soon leads them to prove themselves weak as individuals too.* The respect for form is very favorable to the maintenance of law, but this respect, as it exists in Germany, instils the habit of such punctual and exact procedure that they do not even know how to open a new path to reach a goal that is just before them.

While fully recognizing that German philosophy is inadequate by itself to mold the nation, we must admit that the followers of the new school are much closer than all the others to having strength of character. They conceive of it, dream of it, desire it, yet it often escapes them. There are very few men in Germany who can even write on politics. Most of those who dabble in it are doctrinaire and very often unintelligible. When it comes to transcendental metaphysics, when one tries to plunge into the darkness of nature, no glimpse, however vague, is to be scorned, and every hunch may guide us, every approximation is valuable. But it is different with affairs of this world: it is possible to know them. They must therefore be presented with clarity. When one deals with thoughts that are boundless, obscurity of style is sometimes an indication of the reach of the mind, but obscurity in the analysis of the affairs of life only shows that one does not understand them.

* I beg to remark that this chapter, like the rest of the work, was written in the period of Germany's total subjection. Since then the Germanic nations, awakened by oppression, have lent their governments the strength they themselves lacked to resist the power of French armies and we have seen, by the heroic conduct of sovereigns and nations, the influence of opinion upon the fate of the world.

Chapter XV. Scientific Ethics

Some philosophers in Germany claim to have lent ethics the attributes of a science rigorously proved in its premises as well as in its conclusions, which allows no objection or exception once the basis is adopted.

Philosophers seek a scientific framework for everything; they seem to think that in this way they can fix the future and entirely escape the yoke of circumstances. But what frees us from it is our soul, the sincerity of our inmost love of virtue. The science of ethics can no more show us how to be honest, in all the magnificence of that word, than geometry how to draw or poetics how to invent.

It does not follow from this impossibility of discovering a science of ethics or universal signs from which it can be recognized whether its precepts are observed, that there are no positive duties to serve us as guides. Just as there is constraint and freedom in man's fate, so also must there be order and spontaneity in his conduct. Nothing pertaining to virtue can be entirely arbitrary or entirely fixed.

Part Four. Religion and Enthusiasm

Chapter I. General Considerations on Religion in Germany

The nations of Germanic descent are all naturally religious, and the zeal of this feeling has given rise to several wars among them. In Germany especially, however, people are inclined more to enthusiasm than to fanaticism. The spirit of sect necessarily reveals itself in various forms in a country where thought is exercised more than anything else. But theological discussions there do not usually involve the human passions; the various viewpoints in religion do not go beyond that ideal world where sublime peace reigns.

For a long time they were engaged in the inquiry into the tenets of Christianity; but for the last twenty years, ever since Kant's writings have strongly influenced people, there has arisen a freedom and a scale in the way of conceiving religion that do not require or reject any particular form of worship but make divine things the dominant element of life.

The expression *it is divine,* which has become customary in praising the beauties of nature and art, is an article of faith among the Germans. They are tolerant not out of indifference but because of their universality in the way they feel and conceive of religion. Indeed, every man can find among the marvels of the universe the one that speaks most powerfully to his soul. One person admires the divine in the character of a father, another in the innocence of a child, another in the heavenly look of Raphael's virgins, in music, in poetry, in nature—it does not matter; everyone is in agreement if animated by the rule of religion, the genius of the world and of every human being.

Religion is nothing if it is not everything, if it does not pervade existence, if we do not constantly sustain in our soul this belief in the invisible, this devotion, this elevation of desire that must triumph over the base inclinations to which our nature exposes us.

Chapter II. Protestantism

When we read the details of the deaths of John Huss and Jerome of Prague, the precursors of the Reformation, we see a striking example of what characterizes the leaders of Protestantism in Germany: the union of a lively faith with the spirit of inquiry. Their rationality did not harm their faith, nor their faith their rationality; their faculties of mind acted together.

Of all the great men Germany has produced, Luther is the one whose character was the most German: his firmness was a bit crude; his conviction reached the point of obstinacy; courage in spirit was in him the basis of courage in action. His passions did not divert him from abstract study; and though he attacked certain abuses and dogmas as prejudices, it was not philosophical unbelief but his own fanaticism that inspired him.

Nevertheless, the Reformation introduced religious inquiry into the world. For some, skepticism has resulted from it, but for others a firmer belief in religious truths: the human mind had reached an era when it had to inquire in order to believe. The discovery of printing, the increase in knowledge, and the philosophical investigation of the truth no longer allowed that blind faith that formerly suited people so well. Religious enthusiasm could not revive except through inquiry and thought.

It is essential to assert this above everything: that if Northern Germany is the country where theological issues were the most stirred up, it is at the same time the one in which religious feelings are the most universal. The national character bears their impression, and artistic and literary genius draws all their inspiration from them. Finally, religion in Northern Germany has, among the common people, an ideal and gentle character that is surprising in a country whose customs are generally thought to be very crude.

Chapter IV. Catholicism

The Catholic religion is more tolerant in Germany than in any other country. The Peace of Westphalia having fixed the rights of the various religions, they no longer fear mutual encroachments; moreover, the mixture of religions in a large number of cities has willy-nilly given them the opportunity to know one another.

Protestantism being much more favorable to enlightenment than Catholicism, the Catholics in Germany have adopted a sort of defensive attitude very harmful to the progress of ideas. In countries where the Catholic religion ruled alone, like France and Italy, people knew how to reconcile it with literature and the fine arts, but in Germany, where the Protestants have monopolized literary and philosophical study through their universities and their natural inclination, the Catholics consider themselves obliged to counter with a certain reluctance that virtually extinguishes every means of distinction in the field of the imagination and of thought. Music is the only one of the fine arts raised to a higher level of perfection in Southern Germany than in Northern.

Among the Catholics in Germany there is a genuine, serene, generous piety, but there are no famous preachers or religious writers to mention; nothing there stirs the impulses of the soul. Religion is taken as a matter of fact in which enthusiasm has no part; it might be said that in a religion so well consolidated the afterlife itself becomes a demonstrated truth about which people no longer bother to think.

There are in the human mind two very distinct forces, one inspiring the need to believe, the other the need to inquire. Neither of these faculties should be favored at the expense of the other. Protestantism and Catholicism do not arise from the existence of the Popes and a Luther; to attribute history to accidents is a poor way of considering it. Protestantism and Catholicism both exist in the human heart; they are two social forces that develop in nations because they live in every human being.

Chapter VIII. The Spirit of Sect in Germany

Metaphysical systems are hardly dangerous in themselves; they do not become so until they are combined with the interests of ambition. Thus if one wishes to change the system one must deal with these interests. But people who can eagerly embrace a view independently of the effects it might have are always of a noble character.

The philosophical and religious sects that, under various names, have existed in Germany have had scarcely any connection with political affairs; the kind of talent required to draw men into effective movements is rarely displayed in this country. People may argue about Kant's philosophy, theological questions, idealism, or empiricism without any result but books.

The spirit of sect and the spirit of party differ in many respects. The spirit of party presents views in their most striking concrete form in order to make the populace understand them; but the spirit of sect, especially in Germany, always tends to the most abstract. In the spirit of party, one must recognize the point of view of the populace in order to place oneself in it; the Germans think only of theory and they would follow it even were it to get lost in the clouds. The spirit of party arouses certain common passions in people that unite them in a mass; the Germans subdivide everything through explanation, distinction, and commentary. The spirit of sect aspires only to convince; the spirit of party seeks to rally. The spirit of sect argues about ideas; the spirit of party seeks power over men. There is discipline in the spirit of party but anarchy in the spirit of sect. Authority of any sort has practically nothing to fear from the spirit of sect; it is satisfied by leaving it wide latitude for thought. But the spirit of party is not so easy to satisfy; it does not content itself with intellectual conquests in which each person may create an empire for himself without dispossessing a single occupant.

Three types of religious and philosophical sects in Germany must be distinguished. First, the various Christian denominations which existed, mainly at the time of the Reformation, when people turned toward theological questions. Second, the secret societies. And last, the adepts of some personal doctrines led by one man. The Anabaptists and Moravians must be placed in the first group; in the second, the oldest secret society, the Freemasons; and in the third, the various kinds of visionaries.

Chapter X. Enthusiasm

Many people are prejudiced against enthusiasm. They confuse it with fanaticism, and this is a great mistake. Fanaticism is an exclusive passion whose object is an opinion. Enthusiasm is concerned with universal harmony; it is the love of the beautiful, the elevation of the soul, and the enjoyment of self-sacrifice all combined into one sentiment that has grandeur and tranquillity. The meaning of this word among the Greeks is the noblest definition of it: enthusiasm means *God in us.* Indeed, when man's life is emotionally overflowing it has something of the divine.

Everything that leads us to sacrifice our own comfort or life is almost always related to enthusiasm. For the direct route of selfish reason must be to regard one's self as the object of all one's efforts and to value nothing in the world but health, wealth, and power.

Far from its excesses being feared, enthusiasm probably leads in general to a contemplative inclination that weakens the power to act; the Germans are proof of this. No nation is more capable of feeling and thinking, but when it is time to decide, the very vastness of their ideas impairs their decisiveness of character. Strength of character and enthusiasm differ in many respects. Enthusiasm must guide one's selection of a goal, but character should guide the progress toward it. Thought is nothing without enthusiasm, nor action without strength of character. Enthusiasm is everything for literary nations; character is everything for practical ones. Free nations need both.

Chapter XI. The Influence of Enthusiasm upon Learning

This chapter is in some ways a summary of my whole book, for since enthusiasm is the truly distinctive quality of the German language, its influence upon learning may be judged by the progress of the human mind in Germany.

The philosophers inspired by enthusiasm are perhaps those who are the most precise and patient in their studies. At the same time it is they who dream least of attracting attention; they love science for itself.

It may be said with some reason that enthusiasm leads to a dogmatic spirit. When people are very much devoted to their ideas they want to connect everything to them; but in general it is easier to deal with honest views than with those adopted out of vanity.

Enthusiasm has often been accused of leading to error, but a superficial concern is probably much more misleading; for, to penetrate to the essence of things, we need to be stirred to a passionate consideration of them. I believe it can be affirmed that we shall never find the truth except through elevation of the soul.

Chapter XII. The Influence of Enthusiasm upon Happiness

It is time to speak of happiness! I have very carefully avoided this word because, especially for the last century or so, it has been identified with such material pleasures, such selfish lives, and such narrow calculations that its very image has been profaned. But it may be confidently said that enthusiasm is the sentiment that affords the most happiness, the only one that really affords it, the only one that can enable us to bear our lot in all situations in which destiny may put us.

"Oh, France! land of glory and of love! if one day enthusiasm should be extinguished on your soil, if calculation should govern everything and cold reason alone inspire even contempt for danger, of what use will be your beautiful skies, your brilliant minds, your fertile character? An agile brain, a skillfully managed impetuosity, might make you master of the world but the only trace you would leave upon it would be torrents of sand, as terrible as the waves and as barren as the desert."*

* This last statement is the one that stirred the police to the greatest indignation against my book; but it seems to me that it could not have offended Frenchmen.

Section VIII

England

This Section, bearing my own title, is from Part Six of Considérations sur les principaux événements de la Révolution française, *which Madame de Staël completed in 1816 and which was published posthumously in 1818. The individual chapters retain Madame de Staël's titles.*—Ed.

Chapter III. The Prosperity of England and the Causes That Have Hitherto Increased It
Chapter IV. Liberty and Public Spirit among the English
Chapter V. Learning, Religion, and Morality among the English
Chapter VI. English Society and Its Relation to the Social Order
Chapter VII. The Conduct of English Government Outside of England

Chapter III. The Prosperity of England and the Causes That Have Hitherto Increased It

Reaching England,[1] I was thinking of no particular person: I knew hardly anyone there, but I went with confidence. I was persecuted by an enemy of liberty, so I believed myself certain of honorable sympathy in a country whose every institution was in harmony with my political sentiments. I counted much, also, on the memory of my father to protect me, and I was not deceived. The waves of the North Sea, which I crossed in coming from Sweden, still filled me with terror as I made out from afar the green island that alone had resisted the enslavement of Europe. Those who will not acknowledge the influence of liberty in the power of England constantly repeat that the English would have been conquered by Bonaparte, like all the Continental nations, had they not been protected by the sea. This opinion cannot be refuted by experience. I have no doubt that if, by a stroke of Leviathan, Great Britain had been joined to the European continent, it would certainly have suffered more and its wealth would have diminished. But the public spirit of a free nation is such that it would never have yielded to the yoke of foreigners.

From Harwich to London one travels a highway about seventy miles long bordered almost entirely by country houses to the right and left: a succession of dwellings with gardens, interrupted by towns. Almost everyone is well-clothed, hardly a cottage is in decay; even the animals seem peaceful and thriving, as if there were rights for them, too, in this great structure of social order. The price of everything is necessarily very high, but most of these prices are fixed; there is in this country such an aversion for anything arbitrary that, besides

[1] *In June 1813, while England was at war with Napoleon.*—Ed.

the law itself, a rule and then a custom are established to ensure, as far as possible, in the smallest details, some degree of exactness and stability. The high cost of living resulting from extremely high taxes is of course a disadvantage. But assuming the war was absolutely necessary, what other nation—that is, what other form of government—could be equal to it?

The amount accomplished in England through private contributions is enormous: hospitals, educational establishments, missions, Christian societies were not only maintained but increased during the war; and foreigners who underwent disasters from it—the Swiss, Germans, Dutch—constantly received private aid from England, the result of voluntary gifts.

But to what are these miracles of liberal prosperity to be attributed? To liberty—that is, to the nation's trust in a government that makes publicity the first principle of finances, in a government enlightened by discussion and by freedom of the press. The nation, which cannot be deceived under such an arrangement, knows the use of the taxes it pays, and public credit supports the unbelievable weight of the English debt. If something proportionately similar were tried in any non-representative state on the European continent, it would not be able to go far in such an undertaking. Five hundred thousand owners of government bonds constitute a strong guarantee of payment of the debt in a country where each man's opinion and interest is influential.

The government never meddles in anything that private individuals can do just as well. Respect for individual freedom extends to the exercise of everyone's abilities, and the people are so anxious to manage their own affairs, when it is possible, that in many respects London lacks the police necessary for the convenience of the city because the ministers may not encroach upon the local authorities.

Political security, without which there can be neither credit nor capital accumulation, is still not enough to develop all the resources of a nation: emulation must stimulate men to labor, while the law assures them of its fruit. Commerce and industry must be honored, not by rewards to this or that individual—this presupposes two classes in a country, one of which thinks it has the right to reward the other—but by an order of things that allows each man to rise to the highest level if he deserves it. In fact, the absurd prejudice that forbade the nobility of France to go into business did more harm to the growth of French fortunes than any other abuse of the Old Regime. In England peerages have been recently granted to leading businessmen. Once peers, they do not remain in commerce, because they are expected to serve the country in another way; but it is their function as government officials, and not the prejudices of caste, that divorces them from business, into which the younger sons of the highest nobility enter without hesitation when circumstances call them to it. The same family often has peers on one side and on the other the most ordinary merchants of some provincial town. This political order enhances all the faculties of every individual, because there are no limits to the advantages that wealth and talent can bring, and because the lowest English citizen, if he is worthy of being the highest, is barred from no marriage, employment, society, or title.

All classes of well-bred men in England meet often in various committees engaged in some venture or charity supported by private contributions. Publicity in all matters is a principle so widely accepted that, though the English are by nature the most reserved of men and the most reluctant to speak before others, there are almost always, in the rooms where the committees meet, seats for spectators and a platform from which the speakers address the assembly.

I attended one of these discussions, in which the reasons

calculated to stimulate the listeners' generosity were forcefully presented. It concerned the sending of help to the people of Leipzig after the battle fought beneath its walls. The first speaker was the Duke of York, second son of the king. After the Duke of York, the Duke of Sussex, the fifth son of the king, who expresses himself with much elegance and ease, also spoke in his turn; and the most beloved and respected man in all of England, Mr. Wilberforce,[1] could hardly make himself heard above the applause. Humble men, and with no other status in society than their wealth or devotion to humanity, followed these illustrious names. The listeners contributed as they left, and considerable sums were the result of this meeting. Thus are formed the ties that strengthen the unity of the nation and thus the social order bases itself upon reason and humanity.

The object of these worthy assemblies is not merely to encourage works of charity; some of them serve especially to strengthen the union of the nobility and the businessmen, the nation and the government.

Chapter IV. Liberty and Public Spirit among the English

The greatest support of liberty is individual security, and nothing is finer than English legislation in this respect. A criminal trial is a horrible spectacle anywhere. In England the excellence of the procedure, the humanity of the judges, the precautions of every kind taken to protect the lives of the innocent, and the means of defense of the guilty inject a feeling of admiration into the anguish of such a trial. The ad-

[1] *William Wilberforce (1759–1833), British statesman and reformer, was a leader in the movement to abolish the slave trade.*—Ed.

mirable institution of the jury, which goes back in England to remote antiquity, introduces equity into justice.

English civil law is much less worthy of praise; the trials are too costly and too long. It will certainly be improved with time, as it already has been in several respects, for what distinguishes English government above all is the possibility of orderly improvement.

"Very well," exclaim the enemies of all public virtue, "even if praise of England were fully warranted, it would only mean that it is a skillfully and wisely governed country, just as any other country might be. But it is not free in the way that the *philosophes* understand freedom, for the ministers are the masters of everything, there as elsewhere. They buy the votes of Parliament in such a way as always to assure themselves a majority, and the whole English constitution of which people speak with admiration is nothing but the art of putting political venality to work."

Can anyone honestly convince himself that the English ministers give money to the members of the House of Commons or of the higher chamber to vote with the government? How could the English ministers, who account for public funds so exactly, find sums large enough to corrupt men of such great wealth, to say nothing of their character?

Fidelity to party is one of the virtues based upon public spirit, from which comes the greatest advantage for English liberty. If tomorrow the ministers with whom one voted go out of office, those to whom they have given posts leave with them. A man would be disgraced in England if he parted from his political allies for his private interest. One never hears the same mouth uttering two opposite opinions; but in the present state of things in England differences are a matter of shades rather than colors. The Tories, it has been said, approve liberty and love the monarchy, while the Whigs approve the monarchy and love liberty. But between these two parties there is no question as to a republic or a monarchy, the old or the new dynasty, liberty or servitude.

For nearly fifty years the members of the Opposition[2] have held ministerial office only three or four years, yet their fidelity to party has not been shaken.

The existence of a Government party and an Opposition party, though it cannot be prescribed by law, is an essential support of liberty based on the nature of things. In every country where you see an assembly of men always in agreement, be certain that there is a despotism, or that despotism will be the result of unanimity if it is not the cause of it. Now, since power and the favors it disposes have attraction for men, liberty could exist only with this fidelity to party which imposes, so to speak, a discipline of honor in the ranks of the deputies enrolled under various banners.

But if opinions are settled in advance, how can truth and eloquence influence the assembly? How can the majority change when circumstances require it to do so, and of what use is debate if no one can vote according to his conviction? That is not the situation. What is called fidelity to party means that one must not separate one's personal interests from the interests of one's political allies, nor deal separately with the men in power. But it often happens that circumstances or arguments influence the bulk of the assembly and that the considerable number of neutrals, that is, those who do not play an active role in politics, are able to change the majority. It is in the nature of English government that the ministers cannot stay in office without this majority in their favor. Yet Mr. Pitt, though he temporarily lost it at the time of the King's first illness, could remain in office because public opinion, which was favorable to him, enabled him to dissolve Parlia-

[2] *The Whigs.*—Ed.

ment and to resort to a new election. In short, opinion rules in England; it is this that establishes the liberty of a state.

Enlightenment and the strength of public spirit are a more than adequate answer to the arguments of those who maintain that, if England were a Continental power, the army would encroach upon its liberty. It is undoubtedly an advantage to the English that their strength lies in the navy rather than in ground forces. It requires greater knowledge to be a captain of a ship than a colonel, and the habits acquired at sea do not lead to the desire to interfere in the internal affairs of one's country. But if nature, turned lavish, created ten Lord Wellingtons and if the world saw ten more Battles of Waterloo, it would not occur to those who so readily give their lives for their country to turn their power against it; if they did, they would face an insuperable obstacle in men just as brave as themselves and more enlightened, who detest the military spirit though they admire and practice warlike qualities.

The kind of prejudice that convinced the French nobility that they could serve their country only in a military career does not exist at all in England. A great many sons of peers are lawyers; the bar shares the respect felt for the law, and in all walks of life civil occupations are respected. In such a country people need not yet fear the inroads of military power; only unenlightened nations have a blind admiration for the sword.

Chapter V. Learning, Religion, and Morality among the English

Sound political ideas spread among all the classes and a general training in the sciences and literature constitute a nation's knowledge. In the first of these respects, the English have no rival in Europe. In the second, I do not know of anyone but the North Germans who can be compared to them. But the English have an added advantage, which can arise only from their institutions: the leading class of society devotes itself to learning as much as does the next one.

In England the institutions favor all kinds of intellectual progress. Juries, the administration of counties and towns, elections, and the newspapers afford the whole nation a large share of concern in public affairs. From this it follows that the nation is better informed and that, taken at random, it would be more worth while to discuss political issues with an English farmer than with most men, even the most enlightened, on the Continent. This admirable common sense, based on justice and security, is found nowhere but in England or in the country that resembles it, America. Thinking must remain foreign to men who have no rights; for as soon as they saw the truth they would be unhappy and soon after rebellious. It must also be admitted that in a country where armed might has almost always rested in the navy, and where commerce has been the leading occupation, there is necessarily greater knowledge than where national defense is entrusted to line troops and industry is almost entirely directed toward the cultivation of the earth. Commerce, linking men to the whole world's interests, broadens one's ideas, exercises one's judgment and, through the multiplicity and variety of transactions, makes one constantly appreciate the necessity for justice. In countries where there is nothing but agriculture, the bulk of the population may well be composed of serfs attached to the soil and bereft of all education. But what good are enslaved and illiterate businessmen? A maritime and commercial country is thus by its nature more learned than any other. Yet there is still much to be done to provide the people of England with an adequate education. A large portion of the lower class cannot yet read or write. It is, very likely, in order to remedy this evil that the new methods of Bel and Lancaster[3] are so eagerly received, because they may well put education within the reach of the poor. The ordinary people are perhaps better educated in Switzerland, Sweden, and in several states of Northern Germany, but there is in none of these countries the strength of liberty that will save England, we must hope, from the reaction produced by the Revolution in France.

Thanks to tolerance, political institutions, and freedom of the press, there is more respect for religion and morals in England than in any other country in Europe. In France people like to say that it is out of respect for religion and morals that there have always been censors. Yet it is enough to compare the character of literature in England since freedom of the press was established there with the various writings that appeared under the arbitrary rule of Charles II, and of the Regent or of Louis XV in France. Licentiousness in writings was carried to a horrifying degree among the French during the last century. It is the same in Italy, where the press has nevertheless been subjected to the most burdensome restrictions. Ignorance in the general population and a dissolute independence among the superior minds is always the result of coercion.

English literature is certainly the one with the most works of a philosophical nature. Scotland to this day still has very powerful writers in this *genre;* the leading one is Dugald Stewart, who in retirement does not flag in the search for truth. Literary criticism is carried to the highest point in the reviews, especially that of Edinburgh, where writers who may

[3] *Sic. Andrew Bell (1753–1832) and Joseph Lancaster (1778–1838) were British educators who devised inexpensive systems to teach the poor, using "monitors" already taught to help the teachers.*—Ed.

be famous in their own right—Jeffrey, Playfair, Mackintosch[4] —do not disdain to enlighten authors by the judgments they make upon them. The most informed writers on questions in jurisprudence and political economy, such as Bentham, Malthus, and Brougham,[5] are more numerous in England than anywhere else, because they have the justified hope that their ideas will be put into effect.

English poetry, which is fostered neither by irreligion or the spirit of faction, nor by license in morals, is nevertheless rich and lively and does not experience the decline that successively threatens almost every literature in Europe. Sensibility and imagination preserve the immortal youth of the soul. We see a new age of poetry arising in England because enthusiasm is not extinguished and because nature, love, and fatherland still exert great power there. Earlier Cowper, and now Rogers, Moore, Thomas Campbell,[6] Walter Scott, Lord Byron, in various *genres* and degrees, are preparing a new age of glory for English poetry. Whereas everything on the Continent is in decline, the eternal spring of beauty still flows from free earth.

In what realm is Christianity more respected than in England? Where is more attention paid to its propagation? From where else do so many missionaries leave for all parts of the world?

The Reformation, among the English, put enlightenment in perfect harmony with religious sentiments. That is a great advantage for this country; the high degree of piety people can

[4] *Sic. Sir James Mackintosh, philosopher and lawyer, whose company Madame de Staël enjoyed very much in London; Francis Jeffrey (1773–1850), a founder and editor of the* Edinburgh Review; *John Playfair (1748–1819), scientist, philosopher, contributor to the Review.*—Ed.

[5] *Henry Peter Brougham (1778–1868), British lawyer and statesman, a founder of the* Edinburgh Review.—Ed.

[6] *William Cowper (1731–1800), Samuel Rogers (1763–1855), Thomas Moore (1779–1852), Thomas Campbell (1777–1844).*—Ed.

reach there always leads to strictness of morality but hardly ever to superstition.

In a religious country there must also be good morals, yet the passions of the English are very strong; it is a great error to believe they have a calm disposition merely because they have habitually cold manners. No people are more impulsive in the great affairs of life; but they resemble the dogs of Albania, sent by Porus to Alexander, who were too proud to fight any adversary but the lion.[7] The English take leave of their apparent calm and surrender to excesses of every kind. They seek out dangers, try to do extraordinary things, and want to experience strong feelings. Liveliness of imagination and restraint of customs make such excesses necessary; but these customs themselves are based upon a great respect for morality.

Freedom of the press, which some people would represent to us as contrary to the refinement of morals, is one of its most efficacious causes. Everything in England is known so well and discussed so much that the truth is bound to be reached in all things. One might submit to the judgment of the English public as to that of a friend who might share the intimacies of one's life and the *nuances* of one's character in order to weigh every action fairly according to each individual's condition. The more power public opinion has in England, the more boldness one needs to become free of it. So the women

[7] *The region we know as Albania was famous in classical times for its large Mollosian dogs. But Madame de Staël seems to have confused them with a powerful breed of Indian dogs mentioned by several classical writers. These dogs, believed to come from tigers, were said to prefer to fight only lions in order to prove their pedigree. Alexander was given such dogs as a gift not by Porus, as Madame de Staël says, but by Sophytes, another Indian king whom he conquered.* (*See J. W. M'Crindle,* The Invasion of India by Alexander the Great as described by Arrian, Q. Curtius, Diodoros, Plutarch and Justin, *New Edn., London, 1896, pp. 280, 363–64.*)—Ed.

who defy it do so dramatically. But this is rare even in the upper class, the only one that sometimes affords examples of it. On the second level, among the people of the provinces, there are only happy marriages and private virtues.

Chapter VI. English Society and Its Relation to the Social Order

Although England has the most enlightened men and the most interesting women, the delights of society are seldom found there. If a foreigner understands English well and is admitted to small parties made up of superior men, he tastes, if he deserves them, the highest pleasures that communication with thoughtful beings can afford. But society in England does not consist of these intellectual treats. In London people are always invited to immense gatherings, where they elbow one another as in the pit. Women are the majority there, but usually the crowd is so large that even their beauty has not enough space to be seen, let alone any pleasure of the mind.

Such gatherings come from the necessity of admitting a very large number of persons to the circle of one's acquaintances. The number of social callers an English lady receives is sometimes twelve hundred persons. French society was infinitely more exclusive. The aristocratic spirit that governed the formation of groups was favorable to elegance and amusement but not at all in harmony with the nature of a free state.

The wealthy English landlords, for the most part, perform public functions on their estates. Wishing to be elected members of Parliament, or to influence the election of their relatives and friends, they spend eight or nine months in the countryside. The result is that the practices of society are entirely suspended for two thirds of the year. Familiar and agreeable relations are established only when people see one another constantly. In the part of London where high society lives there are months in summer and fall when the city is so empty that it seems to have been struck by a contagious disease.

When the business of the state comes within everyone's province, the conversation that necessarily attracts people most is the one whose subject is public affairs. In that subject, what matters is not mental agility but the genuine importance of things. In France the art of being pleasant consisted of never exhausting a subject and never dwelling on those that did not interest women. In England, women never actively join a conversation; men have not accustomed them to take part in general conversation. A mistress of the house, unlike among the French, does not think she is obliged to direct the conversation or to take care that it does not flag.

In the country with the most publicity, state secrets are better guarded than anywhere else. There are no intermediaries, so to speak, between the newspapers and the Cabinet, and the Cabinet is the most discreet in Europe. There is no case of a woman having learned—or at least having revealed—what was to be done. In a country where domestic morals are so strict, married men do not have mistresses—and it is only mistresses who know secrets and, especially, who reveal them.

It is difficult to explain fully what is called *mauvaise honte* (*shyness*) in England, that is, the hesitation that suppresses the expression of natural good will; one often meets the coldest manners in persons who would prove to be most generous toward you if you needed them. The English are at least as ill at ease among themselves as among foreigners. They address one another only after having been introduced; familiarity becomes established only after a long time. In England sons and daughters, after marriage, almost never live in the same house as their parents. The *chez soi* (*home*) is the preference of the English, and perhaps this inclination has helped to make them hate any political system that permits exile or arbitrary arrest. Every household has its separate dwelling, and London is composed of a great number of small houses shut tight like boxes, which are scarcely easier to penetrate. There are not even many brothers and sisters who go to dine at each other's houses without being invited. This formality does not make life very amusing. The English people's taste for travel is partly the result of their desire to escape from the restraint of their customs as well as of the need to flee their region's fog.

It cannot be denied, however, that all these honorable motives are mixed with some faults, the natural result of every large association of people. First, though there is more pride than vanity in England, people rather like to distinguish by manners the social classes that most institutions bring together. There is some selfishness in behavior and sometimes in character. Wealth and the tastes it brings are the cause of it: so well can they manage everything, that people are unwilling to inconvenience themselves in anything. Family ties, so intimate in marriage, are much less so in other relations because the entails give eldest sons too much freedom from their parents, and also separate the interests of the younger brothers from those of the heir of the fortune. The entailed property necessary to maintain the peerage should perhaps not be extended to other classes of owners; it is a vestige of feudalism whose unfortunate consequences should, if possible, be reduced. Another result of it is that most women are without a dowry and that, in countries where the institution of convents cannot exist, there are a number of young ladies whose mothers have a great desire to marry them off and who may with reason be anxious about their future. This disadvantage, produced by the unequal apportioning of wealth, is felt strongly in society; unmarried men unduly occupy the attention of women; and wealth in general, far from increasing the pleasure of society, necessarily injures it.

In a nation where everything is strongly marked, as in England, the contrasts are all the more striking. Fashion has a remarkable influence upon the habits of life, yet there is no nation in which there are so many examples of what is called *eccentricity,* that is, an entirely original way of life, one that disregards the opinions of others. They do nothing by halves and pass suddenly from servitude toward the least important practices to the most complete indifference toward what will be said of them. Yet the fear of ridicule is one of the main causes of the coldness that prevails in English society. In this country where people are most attached to freedom of the press and least troubled by newspaper attacks, the jests of society are very much dreaded. This is why people put themselves forward as little as possible in the presence of others. In no country in the world, I believe, have reserve and silence been carried so far as in some circles in England; and if one falls into these circles it is very easy to understand how an aversion for life can seize those confined to them. But outside of these frozen circles, what satisfaction of the soul and mind can one not find in English society if one is well placed there!

Chapter VII. The Conduct of English Government Outside of England

In expressing, so far as I have been able, my profound admiration for the English nation, I have continually attributed its superiority over the rest of Europe to its political institutions. It remains for me to present an unfortunate proof of this statement: where these institutions do not govern, the English government warrants the same reproaches that absolute power has always merited upon this earth. When the English carry out military or diplomatic functions on the Continent, it is still likely that men brought up in the atmosphere of all the virtues act there as individuals. But it is possible that power, which corrupts almost all men when they go beyond the circle ruled by law, has misled many Englishmen when they have been accountable for their conduct abroad only to ministers and not to the nation. Indeed, that nation, so enlightened otherwise, is ill-informed about what happens on the Continent. It lives within the bosom of the fatherland, if we may put it that way, like each man in his house; and only in the course of time does it learn through its blood and treasure the history of Europe, in which its ministers often play only too big a role. So we must conclude from this that every country must always protect itself from the influence of foreigners, whoever they may be. For nations that are most free at home may have leaders who are very envious of the prosperity of other states and so may become the oppressors of their neighbors if they find a favorable opportunity for it.

But let us see how much truth there is in what is said about the behavior of the English outside their country. When they were obliged, unfortunately for themselves, to send troops to the Continent, those troops observed the most perfect discipline. The honesty of the English army cannot be disputed; they have been known to pay their bills in the enemy's country even more reliably than the enemy did in his own country, and they never neglect to mix the solicitude of humanity with the misfortunes of war. The splendor of English bravery, it must be recognized, is never dimmed by cruelty or pillage.

The military force transported to the colonies, and especially to India, should not be held responsible for the acts of authority that may be justly criticized. It is the civil servants who were to blame for enriching themselves by illegal means. Indeed, their conduct, in the early years of the conquest of India, deserves the greatest censure and provides another proof of what cannot be too often repeated—that every man entrusted with the command over others obeys nothing but his passions if he himself is not subject to the law. But since the trial of Mr. Hastings,[8] the eyes of the English nation being directed toward the horrible abuses tolerated in India until then, public opinion has obliged the government to attend to them.

England has adopted the principle of governing the inhabitants of the country according to their own laws. It may be hoped that the example of the English will sufficiently form these people so that they may one day claim independence. All enlightened men in England would approve the loss of India through the very benefits the government has bestowed there. It is one of the prejudices of the Continent to regard English power as dependent upon the possession of India. This Oriental empire is virtually a luxury; it contributes more to splendor than to real strength. England lost its American provinces, and its trade has been increased by it. If the colonies still remaining to them declared themselves independent, it would still maintain its naval and commercial superiority, because it has within itself a source of action, progress, and endurance that always puts it above external circumstances.

[8] *Warren Hastings (1732–1818) was the first governor general of British India. His trial, which began in 1787, lasted a long time and involved some of the leading statesmen in England. He was acquitted in 1795.*—Ed.

Section IX

Russia

The following observations on Russia are translated from Part Two of Madame de Staël's Dix années d'exil. *Her son was the first to edit and publish this work, with his own omissions, additions, and division into chapters; I have retained this division and the titles of the chapters as well. For a long time his edition remained the only one; see, for example, Madame de Staël's* Oeuvres Complètes, *Vol. 3, pp. 335 ff. The following translation of the work, however, is made from the text re-established from the original manuscripts by Paul Gautier. The only serious discrepancy between the two versions that arises in these excerpts is indicated below in a footnote to the last sentence in the first paragraph of Chapter XVII.*—Ed.

Chapter X. Arrival in Russia
Chapter XI. Kiev
Chapter XII. The Road from Kiev to Moscow
Chapter XIII. Appearance of the Country. Character of the Russian People
Chapter XIV. Moscow
Chapter XVII. The Imperial Family

Chapter X. Arrival in Russia

People are hardly accustomed to regarding Russia as the freest state in Europe, but the yoke the Emperor of France imposes upon all the states of the Continent is such that one thinks he is in a republic upon arriving in a country where Napoleon's tyranny can no longer make itself felt. It was on the fourteenth of July that I entered Russia; this anniversary of the first day of the Revolution struck me with special force: thus, for me, the circle of French history that began on the fourteenth of July, 1789, was closed.[1]

In the Russian empire, so falsely labeled barbarous, I had impressions of only nobility and gentleness. May my gratitude draw down further blessings upon this nation and its sovereign! I entered Russia at a moment when the French army had already penetrated very far into Russian territory,[2] yet no persecution or restraint impeded the foreigner for an instant. Neither I nor my companions knew a word of Russian; we spoke only French, the language of the enemy who was devastating the realm. Well, in this state our journey was safe and easy, so great is the hospitality of the nobility and the populace in Russia!

The French army was making rapid progress, and one is so accustomed to seeing the French victorious over all abroad, though at home they cannot resist any kind of yoke, that I

[1] *Madame de Staël entered Russia on Bastille Day, 1812. On the same day, five years later, she died. It was on July 14, 1789, marking the beginning of the French Revolution, that the Bastille was stormed because of popular outrage at the dismissal of Jacques Necker, Madame de Staël's father, from his post as director general of finances under Louis XVI. He was recalled and then resigned permanently in 1790.*—Ed.

[2] *Napoleon and his Grand Army entered Russia in June 1812, several weeks before Madame de Staël. He reached abandoned Moscow on September 14, a week after she had left St. Petersburg for Finland.*—Ed.

could reasonably fear to run into them on the very road to Moscow. What a strange destiny for me—first, to flee from the French, among whom I was born and who had carried my father in victory, and then to flee from them even to the borders of Asia!

Chapter XI. Kiev

Determined to continue my journey through Russia, I entered the Ukraine, of which Kiev is the capital. It had already been the capital of Russia, for that empire began by establishing its capital in the South. At that time the Russians had continual contact with the Greeks established at Constantinople and in general with the peoples of the Orient, whose customs they have assumed in many respects. The Ukraine is a very fertile country but not at all pleasant: you see great plains of wheat which seem to be cultivated by invisible hands, so rare are the houses and the inhabitants. In approaching Kiev or most of what are called cities in Russia, one must not expect to see anything like the cities of the West; the country roads are not better maintained and the cottages do not portend a more populated area. On arriving in Kiev, the first thing I set eyes on was a cemetery: this is how I learned that I was near a place where men were gathered together. Most of the houses in Kiev look like tents, and from afar the city resembles a camp. One cannot help thinking that the movable dwellings of the Tartars were the model for the construction of these wooden houses, which do not appear to be very solid either. In the midst of these huts, however, palaces rise, particularly churches whose green and gilded cupolas strike the eye especially.

The Russians never pass in front of a church without making the sign of the cross, and their long beards add much to the religious expression of their faces. They mostly wear a large blue robe tightened around the waist with a red sash; women's clothes also have something Asian about them, and one notices the taste for lively colors that comes to us from countries where the sun is so beautiful that people like to enhance its brilliance with things it shines upon. I quickly took such a liking to this Oriental clothing that I regretted seeing Russians dressed like other Europeans. It seemed to me then that they were about to enter that vast uniformity of Napoleon's despotism, which first presents every nation with conscription, then war taxes, then the Napoleonic Code, in order to govern entirely different nations in the same way.

The Russians, as I see it, have much more in common with the peoples of the South, or rather the Orient, than with those of the North. Their European traits pertain to the manners of the Court, which are the same in every country. But their nature is Oriental. One feels oneself, in Russia, at the gate of another land, close to the Orient from which so many religious creeds have emerged, and which still contains within its bosom incredible stores of perseverance and contemplation.

Chapter XII. The Road from Kiev to Moscow

I have seen nothing barbaric in these people. On the contrary, their manners have something elegant and gentle that is not found elsewhere. I am quite aware that one may reasonably raise, in objection to my view, the great atrocities found in Russian history. But, first, I should place the blame for them upon the Boyars, depraved by the despotism they practiced or suffered, rather than upon the nation itself. Moreover, political dissension, in all places and times, perverts the national character. Nothing in history is more deplorable than a succession of masters elevated and overturned by crime. But such is the inevitable condition of absolute power upon this earth.

If tyranny had on its side only its fully convinced advocates, it could never maintain itself. The astonishing thing, which more than anything else reveals human wretchedness, is that most ordinary men are at the service of success. They do not have the power to think beyond a bare fact, and when an oppressor has triumphed and a victim is destroyed, they hasten to justify not the tyrant, precisely, but the fate of which he is the instrument. Weakness of mind and character is no doubt the cause of this servility, but there is also in man a certain need to justify fate, whatever it may be, as if that were a way to live in peace with it.

Everywhere in Europe one sees the contrast between wealth and poverty, but in Russia neither the one nor the other, so to speak, is conspicuous. The populace are not poor; the upper class can, when necessary, lead the same life as the populace. What characterizes this country is the mixture of the severest hardships and the most exquisite pleasures. Those very noblemen whose houses combine the most striking luxuries from various parts of the world live, while traveling, on much worse food than do our French peasants and can endure a very disagreeable physical existence not only in war but in many circumstances of life. The severity of the climate, the marshlands, forests, and deserts, which make up a large part of the country, put man in a struggle against nature. What the English call *comfort,* and what we call *l'aisance,* is hardly to be found in Russia. You will find nothing of any kind perfect enough to satisfy the fancy of the Russian nobles. But when this poetry of abundance falls short, they drink hydromel, sleep on a plank, and travel day and night in an open carriage without missing the luxury to which one would think them accustomed. They love wealth for its magnificence rather than for the pleasures it affords; in this too they are like Orientals, who practice hospitality toward strangers, overwhelm them with presents, and often neglect their own ordinary comfort. This is one of the reasons that explain the great courage with which they have borne the ruin inflicted upon them by the burning of Moscow. More accustomed to external pomp than to solicitude for themselves, they are not debilitated by luxury; to give away money satisfies their pride as much as or more than lavish spending. A gigantic quality in all things characterizes this nation; ordinary dimensions do not at all apply to it. I do not mean by this that neither true greatness nor stability are to be found in it. But the boldness, the imagination, of the Russians knows no bounds. Among them everything is colossal rather than proportional, audacious rather than thoughtful, and if the target is not hit it is because it is overshot.

Chapter XIII. Appearance of the Country. Character of the Russian People

On the eve of my arrival in Moscow, I stopped, the night of a very warm day, in a pleasant enough meadow. Some peasant women, dressed picturesquely in accordance with the habit of the locality, were returning from their labors singing Ukrainian tunes whose words praise love and liberty with a kind of melancholy akin to regret. I asked them to dance and they consented to do so. I was struck by the gentle gaiety of these peasant women, as I had been by that of most of the common people I met in Russia. I can well believe that they are terrible when their passions are aroused; and as they have no education, they do not know how to curb their violence. As a result of this ignorance, they have few moral principles, and theft is very frequent in Russia, but so is hospitality. They give to you as they take from you, according to whether trickery or generosity strikes their fancy; both arouse the admiration of this nation. There is a little resemblance to uncivilized people in this way of living, but it seems to me that at present the only vigorous European nations are those that are called either barbarous—that is to say, unenlightened—or free.

One thing worth noting is the degree to which public spirit is marked in Russia. The reputation for invincibility which a great many successes have given this nation, the pride natural to the nobility, the self-sacrifice ingrained in the character of the nation, the profound influence of religion, the hatred of foreigners which Peter I tried to destroy in order to enlighten and civilize his country but which remains nonetheless in the blood of the Russians and is occasionally aroused—all these causes combine to make this nation a very energetic one. Some wretched anecdotes about earlier reigns, some Russians who ran up debts in Paris, and some *bon mots* of Diderot[3] put it into the heads of Frenchmen that Russia consisted only of a corrupt Court, officers and chamberlains, and a population of slaves. This is a great error.

The welcome the Russians extend is so kind that from the first day one thinks he is intimate with them, but very likely one would not really know them even after ten years. Russian silence is absolutely extraordinary; it is induced only by what arouses their deep interest. Of everything else, they talk as much as one would like, but their conversation reveals only their politeness: it betrays neither their feelings nor their opinions. Moreover, as they are in general not highly educated,

[3] *Near the end of Ch. XIV (p. 313 of Gautier's edition of* Dix années d'exil), *in a portion of the text I have omitted, Madame de Staël cites Diderot as the source of a remark sometimes attributed to others: "The Russians became rotten before they grew ripe."*—Ed.

they find little pleasure in serious conversation and do not take pride in scintillating by the wit that may be displayed in it. Poetry, eloquence, and literature are not found in Russia. Luxury, power, and courage are the main goals of pride and ambition; all other ways of distinguishing oneself still seem effeminate and hollow to this nation.

But, it will be said, the people are slaves. What kind of character can they be credited with? I certainly do not have to point out that all enlightened people hope that the Russian nation will emerge from this condition, and the one who probably desires it most is Emperor Alexander. But this Russian slavery does not resemble the kind we are familiar with in the West. It is not, as under the feudal *régime*, a matter of conquerors who imposed their harsh laws upon the conquered. The relationship between the nobles and the populace is more like what was called the family of slaves among the ancients than the status of serfs among the moderns. There is no third estate in Russia. This is a great hindrance to the progress of literature and the fine arts, for it is usually in this middle class that learning is developed. But the result of this absence of an intermediary between the nobility and the populace is that they have greater affection for each other. The distance between the two classes seems the greater because there is nothing between these two extremes, but in actual fact they are the closer to one another for not being separated by a middle class. This is a social organization entirely unfavorable to the enlightenment of the upper classes but not to the happiness of the lower. Moreover, where there is no representative government, that is, in countries where the monarch still decrees the laws he is to execute, men are often more degraded by the loss of their reason and their character than in this vast domain where a few simple religious and patriotic ideas govern a large mass guided by a few leaders. The immense extent of the Russian realm also prevents the despotism of the nobles from bearing heavily upon the people in everyday affairs. Finally, above all, the religious and military spirit is so predominant in the nation that many faults may be forgiven in consideration of these two great sources of noble deeds.

Chapter XIV. Moscow

Gilded cupolas announced Moscow from afar; yet, as the surrounding country is only a plain like all of Russia, one can reach that large city without being impressed by its extent. Someone has said with reason that Moscow is rather a province than a city. Indeed, one sees there huts, houses, palaces, a bazaar as in the Orient, churches, public buildings, bodies of water, woods, and parks. The diversity of manners and of nations that make up Russia is revealed in this vast region. I was asked: Would you like to buy some Kashmir shawls in the Tartar district? Have you seen Chinatown? Asia and Europe are combined in this immense city. People in it enjoy more liberty than in Petersburg, where the Court necessarily exercises great influence. The nobles settled in Moscow do not strive for high places; but they show their patriotism by large gifts to the state, whether for public purposes in time of peace or for relief in time of war. The colossal fortunes of the Russian nobles are used for building up collections of all kinds, for commercial enterprises, and for entertainments modeled after the *Thousand and One Nights,* and these fortunes are also very often lost through the unrestrained passions of their owners.

When I arrived in Moscow, there was talk of nothing but the sacrifices made for the war.

No sooner does a Russian become a soldier than his beard

is cut, and from this moment he is free. People wished that everyone who served in the militia would also be regarded as free, but then the whole nation would have been free, for it rose up almost in its entirety. Let us hope that this liberation, so much desired, will be brought about peacefully. But, in the meantime, one wishes the beards would be preserved, so much strength and dignity do they lend the face.

The Kremlin, that citadel where the emperors of Russia defended themselves against the Tartars, is surrounded by a high wall crenelated and flanked with turrets whose unusual shapes recall a Turkish minaret rather than a fortress like most of those in the West. But though the external character of the city's buildings is Oriental, the imprint of Christianity is found in the multitude of churches, so revered, which attract one's notice at every step.

The Russians played no role in the Age of Chivalry; they were not involved in the Crusades. Constantly at war with the Tartars, Poles, and Turks, the military spirit took shape among them in the midst of atrocities of all kinds brought about by the barbarity of the Asian nations and of the tyrants who governed Russia. In social relations, which are so new to them, the Russians do not distinguish themselves by the spirit of chivalry as the peoples of the West conceive it; rather, they have always shown themselves to be unmerciful toward their enemies. So many massacres took place in the interior of Russia down to and after the reign of Peter the Great that the morality of the nation, and especially that of the nobility, necessarily suffered much from them. These despotic governments, whose only limit is the assassination of the despot, overthrow the principles of honor and duty in the minds of men. But patriotism and attachment to religious beliefs have maintained themselves in all their strength through the wreckage of this bloody history, and the nation that preserves such virtues may yet astonish the world.

In Moscow I saw the most enlightened men in the field of the sciences and literature. But there, as at Petersburg, almost all the professorial posts are filled by Germans. There is a great scarcity of educated men in every field in Russia. The young people, for the most part, do not go to the university except to enter the military profession sooner. Civil offices in Russia confer a rank corresponding to a grade in the army; the spirit of the nation is entirely directed toward the war. In everything else, in administration, political economy, public education, etc., the other nations have until now surpassed the Russians. They are, however, making attempts in literature. The softness and vividness of the sounds of their language are obvious even to those who do not understand it; it should be well suited to music and poetry. But the Russians, like so many other nations on the Continent, make the mistake of imitating French literature which, by its very beauty, is appropriate only to the French. It seems to me that the Russians should find their literary heritage in the Greeks rather than in the Latins. The letters of Russian script, which are so much like those of the Greeks, the former connections between the Russians and the Byzantine empire, their future destinies, which may lead them toward the illustrious monuments of Athens and Sparta—all this should induce the Russians to study Greek. But above all their writers must draw their poetry from the deepest source in their own souls. Their works, until now, have been composed, so to speak, only from their lips, but so vigorous a nation can never be stirred by such weak notes.

Chapter XVII. The Imperial Family

At last I saw that monarch absolute by law as well as by custom but moderate by his own preference. As I was speaking with the Empress, the door opened and Emperor Alexander did me the honor of coming to speak with me. What first struck me about him was such an expression of goodness and dignity that these two qualities appeared inseparable and to have become one in him. I was also very much affected, from the first words he was pleased to address to me, by the noble simplicity with which he approached the great problems of Europe. I have always regarded as a sign of mediocrity that dread of discussing important matters that has been instilled in most sovereigns of Europe. They are afraid to utter a word that might have real meaning. The Emperor Alexander, on the contrary, spoke with me as would English statesmen, who rely upon their own strength and not upon the barriers with which they may be surrounded. Emperor Alexander, whom Napoleon has tried his best to belittle, is a man of remarkable understanding and education, and I do not believe that he would find in his empire a minister abler than himself in anything concerning the judgment and direction of public affairs. He did not conceal from me the admiration he had felt in his relations with Napoleon.[4]

Emperor Alexander, however, very shrewdly described the effect upon him of these conversations with Bonaparte in which he said diametrically opposite things as if one ought to be astonished by each one without considering the contradic-

[4] *In the version of this work edited by Madame de Staël's son (see my note at the beginning of this Section), this sentence reads:* He did not conceal from me that he regretted the admiration he had felt in his relations with Napoleon.—Ed.

tion. He also told me about the Machiavellian lessons Napoleon thought it appropriate to give him. While being convinced of Alexander's honesty in his relations with Napoleon, I was at the same time certain that he would not follow the example of the unfortunate sovereigns of Germany and sign a peace with the man who is as much the enemy of peoples as of kings. A noble soul cannot be deceived twice by the same person. The Emperor talked to me enthusiastically about his people and their potentialities. He expressed to me the desire, which everyone knows he has, to improve the condition of the peasants still subject to slavery.

In Petersburg, especially, the nobles are less liberal in their principles than the Emperor himself. Accustomed to being the absolute masters of their peasants, they would in turn like the monarch to be omnipotent in order to maintain the hierarchy of despotism. The middle class does not yet exist in Russia, though it is beginning to take shape. The sons of priests and merchants, and some peasants who have obtained from their lords the freedom to become craftsmen may be considered a third estate. The Russian nobility, moreover, is not like Germany's or France's; one becomes a noble in Russia upon obtaining military rank. No doubt the great families will always have the highest status in the realm, but it is no less true that the advantages of aristocracy accrue to some men whom the sovereign's will has made nobles in a day; so the whole ambition of the middle class is to make their sons officers so that they may join the privileged class. The result is that schooling is finished at the age of fifteen; one rushes into a military career as soon as possible and everything else is neglected.

For Product Safety Concerns and Information please contact our EU
representative GPSR@taylorandfrancis.com
Taylor & Francis Verlag GmbH, Kaufingerstraße 24, 80331 München, Germany

www.ingramcontent.com/pod-product-compliance
Lightning Source LLC
Chambersburg PA
CBHW071933130726
47908CB00015B/285

* 9 7 8 0 7 6 5 8 0 6 4 5 1 *